Bion and Contemporary Psychoanalysis

This book examines the importance and continued relevance of *A Memoir of the Future* in understanding and applying Bion's work to contemporary psychoanalysis. Bion continued to innovate throughout his life, but the *Memoir* has been largely overlooked.

Focusing on *A Memoir of the Future* is not only of deep interest in terms of the author's biography, or even only in function of a better understanding of his theoretical concepts, but can also be considered, for all intents and purposes, the final chapter of an ingenious creative enterprise. While by some it was thought of as the evidence of Bion's presumed senility, this book challenges that perspective, arguing that it represents the last challenge he issued to the psychoanalytic Establishment. In each chapter, the contributors explore this notion that *A Memoir* forms an essential part of Bion's theory, and that in it he establishes a new 'aesthetic' psychoanalytic paradigm.

With an international list of distinguished contributors, this is a key book for any analysts interested in a comprehensive understanding of Bion's work.

Giuseppe Civitarese, psychiatrist, PhD in psychiatry and relational sciences, is a training and supervising analyst in the Italian Psychoanalytic Society (SPI), and a member of the American Psychoanalytic Association (APsaA) and of the International Psychoanalytic Association (IPA). Previous work includes, *The Intimate Room: Theory and Technique of the Analytic Field, The Violence of Emotions: Bion and Post-Bionian Psychoanalysis, Truth and the Unconscious in Psychoanalysis* and, with co-author Howard Levine, *The W. R. Bion Tradition Lines of Development – Evolution of Theory and Practice over the Decades*.

Psychoanalytic Field Theory Book Series

The Routledge Psychoanalytic Field Theory Book Series was initiated in 2015 as a new subseries of the Psychoanalytic Inquiry Book Series. The series publishes books on subjects relevant to the continuing development of psychoanalytic field theory. The emphasis of this series is on contemporary work that includes a vision of the future for psychoanalytic field theory.

Since the middle of the twentieth century, forms of psychoanalytic field theory emerged in different geographic parts of the world with different objectives, heuristic principles, and clinical techniques. Taken together they form a family of psychoanalytic perspectives that employs a concept of a bi-personal psychoanalytic field. The Psychoanalytic Field Theory Book Series seeks to represent this pluralism in its publications. Books on field theory in all its diverse forms are of interest in this series. Both theoretical works and discussions of clinical technique will be published in this series.

The series editors are especially interested in selecting manuscripts which actively promote the understanding and further expansion of psychoanalytic field theory. Part of the mission of the series is to foster communication amongst psychoanalysts working in different models, in different languages, and in different parts of the world. A full list of titles in this series is available at: https://www.routledge.com/Psychoanalytic-Field-Theory-Book-Series/book-series/FIELDTHEORY

Bion and Contemporary Psychoanalysis

Reading *A Memoir of the Future*

Edited by
Giuseppe Civitarese

Routledge
Taylor & Francis Group

LONDON AND NEW YORK

First published 2018
by Routledge
2 Park Square, Milton Park, Abingdon, Oxon OX14 4RN

and by Routledge
711 Third Avenue, New York, NY 10017

*Routledge is an imprint of the Taylor & Francis Group, an informa
business*

© 2018 selection and editorial matter, Giuseppe Civitarese;
individual chapters, the contributors

British Library Cataloguing-in-Publication Data
A catalogue record for this book is available from the British
Library

Library of Congress Cataloging-in-Publication Data
Names: Civitarese, Giuseppe, 1958– editor.
Title: Bion and contemporary psychoanalysis: reading A memoir
of the future / edited by Giuseppe Civitarese.
Description: Abingdon, Oxon; New York, NY: Routledge, 2018. |
Series: Psychoanalytic field theory book series | Includes
bibliographical references and index.
Identifiers: LCCN 2017003252 | ISBN 9781138038844 (hardback) |
ISBN 9781138038851 (pbk.)
Subjects: LCSH: Bion, Wilfred R. (Wilfred Ruprecht), 1897–1979. |
Bion, Wilfred R. (Wilfred Ruprecht), 1897–1979. Memoir of the
future. | Psychoanalysis.
Classification: LCC BF173 .B49185 2018 |
DDC 150.19/5092—dc23
LC record available at https://lccn.loc.gov/2017003252

ISBN: 978-1-138-03884-4 (hbk)
ISBN: 978-1-138-03885-1 (pbk)
ISBN: 978-1-315-17708-3 (ebk)

Typeset in Times New Roman
by codeMantra

Contents

Contributors

Adela Abella is a psychiatrist and psychoanalyst working with children, adolescents and adults. Training analyst of the Swiss Psychoanalytical Association (SSPsa/SGPsa). She is past-president of the Centre de Psychanalyse de la Suisse Romande. Member of the board of the *International Journal of Psychoanalysis*. Amongst her publications: papers on the interface between psychoanalysis and art, interdisciplinary and theory of technique, and books such as *La construction en psychanalyse. Récupérer le passe ou le réinventer?* (with J. Manzano, 2011), *Précis de technique psychanalytique,* (with J. Manzano and F. Palacio Espasa, 2016), and *Conviction, séduction, suggestion* (in press).

Avner Bergstein is a faculty member and training and supervising psychoanalyst with the Israel Psychoanalytic Society. He is in private practice with adults, adolescents and children, and has worked for some years at a kindergarten for children with autism. He is the author of several papers elaborating on the clinical implications of the writings of Bion and Meltzer. He has also translated and co-edited the Hebrew translations of a number of psychoanalytic books, including works by Bion, Tustin and Ogden.

Sara Boffito is a psychologist and a candidate at the Italian Psychoanalytical Society (SPI), works in private practice with children, adolescents and adults in Milano. Her theoretical interests touch the relationship between adult and children psychoanalysis and Contemporary Art, Cinema and Literature. She published many works in Italian and international journals and collected books. Among them are papers on aesthetics and contemporary art co-authored with Giuseppe Civitarese (*Losing Your Head: Abjection, Aesthetic Conflict, and Psychoanalytic Criticism*, 2015) and on Nina Coltart's contribution to psychoanalysis published in *American Imago* and in the book *Her Hour Come Round at Last. A garland for Nina Coltart* (2011). She collaborates with the *Rivista di Psicoanalisi* and translates into Italian several Anglo-Saxon psychoanalytic authors.

Duncan Cartwright, PhD, is head of the Centre for Applied Psychology, Psychology, University of KwaZulu-Natal, Durban, South Africa. He serves on the editorial board of *Psycho-analytic Psychotherapy in South Africa* and is a member of SAPC. He is the author of *Murdering Minds: Psychoanalysis, Violence and Rage-Type Murder* (2002), and *Containing States of Mind: Exploring Bion's Container Model in Psychoanalytic Psychotherapy* (2010).

Giuseppe Civitarese, MD, PhD, is a training and supervising analyst and member of the Italian Psychoanalytic Society (SPI), of the American Psychoanalytic Association (APsaA) and of the International Psychoanalytic Association (IPA). He lives, and is in private practice, in Pavia, Italy. He is the past-editor of the *Rivista di Psicoanalisi*, the official journal of the Italian Psychoanalytic Society. He has published several books, which include *The Intimate Room: Theory and Technique of the Analytic Field* (2010), *The Violence of Emotions: Bion and Post-Bionian Psychoanalysis* (2012), *The Necessary Dream: New Theories and Techniques of Interpretation in Psychoanalysis* (2014), *Losing Your Head: Abjection, Aesthetic Conflict and Psychoanalytic Criticism* (2015), *The Analytic Field and Its Transformations* (with A. Ferro, 2015), and *Truth and the Unconscious* (2016). He has also co-edited *L'ipocondria e il dubbio: L'approccio psicoanalitico* [Hypochondria and doubt: the psychoanalytic approach] (2011), *Le parole e i sogni* [The words and the dreams] (2015), *The W. R. Bion Tradition: Lines of Development—Evolution of Theory and Practice over the Decades* (2015), and *Advances in Psychoanalytic Field Theory: International Field Theory Association Round Table Discussion* [with M. Katz and R. Cassorla)] (2016).

Giovanni Foresti, MD, PhD, lives in Pavia, Italy. He is a training and supervising analyst of the SPI (Italian Psychoanalytic Society), works in private practice as psychoanalyst, psychiatrist and organizational consultant, and teaches at the State University of Milan (School of Psychiatry), at the Milan Catholic University (Psychology of Organizations and Marketing) and at the SPI National Institute for Training. He is member of OPUS, London, and the Scientific Committee of IL NODO group, Turin. Co-chair for Europe of the Committee 'Psychoanalysis and the Mental Health Field', he is now in the IPA Board as European Representative. His interests are focused on clinical issues, institutional functioning and group dynamics.

Mauro Manica is a psychiatrist and psychoanalyst, and is a full member of the SPI (Italian Psychoanalytic Society) and the IPA (International Psychoanalytic Association). He published several books: *Guardare nell'ombra. Saggi di psichiatria psicoanalitica* (1999), *Psicoanalisi in situazioni estreme* (2004), *Il suicidio. Amore tragico, tragedia d'amore* (with E. Borgna and A. Pagnoni, 2006), *La musica della psicoanalisi* (Rome 2007), *Fare psicoanalisi, vivere la clinica, sognare la teoria* (2010), *Ogni angelo è tremendo. Esplorazioni ai confini delle teoria e della clinica psicoanalitica* (2013), *Intercettare il sogno. Sviluppi traumatici e progressione onirica nel discorso psicoanalitico* (2014), and *L'arte di guarire. Breviario di psicoanalisi contemporanea* (2016).

Antonino Ferro is a psychiatrist, psychoanalyst, past-president of the Italian Psychoanalytic Society (SPI) and member of the American Psychoanalytic Association (APsaA) and the International Psychoanaltytic Association (IPA). He supervises and gives lectures internationally. His publications include *Psychoanalysis and Storytelling* (London 2006), *Mind Works* (London 2009), *Avoiding Emotions, and Living Emotions* (2011), and *Torments of the Soul* (2014). In 2007, he received the Mary Sigourney Award.

Clara Mucci is a psychoanalytically oriented psychotherapist practicing in Milan and Pescara, Italy. She is Professor of Clinical Psychology at the University of Chieti, where she has been until recently Full Professor of English Literature and Shakespearean Drama. She received a PhD in Literature and Psychoanalysis from Emory University, Atlanta, USA, and was a Fellow, in 2005–2006, at the Personality Disorder Institute directed by Otto Kernberg, in

New York. She is the author of several monographs on Women's Literature, Shakespearean drama and literary theory; more recently she has published on trauma and its intergenerational transmission: *Beyond Individual and Collective Trauma. Intergenerational Transmission, Psychoanalytic Treatment and the Dynamics of Forgiveness* (2013).

Benjamin H. Ogden is Assistant Professor of literature and humanities at Stevens Institute of Technology. He is co-author, with Thomas H. Ogden, of *The Analyst's Ear and the Critic's Eye: Rethinking Psychoanalysis and Literature* (2013). He is completing his second book on the intersection of psychoanalysis and literature, entitled *Where We Most of the Time Are: Writing and Thinking between Disciplines.*

Violet Pietrantonio is a psychologist, specialized in Clinical Psychology; psychoanalyst; and member of the Italian Psychoanalytical Society (SPI) and of the International Psychoanalytic Association (IPA). She lives and works in Bologna, Italy. She is particularly interested in clinical and theoretical developments of the oneiric model of the mind as proposed by Bionian Field Theory. Among her publications are as follows: 'At the Origin of Psychic Life: In a Grain of Sand the First α Wailings of a Newborn Dreamer', *Ital. Psychoanal. Annu.*, 9:25–49; 'Borderline' (pp. 131–159) and 'Gelosia: la perfidia di una sorella dimenticata' (pp. 283–303), both in A Ferro, ed., *La clinica psicoanalitica oggi*, Rome, 2016.

Lissa Weinstein is a professor in the Doctoral Program in Clinical Psychology at the City College of New York and the Graduate Center, a faculty member of the New York Psychoanalytic Institute, and a fiction writer. Her interests include the interrelationship of neurobiology and psychoanalysis, the function of repetition, as well as film and literature studies. She won the Heinz Hartmann Jr. Award winner with Dr. Arnold Wilson for their papers on the work of Lev Vygotsky and psychoanalysis and was given the Margaret Marek award from the International Dyslexia Association for *Reading David: A Mother and Son's Journey through the Labyrinth of Dyslexia* (2003). Recent publications include *The Neurobiology of Personality Disorders: Implications for Psychoanalysis* and *Personality Disorders, Attachment and Psychodynamic*

Psychotherapy, both with Larry Siever, *Physiological and Developmental Contributions to the Feeling of Reality*, and *Towards a Clinical Integration of Theoretical Perspectives* with Steven Ellman, PhD, and *Between Forgetting and Remembering: Two Films of Alain Resnais*.

Acknowledgements

Chapter 1 is based on 'Why Bion? Why Now? Novel Forms and the Mystical Quest', by L. Weinstein, Reprinted by permission of *Rivista Psicoanal.*, 61: 93–118, 2015.

Chapter 2 is based on '"Psychoanalysis, I Believe" in Wonderland. Reading and Literature in *A Memoir of the Future*', by S. Boffito, http://www.funzionegamma.it/psychoanalysis-believe-wonderland-reading-literature-memoir-future/

Chapter 4 is based on '*A Memoir of the Future* and Memoir of the Numinous', by M. Manica, http://www.funzionegamma.it/memoir-future-memoir-numinous/. This chapter was translated from Italian by Andrew Ellis.

Chapter 5 is based on '*A Memoir of the Future* and the Defence against Knowledge', by A. Ferro, http://www.funzionegamma.it/memoir-future-defence-knowledge/

Chapter 6 is based on 'Wilfred's Razor: A Reading of W.R. Bion's *A Memoir of the Future*', by G. Foresti, http://www.funzionegamma.it/wilfreds-razor-reading-w-r-bions-memoir-future/. This chapter was translated from Italian by William Cooke.

I thank Claudio Neri for having inspired this book.

Introduction

Giuseppe Civitarese

There is a growing interest in Wilfred R. Bion, as demonstrated by the increasing number of papers in the best psychoanalytic journals, meetings and books about his thinking, but there is not much on *A Memoir of the Future*.[1] So, the idea of a book on this topic is to fill a void in the area of Bion's studies. *MF* is exceptionally interesting because, while by some it was thought to be evidence of Bion's presumed senility, on the contrary it represents the last challenge he issued to the psychoanalytic Establishment. The three books that make up *MF* are admittedly the recounting of a long uninterrupted dream in which Bion deals with very important theoretical matters in a narrative way, showing once again how he was establishing a new paradigm in psychoanalysis, which can be named 'aesthetic'.

Focusing on *MF* means the undertaking of a theoretical activity. *MF* is not only of deep interest in terms of the author's biography, or even only in function of a better understanding of his theoretical concepts, but rather can be considered, for all intents and purposes, the final chapter of an ingenious creative enterprise – not a mere summary or appendix, but a whole new chapter. In *MF*, Bion once again shows his diabolical ability to disorient his readers, forcing them to wrack their brains and thus to think with their own minds. 'Diabolical' because, in this tenaciousness there is something infernal, a quality that psychoanalysis must always possess, and also something provocative – but what Bion aims to generate is *courage*.

We must always remember this key aspect in his thinking – a thinking that is never static – all the more so now that it has finally started to be embraced (and even normalised). There is always the risk of making it into a sterile collection of formulas, with the resulting loss of its pervasive deconstructive impetus. Thus, what *MF* highlights is the notion of the dream as a narrative activity. We are called upon to dream with him in a swirling vortex of images, stories, characters and quotations. It is the mind at work, the space of dream, peopled with presences, at once shadowy and hyper-luminous.

Both conceptual thinking and imagination protect the individual from the terror provoked by the immense forces of nature. As in any Romanticist painting inspired on the sublime, while never ceasing completely to cause some anguish, these forces are now at a safe distance. The subject can contemplate them without being overwhelmed by fright.

Nevertheless, if we judge the text according to the categories of fictional narrative, we could not consider it successful. The echoes of Beckett, in some places inspiring, are not enough. On the other hand, if we read it as analysts, i.e., as persons with a passion for the field of science invented by Freud (analysis, Ogden (2005b) writes, is a form of human relating that did not previously exist, something both simple and enormous), these pages become an infinite fount of precious suggestions. The field of psychoanalysis feeds deeply on writings, but it is also the empirical field of encounter and of a caring practice, and cannot do without this duality. If we stop and think about it, the purely narrative works of even famous analysts almost always bore and disappoint us because they are not nurtured *directly* on the analysts' lifeblood, their experience or efforts to frame that experience in theory – that lifeblood that, on the other hand, circulates abundantly in *MF*.

In the first chapter, 'Why Bion? Why now? Novel forms and the mystical quest', Lissa Weinstein writes that Bion's elegant, complex and 'bottomless' memoir perfectly melds form with function, using the form of a postmodern novel to offer the reader a living experience of the function of reverie and the need to tolerate not knowing during the meandering, often confusing path of an in-depth psychoanalytic exploration. The paper offers a more personal and affective reaction to the material than is usually presented in a scholarly work, attempting not so much to explicate the text as to *respond* to it through linking several seemingly disparate literatures – Bahktin's work on novel structure, postmodern literature, and mysticism. Weinstein argues that Bion's choice of a novel format and the use of a radical, 'precisely obscure' language are necessitated by his concept of O, which differs significantly from the Freudian unconscious. It is only through a multi-voiced context that the 'real' of the affective contents of O and their ultimately mystical nature can be approached.

Instead of calling his trilogy *MF*, writes Sara Boffito in her '"Psychoanalysis, I believe" in Wonderland. Reading and literature in *A Memoir of the Future*', Bion has chosen to call it *A Memoir*. The word used for the Italian translation, *memoria*, is more ambiguous and omits the distinction. In English, the title alerts the reader as to what is to come – a *memoir* – that is, an account of personal recollections. If we investigate what exactly a memoir is as a literary genre, the paradox merely gets deeper. For instance, G. Thomas Couser has devoted several publications to defining the genre, starting with his *Memoir: An Introduction* (2011), in which he expounds on the differences between novel and autobiography, identifying one of the distinctive traits of the memoir as a 'commitment to the real', and adds that such a genre indicates the fundamental human activity of narrating our life story on its own terms.

Just what constitutes reality and truth, and what might right be considered 'facts', is one of the chief arguments underpinning the dialogues between the characters of the *Memoir* and involving the reader so deeply. It may seem paradoxical, but the author reckons we can surmise that Bion wrote these books for reasons akin to this 'commitment to the real', even if the reality to which he felt committed is neither historical nor material but psychic, emotional truth, and the 'facts' and 'actual events' under discussion are far more complex than those that may be observed with one's eyes. From this starting point in this paper, Boffito explores further Bion's relationship with narration and literature.

Literature is also the perspective chosen to approach *MF* by Benjamin Ogden (in 'Bion and the apes: the bridging problem of *A Memoir of the Future*'). *A Memoir of the Future* is difficult on its readers. It asks them not only to figure out what the book means, but also how it can be fairly evaluated. On what criteria is it appropriate to judge the merits and failures of *A Memoir of the Future*? How does one read, or write critically about, a work that was plainly written to frustrate attempts at making sense of it? The goal of this paper is to establish criteria for evaluating Bion's least understood work. It does this by demonstrating that Bion's theory of thinking is in many ways similar to the theory of thinking developed by Wolfgang Köhler while studying the behaviour of apes on the island of Tenerife, described in his monograph *The Mentality of Apes*. In *Elizabeth Costello*, the novelist J.M. Coetzee discusses Köhler's experiments and in doing so proposes some ways of evaluating not only Köhler's work, but also *A Memoir of the Future*. Much as Köhler tried to cross the bridge from psychology into the 'poetics' of thinking, Bion tried to cross the bridge from psychoanalytic epistemology into literary aesthetics. This paper considers these crossings, drawing from Coetzee's insights.

In his '*Memoir of the Future* and memoir of the numinous', Mauro Manica starts with the comparison between Jung's *Red Book* and Bion's *MF* trilogy. He suggests the hypothesis that similarly to what happens for the individual personality – where the eruption of underground experiences confronts us with the emergency of parts of the mind that have not fully come into being or have been precociously miscarried, as they have not found any space within the mind of the object – there seem to be models and theories that did not find enough space in Freud's mind or in that of the scientific community he created and thus sank into the underground galleries and dungeons of psychoanalytic conceptualisation. In Jung's reflection, the contexts that anticipated the most current developments of post-Freudian psychoanalysis seem to have been split or dissociated and stored there – that is to say, he offered a further perspective on the unconscious that was not only formed as a depository of repressed childhood memories, but could also overlook the infinite (Matte Blanco, 1975), as it is driven by the truth instinct (Bion, 1977a), an impulse to representation (Bollas, 2009) and the knowledge instinct (Odgen, 2011).

We would have plausible reasons to think that Jung's *unknown* has been absorbed, in Bion's reflection, in the empty concept of *O* and in its numinous definition: fascinating (as it refers to *fascinosum*) and dreadful (as it concerns the *tremendum*). However, in Bion's version, the concept of *O*, the *unknown*, seems to have expanded and allowed for an evolution of the model of the mind to which we can refer. In extending and overcoming Freud's and Jung's conceptions, Bion seems to have succeeded in conceiving a mind that overlooks the repressed and the numinous but is forced to be confronted, since its origin, with the nothingness of *O*, its lack of meaning.

In his paper '*Memoir of the Future* and the defence against knowledge', Ferro seeks to show how psychoanalytic work allows the continuous opening of different possible worlds and the threat of dogmatism.

For his part, Foresti claims that *MF* is a text that through aesthetic and narrative means develops the reform that conceptually had already been introduced in *Experience in Groups* and in *Learning from Experience*. The epistemological continuity between the Bionian texts is seen as a realisation of the theoretical precautions and the methodological preoccupations that have been peculiar of nominalism and British empiricism: the avoidance of speculative excesses and the ontological distance between objects and concepts.

In a very creative contribution, 'Memories of the future, realisations in the present. The oneiric destiny of pre-conceptions that turn up in the minds of dreamers', Violet Pietrantonio not only tells us about *MF*, but also shows what it means to take Bion seriously. In the *après-coup* of Contemporary Psychoanalysis, *MF* could reveal itself as a sort of Guernica, an avant-garde manifesto that calls Psychoanalysis to new tasks; it would incarnate new languages necessary to give psychic figurability to what remains still unnamed in psychoanalytic common sense. The author tries to show how this phantasmagorical work can serve as a sort of reference book of a future psychoanalysis, in which it is possible to trace, in the form of intuitions and preconceptions, the seeds of many elements that make up contemporary theories. In the brood of newness that swarms between chapters and lines of this futuristic mythopoetic text, it is possible to breathe and experience the analytic method O → K, to glimpse blossoms of those oneiric properties of narrative function developed in all the work of Antonino Ferro, to detect innovative analytic concepts that help analysts to become receptive to the psychic facts that emanate from the so-called inaccessible unconscious.

According to Avner Bergstein ('The ineffable'), Bion often addresses the paradoxical nature of the relationship between language and truth whereby linguistic expression is the path by which truth can be glimpsed, while at the same time hiding and distorting it. In a trance-like state, Bion seems to try to seize the multidimensional, elusive truth through the multitude of characters portrayed in the *Memoir*. Reading the *Memoir* is an emotional experience of capturing glimpses of an ineffable, hidden reality, and awakening the realm of noumena, the juxtaposition between psychoanalytic thinking and mysticism. In fact, Bion drew a parallel between psychoanalytical and mystical states of mind. Mystical thinking maintains that truth is hidden from the senses, from language and from thought. It is concerned with the unknown, concealed, and zero-ness. Bion borrows words such as God and Godhead, to try to depict an emotional truth, or ultimate reality, existing beyond the possibility of human knowledge and consciousness. Throughout the *Memoir*, P.A. and PAUL/ PRIEST (representing both religion and the mystical tradition) come to realise the affinities between them. The present paper explores this affinity, suggesting that the mutual work of analysis facilitates the development of an intuitive, mystical capacity in both analyst and analysand.

In her 'Psychoanalysis "at the mind's limits"': trauma, history, and paronomasia as "a flower of speech" in *A Memoir of the Future*', the following chapter, Clara Mucci tries to prove that there is a parallel between the explosion of language (in the sense of paronomasia, as explained by Roman Jakobson, 1960, about poetic language) in *MF* and the traumatic scenery on the ruins of which Bion is writing. A parallel is also shown in the psychoanalytic theory Bion is taking to its extreme, between 'wakeful dream thinking' and the language of disguise typical of poetry and literature, i.e., figurative language (defined as a 'flower of language' in *MF*), in so far as they are structurally similar expressions of a kind of traumatic reality, therefore by definition ineffable and at the margins of representation.

Therefore, in *MF*, Bion provocatively acts out what happens 'at the mind's limits', to echo Jean Amery's book on his survival after the trauma of Auschwitz. The deconstructive language of the pun, or paronomasia, eludes and escapes one-to-one correspondences to privilege the multiplicity of references and resonances, so that, in the wake of Freud's model of the joke, is the perfect correlative of a world where 'the center does not hold', to echo W.B. Yeats.

In the next chapter, 'The "*Memoir*" experienced from the standpoint of contemporary art: a chronicle of a death foretold', Adela Abella states that a striking convergence is described between the *Memoir* and some trends in contemporary art, best represented by Marcel Duchamp, John Cage and Christian Boltanski. This artistic trend seeks to question traditional boundaries and accepted taste in order to open up new ways of perceiving and thinking about the world, enhancing the personal appropriation and creativity of both the artist and the public. Nevertheless, with the passage of time, the enlivening capacity of works of art is irremediably used up, leading to its death through habit, idealisation and canonisation. The author suggests that this might also be the fate of Bion's *Memoir*.

The next chapter seems to be a comment on, as well as an answer to, this issue. In 'Reflections on "nonsense" in *A Memoir of the Future*', Duncan Cartwright sustains that reading Bion is as much an experience as it is an attempt to grapple with his ideas. Perhaps like no other psychoanalytic author, Bion engages his audience in a way that provokes and challenges the reader to seek 'personal truth' as an essential part of reading or learning. In this way, it could be said that he is more concerned with 'infecting' the reader or interlocutor with the problem itself – the experience rather than the accumulation of facts or rationalisations.

MF represents Bion's final and most audacious attempt to explore the nature of psychic reality as a here-and-now living experience. To do so, he employs a host of literary devices, characters, personages, presences and registers of experience to represent a 'science fiction' of psychoanalytic experience. From the beginning, the reader is plunged into a world of multiple reciprocal relationships, unresolved paradoxical tensions and reversed perspectives that generate confusion, unease, disorientation and turmoil. The provocative narrative and style appears to contain an implicit imperative: dismiss the trilogy as nonsense or engage, fall to sleep or tolerate 'something' that is unknown but 'becoming', choose oblivion or wisdom. From this perspective, the trilogy is framed by an appeal to 'not understand' and an attack on comfortable certainties, both generally and within psychoanalysis.

Taking this as one of many possible perspectives on *MF*, this chapter explores the trilogy as a meditation on 'non sense' – psychic reality – and its interminable, unresolvable, relationships with the sensory world, facts and articulate language. As a 'true' representation of psychic reality, the work is necessarily unsuccessful, deliberately obscure and unresolved, a platform that creates the 'roughness' for dreaming one's own dreams against the background of the formless infinite. As well as exploring entangled representations of facts and fiction in the trilogy, Cartwright explores Bion's appeal to not understand him in the context of the trilogy. He also explores some of the trilogy's 'evocations' or 'dream thoughts' in terms of our most recent 'fashionable' solution to psychic uncertainty: cyberspace. Here, the immediacy of 'making sense' poses new challenges in the journey towards 'mental oblivion' or wisdom.

Will the reader make the mental effort, take the time, to *not* understand? As a largely dismissed piece of work, perhaps Bion's intensions remain as alive today as they ever were, still awaiting a thinker.

Note

1   From now on indicated as *MF*.

Chapter 1

Why Bion? Why now? Novel forms and the mystical quest

Lissa Weinstein

Introduction

I order my copy of *A Memoir of the Future* on a Tuesday night last February, having been asked to write something by September. Knowing little about it, I vow, with true superego severity, not to read too much of Bion's other writings, not to dig into secondary texts or the more directly autobiographical memoirs, but rather to approach the text as one does a patient—without memory or desire. I wonder, is it even possible to forgo the comfort of theory?

'Beckett-y,' friend Jamieson tells me. 1000 pages.

Expensive. Even on *half.com* at eBay, over 100 dollars. I buy it used from someone in the States, not wanting to wait for Karnac to ship from England. To my astonishment, it arrives by the next afternoon, left in a plain brown wrapper, like pornography, in my vestibule. Looking at the package with no return address, the dreamy fog of reverie already clouding the corners of my eyes, I imagine the person who wanted to get rid of it. Quickly. Perhaps it has driven him or her mad. Uncannily unable when people ask, to remember the work's proper, though paradoxical, title. *A Memoir for the Future? Of the Future? The Past of the Future?*

I find myself simply calling it 'The Book,' after Bruno Schulz's (1937) story in which a boy remembers, the 'Authentic,' a book so magical that the *Bible* is only a mere 'clumsy falsification,' a book whose script 'unfolds while being read, its boundaries open to all currents and fluctuations.' Although told by his father that the book is a myth children believe and then forget, the boy knows that it is both 'a postulate and a goal.' Finding evidence of its pages in some wrinkled, discarded papers used to wrap meat at the butcher, he understands that within the imperfect fragments he has retrieved, one can still find 'the faded silvery imprints of the bare feet of angels' (p. 13).

I decide to engage the *Memoir* in the manner Schulz advises one to approach the 'Authentic,' with 'imagination and vicarious being' (p. 14). Recent writing on the constructivist nature of reading (Bruner, 1986; Ferro, 2006; Ogden TH and Ogden BH, 2013; Greene and Duisit, 1980) allow me the leeway to author the *Memoir* as well as read it, to treat it as 'scriptable' as opposed to a 'lisable' text (Barthes, 1975) and to absorb its form as well as its content. In this paper, a record of my journey with Bion, reactions to, reveries about, and struggles to 'be' with the text are inseparable from my understanding. Given Bion's equation of fact with feeling in the analytic situation, I imagine that he would have approved, as it mirrors his choice of an artistic rather than an expository format, one in which the sense and rhythms of words and the affects they evoke as well as their dictionary meaning could be contained.

This approach, however, dictated a rather meandering path for a scholarly paper, an emotional response to the *Memoir* before attaching these reactions to a wider context, in this case an attempt to understand the necessity of a novel format as the way for Bion to express his ideas about O as they differ from Freud's unconscious. A reversal of sorts, thesis last not first, a paper that will not so much provide answers as attempt to bring a few seemingly disparate literatures into conjunction, in this case a Bahktinian perspective on the novel, postmodern theory, and the search for a mystical and unifying experience. Like Bion, we will start in the middle with intuition and only later find concepts.

There are, undoubtedly, numerous other productive ways to approach this complex and 'bottomless' text whose structure mirrors the ultimate unknowability of O, for example, as self-analysis (Harris Williams, 1983), an autobiographical resolution of Bion's war experiences or as metaphor for a revolutionary effort to shake up the complacency of psychoanalytic theory. However, the focus of my reading will not be on the content of Bion's self-examination except insofar as it exemplifies his search for a universal discoverable only through examination of the particular; nor will the cogent discussions of analytic morality and technique that flow through the third section receive their due. No attempt will be made to provide a sequential summary of *Memoir*'s plot or explication of the characters. Instead, my reading will focus primarily on the first section as it is within *The Dream* that one sees most clearly Bion's discontent with articulate language and his efforts to traverse the caesura between language and the event. Both the struggle and his disappointment determine Bion's search for a new expressive form rather than the use of the standard expository presentation common to analytic papers, engendering *Memoir*'s stylistic and substantive similarities to postmodern fiction. A final section will attempt to understand the renewed interest in Bion and *Memoir* in particular.

Entering the text

The dream

A brief introduction warns the reader of what is ahead—we will understand some meanings that are 'obvious, communicated and interpretable according to the rules of grammar and articulate speech'; we will come to understand other things if we try hard to ascertain subtle changes in rhythms, and then there will be 'modes of thinking to which no known realization has so far been found to approximate' (*MF*, p. ix) and so may remain unobserved, like a star that exists far from the purview of our most powerful instruments.

We begin *in media res*, told only that it is a fictitious account of psychoanalysis including an artificially constructed dream. However, the superior reality of artifice is immediately evoked as we are asked to consider whether a well-drawn fictitious character is not more 'real' than the drab and conventional unlived lives that surround us. The question of the authenticity of imagined characters will preoccupy Bion, just as it has Pirandello (1921) and Unamuno (1928) before him; for Bion, the existence of realer-than-real imagined characters will encapsulate his belief in psychic reality. As in Ferro's (1992a) play on the title of Pirandello's *Six Characters in Search of an Author*, Bion is an author in search of characters that will allow him to articulate his history and trace processes of development. A bidirectional process between author and text, the creation of characters, and their reality will inevitably touch on questions of identity:

> Every novel, every work of fiction, every poem when it is live is autobiographical. Every fictional being, every poetic personage whom an author creates helps create the author himself.
>
> (Unamuno, 1928, p. 415)

In truth, Bion is already a character created by his minions. Like Jorge Luis Borges who documents this dissociation in *Borges and I* (1960), Wilfred Bion is a different being from the public Bion, the recipient of worship and/or hatred and different still from the psychoanalyst Bion, represented in the memoir by *P.A.* How can he possibly give voice to a disorganized mind, when he is already an icon, reified in the minds of those who look toward him? Only through a fiction, a self-reflexive and self-conscious fiction that allows for the representation of fragments of his identity through numerous characters who can then comment on their own creation.

> The whole of this book is so far printed can be regarded as an artificial and elaborate construct. I myself, here introduced into the narrative can be regarded as a construct artificially composed with the aid of such artistic and scientific material as I can command a and manipulated to form a representation of an author whose name appears on the book and now, for the second time, as a character in a work of fiction. Is a convincing portrait? Does it appear to 'resemble' reality?
>
> (*MF*, p. 86)

The memoir will suggest that there is no answer, or to be more precise, no single answer, only an approximation of the truth as the question is explored from numerous vertices.

My reading starts out pleasurably. After all, it is a novel, with dialogue, interaction, and characters in place of topic headings and dried prose. The characters are vivid enough: the maid, *Rosemary*,[1] with her earthy language and practical wisdom; *Roland*, the weak and desiccated lord of the manor; and his wife, *Alice*. Recognizable characters, roles we can identify, emotions easy to name if not understand—jealousy, competition, cruelty. Mimesis providing its comforting mirror of the real. The sound of distant gunfire, an undefined danger, always enticing, signals that the world that the characters have known is about to be shaken. An auspicious beginning, as it so often seems to be in analysis, the resistances still in abeyance as the new, hoped for object is approached.

As the section progresses, there is a complete dissolution of all structures of temporality and space. A dream, but whose dream? Who is awake? Who asleep? Are we in daytime or in darkness only dreaming of light? Which of the characters named exist in the novel's created external reality and which in our reality? Day–night boundaries abrogated; social positions are quickly reversed; 'fictional' characters mingle freely with internal objects and self-representations, as well as the sensibilities and sounds specific to animals and primitive species. The style is a sharp contrast to Freud's orderly approach to the study of mental phenomena; we are literally 'in' someone's mind. Theoretical concepts, alpha and beta, come alive and mock the reified status of psychoanalytic jargon. As the dream deepens, all boundaries are lost.

> [T]he 'facts' of daytime and night were defective, mutilated. They were having dreams – mutilated dreams – lacking a dimension like a solid body that casts no shadow in light. The world of reality, facts, was no longer distinguishable from dreams, unconsciousness, night. Thoughts with and thoughts without a thinker replaced a universe where discrimination ruled. Dreams had none of the distinguishing characteristic of mind, feelings, mental representations, formulations. The thinker had no thoughts, the thoughts were without thinkers.
>
> (Ibid., p. 33)

A new character, *Paranoid-Schizoid* who is not embodied like the others, complains that the language he hears is excruciating, a babble, leaving him unable to distinguish memory from premonition; perhaps in this universe we have suddenly entered, where time and space no longer provide coordinates of meaning, the two perspectives are identical. Is this how words are perceived by the newborn, not quite a self who can receive meaning as we conceive it from a mature perspective, yet still fully responsive to the stimuli around him? The world of a new *Depressive Position* wonders, 'What are the rules in this domain of pure thought and how can we ever represent the experiences that take place there ... What are the counterparts of disturbances, perturbations, turbulences that are violent, invisible, insensible?' (p. 51). It is clear *Roland* states that 'Time as a concept is as inadequate as topological space to provide a domain for the play of such enormous thoughts as those liberated by freedom from dependence on a thinker' (p. 70) and from the 'polarization of "truth and falsehood."' Communication then becomes a problem of form far more than of repressed content. The task seems almost insurmountable:

> If you think the problems that we have to solve can be solved in a framework where 'things' happen in time and space, with ideas taken from the vocabulary and grammar invented for the senses, we shall fail. It is not unlike solving the problem of joining nine dots, arranged on a plane to form a cube, with four straight lines. You cannot do this *and* stay within the pattern of the cube.
>
> (Ibid., p. 188)

The Dream section is nearly incomprehensible, obstinate in its assault on our usual structures of understanding. No matter what time of day I pick up the book, I fall into a dreamless sleep after reading only a few pages and awaken with no memory. Like an analyst with a psychotic patient, I wonder, 'What did I sign on for? Rudderless, insensible, can't he explain himself? Is it worth all the work it will take to comprehend this?' I search for familiar terms to cover the experience, but Bion has undermined that soothing trick:

> (More bloody metaphors! Who ever could sort out a mass of verbiage like this?) You could try calling it 'Paranoid Schizoid' after–a long way 'after'–Melanie Klein. Good idea. Good dog paranoid schizoid here, here is a nice piece of jargon for you.
>
> (Ibid., p. 59)

I am beginning to truly understand Freud's (1915/1955a) statement that 'Hate, as a relation to objects, is older than love' (p. 139). Instead of thoughts, I have a visceral sense of being tormented by this bizarre, fragmented universe and an aversion to ever opening this book again.

Bion, now entering the narrative as a character (sometimes called *Captain Bion* or alternately *Myself*), suggests that it is a problem of perspective, or from which vertex one is viewing:

> The poet or genius can look at the scientist or genius and the rev-
> elation, as at the opposite ends of the telescope, are too large and
> too small to be tolerable or even to be recognizably related. It
> is felt to be the 'fault' of the instrument that brings such differ-
> ent objects together. But it might be the 'fault' of the objects for
> being so different—or is it the human animal that has to 'use' its
> accumulations of facts, that it has not the experience that would
> enable it to 'understand' what it sees, blind or sightful?
>
> (MF, p. 57)

My capacity for tolerating not knowing is sorely tested. As I type my chosen quotes, they return to the impenetrable, their meaning de-leted, evading my grasp. I begin to feel the dread of the paper due, the terror of my colleagues' reactions. I call upon my analytic faith that it will come to me, that something will come to me; it always does, that terror does not last forever. I think of my analyst remarking that everyone writes a bad paper, most people more than one; a writing teacher who tells me that dread is part of every writing experience, you just have to push through it. But what is the purpose of this book? Autobiography? Something else?

> This book could be hailed as bearing, in itself, resemblance to its
> paternity—that it could not be mistaken for someone else's 'brain
> child'. But I may have a different aim; say, that of writing a de-
> scription of psycho-analysis. To me, that the book bore witness to
> its mental origins might be an unwelcome irrelevance, a feature
> additional to the main component of my wish to communicate
> and your wish to receive.
>
> (Ibid., p. 86)

'Show, don't tell,' the first axiom of every creative writing teacher. If not an answer, the idea of an induced experience at least allows an approach to the material. More than a self-portrait, Bion wants to communicate a mode of thought—the inarticulate, the indescribable. This can *only* be accomplished through the reader's (in this case, my) phenomenological experience of the reception of the disorganized, terrified fragments he presents. Through its artificiality, its lack of fidelity to consensual reality, *Memoir* aims to create a 'real' emotional truth. As incomprehension is at the core of analysis, Bion also wants to convey the practice of psychoanalysis, to immerse the reader in its 'feel, rather than write (another) a paper about psychoanalysis, whose reified terms have lost their life and now function to provide a defense against knowing.

Unable to actively impose a structure I already understood on the material, with little option, I allow a state of passive (or is it active?) receptivity and find myself responding less to content or symbolic meaning, but resonating with fragments, tempos, rhythms, shapes, thoughts without a thinker. After a while, islands of sensibility emerge from the flood. Recurring themes become recognizable, sections repeat accruing new meaning and form rudimentary patterns: the near ubiquitous inclusion of something and its opposite made identical except for their position along a continuum, repeated references to Plato's cave, the concern with the real versus the imagined/created, the difficulty linking one way of thinking to another, the inherent paradox of language—that once communicated, thought is no longer 'alive,' but ossified, hence the need for constant new beginnings, new vantage points once something has been grasped, how every seeming solution brings us to the start of a new problem, the same questions asked again, each time beginning from a new vantage point. If the text does not quite make 'sense,' at least my sense of dread retreats.

I allow myself the freedom of incomprehension that I tolerate when approaching an experimental novel; only this time, it is a novel whose other reality is a way of thinking and not, for example, as in Henry James 'Jolly Corner,' a ghostly world where the self that his current life has eclipsed continues to exist. From this vantage point, each character in *Memoir* need not be understood for his or her individual dynamics, but for the part he or she plays in a larger puzzle, the literary critic's question: why does the author create this character this way? Why now?

Something else happens. I begin to notice the beauty of the language, for example, the passage where *Rosemary* is answering a series of questions repeatedly posed as 'Who are you?' She answers,

I am a funny story. I am a child's book. I am wonderland. I am a children's story. You are laughing in your sleep. You are waking up. The funny story which makes you laugh will make you cry. The child's dream will grow up to become adult, the night mare will carry you, like Shakespeare's sonnet, sluggishly away from home, but fast, back to where you came from: which is the same one you go to.

(Ibid., pp. 37–38)

Why had not I noticed before how poetic and funny some of the writing was? Too busy, as Bion might say, trying to 'catch up with an answer' (ibid., p. 239), listening for, not listening to.

Out of the mist, new characters enter the dream—more real and unreal than ever: *Sherlock Holmes*, his brother the indolent, do-nothing-but-think, brilliant *Mycroft* whose 'specialism is omniscience' (Conan-Doyle, 1893, p. 914). Detectives, followers of arcane clues, tout their superiority both to their creator and to *Bion*, who keeps trying to dismiss them as mere fictions. *Mycroft* will suggest a way that thoughts might find a thinker. Perhaps, as Freud suggested in the *Project* (1895/1955), the mind might be able to perceive psychic quality, and through a process of 'probing and reacting' to the grosser, senses reveal (like an x-ray) previously unnoticed patterns and connections, which could then be transformed. In a long soliloquy, *Myself* reiterates the limitations of the observing instrument to know or to communicate the experience of an event, no better than a photograph that, despite its putative reality, lacks the feeling of the event it is meant to capture, providing, at best, a screen memory. Thus, what we believe we know as analysts, the very structures of our psychoanalytic world view, depicted in already-made jargon that falls authoritatively from our lips (psychosexuality, the Oedipal crisis, hysteria), are only outcroppings of another, more fundamental, truth:

… patterns, configurations, insignificant in themselves, but, if delineated, indicative of an *underlying* reality by their perturbations, regroupings, shifts in pattern and colour; they reflect a category and kind that the human mind cannot formulate or conjecture in their presence ...

(*MF*, p. 112)

They reflect something about the psyche, and it is the psyche that needs to be studied ...

> Psychoanalysis itself is just a stripe on the coat of the tiger. Ultimately, it may meet the Tiger – The Thing Itself O.

(Ibid., p. 112)

How then can language, our central symbolic system, relate to the thing-in-itself, be it the psyche or the unmetabolized sensory images that constitute it?

> It is analogous to expanding the domain of arithmetic to contain irrational numbers, negative numbers, compound conjugate numbers. The domain which is adequate for the operation of natural numbers cannot contain these other numbers.

(Ibid., p. 188)

One possibility is parallelism, a kind of linguistic isomorphism.

> Much in this book has been described in narrative terms. The constructions employed could be understood if the language were known to conform to the conventions of spelling, orthography, print, grammar. Are those rules to be understood as applying only to the domain of articulate speech, or is it possible that they derive from and apply to some domain of which we are unaware? Are the rules to which I conform also to be understood to be a part of the representation to which some yet undisclosed realization approximates?

(Ibid., p. 117)

The problem, however, is more complex. Perhaps a listener is not only hearing the spoken words but is instead primarily responding to the rhythms of breath or changes in prosody; perhaps the words are experienced through another sense, such as vision or proprioception. *Myself* argues that it is more elusive still—even if we assume that there is a mind, perhaps there is a domain 'as approximates to, but is not identical with the mind' (ibid., p. 118)—then the problem is not just between the two people, but also one's ability to apprehend this other domain. Comprehension would require an extension of Freud's theory of consciousness to the whole human mind, and taking whatever lies 'beyond' as an object of attention (ibid.). It is possible that things might appear nonsensical not only because we cannot bear what they represent, that is because of our need to defend and ward off specific contents, but also because what appears as nonsense represents the outcroppings of a different form of thought prior to any language. Making an analogy to the field of mathematics, Bion proposes,

> If the world of conscious thought is not suitable for playing 'Oedipus Rex', the 'universe of discourse' must be enlarged to include such plays. If serious psycho-analytic discussion cannot take place in the domain that Freud found adequate, it must be enlarged. In fact, Freud did enlarge it when he found that he could not believe what his experience with patients seemed to suggest— that they had been all assaulted sexually. He had to entertain the idea that events which had never taken place could have serious consequences. If I cannot 'believe', I cannot act or think. I need 'thoughts without a thinker'.
>
> (Ibid., p. 176)

How then are these unmetabolized elements, these undigested things-in-themselves, sensory elements, transformed into something that can be grasped? One answer is through relationship, through commerce with another mind that can contain the chaos they engender and its related terror. However, aspects of O will remain unknowable, although at moments thoughts can be apprehended at the moment that they develop.

In *Memoir*, Bion depicts his own transformation, as the group of characters, both the actual ones such as *Rosemary* and *Roland*, the creatures Stegosaurus and Tyrannosaurus and the fictitious ones ('This place is thick with fictitious characters,' ibid., p. 122) begin to cohere as a group and function as a container. The characters themselves transform, as *Myself* notes that 'the mental diet of entertaining fictitious characters has contributed greatly to his mental health' (ibid., p. 124). Further, transformation can only occur in the present, and the critical nature of the present, as both past and future are hidden from us, but are *'in fact,* as opposed to verbally and grammatically, not separable from the present.'

We see one example of this transformation as Bion's war experience is mentioned for the first time, in a poignant description of his experience of the loss of fear, the sweet smell of death, and the fact that 'Love had died, love for anyone and anything' (ibid., p. 150). His language has changed; the visual and sensual nature of the scene is clear, as well as the emotion, portraying for the first time in *Memoir* a scene capable of being visualized. Bion is able with the help of the group to begin to think,

> *The darkness deepens. The skull-crushing and sucking object is overwhelmed by depression at the failing supply of nutriment from the dead ♀ and the failure to restore it to life. He formulates in stone an arti-factual representation, easily seen by Plato to be a lying representation of, a substitute for, pro-creation, substitute for creation. The lying substitution is transformed into a prelude to action. This whirling, swirling chaos to infinite and formless darkness becomes luminous, and a Leonardo da Vinci robs the hair, the brooding waste of waters, of its formless chaos.*

(Ibid., p. 161)

The momentary clarity is followed by new confusions, not surprising, as glimpses into this other reality are brief, albeit profound in their implications and life-giving potential. Thought will always oscillate between more integrated understandings of objects and events and the fragmentation that must accompany any new learning.

The problem remains not just the awareness of a visual scene, but also how it relates to the body, to the emotions. Something must be felt as real, and what determines that is the vertex or perspective of observation. Thought, as Bion defines it, is ever changing, free from restraint. But as soon as it is given written or spoken expression, 'freedom of thought has been eroded. The freedom of communicated thought cannot at any time be absolute' (ibid., p. 170).

One possible answer for how to apprehend this other reality lies in the realm of the artistic.

> 'Articulate' communication is the dominant method of communication between the self and the self; insofar as communication takes place between what psycho-analysts call the 'unconscious' levels of different individuals. I think the prevalent methods of communication between painters, poets musicians conform to rules which are very different from those of 'articulate' communication.
>
> (Ibid., p. 208)

Although 'non artistic methods of communication are less accurate than those used by artists' (ibid., p. 110), many do not feel that they have the requisite skill to communicate as poets and artists. *The Dream* section will end with little resolution of the problem, with Bion asking which is more real, Leonardo da Vinci's drawings of hair or the creation of a hairdresser, the evocation of the underlying pattern that is capable of stimulating feeling or the actual hair. Bion will conclude that it depends on the vertex of observation. In addition, it is at least conceivably possible that the observation of mental events changes them, as Heisenberg suggested that observation alters the physical world. For these reasons, language remains a limited system. Yet, despite this, as *Alice* observes, *we* still talk, continuing to behave as though language was serviceable.

The Dream section introduces all of the elements and questions that will be reworked on 'higher' levels in the next two chapters. Bion seems humorously aware of the incomprehensibility of this section and creates a final, impatient character/commentator who admits he has not read the section but is simply looking this far ahead 'to see how it ends.' While these later sections are more comprehensible, *The Dream* section offers the closest look into the other reality by creating an experience of its apprehension in the reader, an invaluable contribution although not necessarily an always enjoyable one.

The past presented; the dawn of oblivion

The title of the second section continues to mirror the inclusion of paradox for which Bion searches in language. Does he mean that the past exists in the present or that the reader will be shown the determinants of prior events? What can pairing the dawn (the beginning) with oblivion (the end) mean? Destabilized, we are forced to create our own meanings. Both sections will alternate between 'sense' and a plunge back into non-sense; episodes that can be comprehended in our usual language are interrupted by a carnival of language, multivoiced dialogues, puns, and jokes. While *The Dream* section depicts the creation of thought, the next section presents interpersonal conflict; *The Dawn of Oblivion* will focus on internalized conflict, guilt, and responsibility. The most immediate shift in the second section is the introduction to time, as *Alice* awakes and immediately attempts to locate herself temporally as well as spatially. Along with this, the group of characters narrows. Dropped are those without any corporality, present or potential, as well as our dinosaur friends; now, the characters have relationships with each other, a history that can be traced, rather than behaving as kinetic molecules that form and re-form, randomly bumping into each other.

The next two sections are far easier; falling asleep reading, I dream of Clarisse's first visit to Hannibal Lecter in *The Silence of the Lambs*, a dangerous meeting, but one that awakens her to the possibilities of transformation. My reveries become more compassionate; I begin to fantasize writing '*Bion and I*,' a parallel to a Borges short story where Borges split into himself and his public persona observes that he can never be free of 'the other one' whose 'sound pages ... no longer belongs to any individual ... but rather to language itself, or to tradition. Beyond that, I am doomed—utterly and inevitably—to oblivion' (Borges, 1960, p. 324). I imagine Bion shrinking horrified from the adulation in which he is held, retreating to the private and magical world he tried to articulate, a source of great terror as well as the fount of his awesome creativity. How hard he struggled to break the barriers of language. By the end of *The Dawn of Oblivion*, I nearly burst out laughing when Bion said that he had failed completely at what he had set out to do—write a book of non-sense. There is no final resolution, no Valhalla at the end of any journey, just a new vertex from which to begin again.

From metapsychology to metafiction

The novel form

Bion has penned an amazing, at times infuriating and hateable, but ultimately exhilarating text, one that demands to be read at least more than once to assure even the slightest chance of understanding (or the false hope of understanding), a book that demands the fortitude and optimism of the analyst who chooses to work with more disturbed patients, patients who do not immediately form a recognizable transference. His book, chaotic and meandering, with its end turned round like a Moebius strip that brings us back to the beginning, stands in contrast to the standard psychoanalytic tome that will reach a clear conclusion after marshaling its arguments in near stultifying outline form.

The first question when confronted with *A Memoir of the Future* is why Bion chose to write a paper on psychoanalytic theory in the form of a novel, soon followed by the second: why this particular form of novel? One of the central problems *Memoir* addresses is the means through which other modes of thinking can be accessed, modes that are critical for our understanding of development, psychotic states, and the psychoanalytic process. Like Schulz, and other experimental writers both before and after him, Bion struggled to communicate the unrepresentable and ineffable, the *ding-an-sich* that can be felt, but not known, graspable only for moments through shadowy fragments, imperfect shards, 'won from the void and formless infinite' (Milton, quoted in *MF*, p. 180). One of these fragments is the very language with which we try to communicate, a paltry tool for understanding primitive elements of thought, as this articulate language was 'elaborated later for other purposes' (ibid., p. 229) and often functions as an opaque shield that precludes *entrée* into this other reality. Complicating the insuperable difficulty of articulation to the self is the further complexity of bridging the gap between two minds, inherent in the polysemic nature of language and the fact that any chosen word shuts out others vying to be heard, literally splitting off alternate coexisting meanings.

These problems necessitated Bion's choice of a novel format because it is only through the use of a multivoiced artificial structure that one can approach the 'real' of the affective contents that form the core of O. Conceptualized this way, the structure of *Memoir* perfectly matches Bion's intention, to use language in a 'precisely obscure' (ibid., p. 191) and ambiguous way to trigger associations and reactions in the reader that may allow a brief light to penetrate the darkness. Further, the dialogic structure of the novel creates an analogue to the process of containment.

Bion's choice of the novel format is best understood within the framework offered by Bahktin (1981a, 1934/1981b, 1986). One could make a number of interesting personal comparisons between Bahktin and Bion, their originality, their strangeness, their interest in dialogue, their tendency to circle back around to consider a question from numerous vantage points and think through problems in multiple texts, a penchant for expressing themselves using a variety of aliases. Despite the fact that Bahktin, a confirmed Marxist, did not share Bion's reverence for psychoanalysis and had, under the name Volosinev, published *Freudianism: A Marxist Critique*, they shared a conceptual framework, as both are deeply relational in their formulation of meaning. In their introduction to Bahktin's *Speech Genres and Other Late Essays*, the editor Michael Holquist notes,

> If there is something like a God concept in Bahktin, it is surely the superadressee, for without faith that we will be understood somehow, sometime by *somebody*, we would not speak at all. Or if we did, it would be babbling.
>
> (1986, p. xviii)

Bahktin posits the novel as the sole still developing literary genre 'that is as yet uncompleted' and still full of plastic possibilities. In contrast to the epic form, whose tradition bound heroes and plot are grounded in the past, the novel 'comes into contact with the spontaneity of the inconclusive present' (Bahktin 1981a, p. 27), where the end of the story has not already been told and is not known to the reader. Using Bion's terminology, the novel takes place fully in the present, the one tense that is capable of being experienced.

In addition to its relationship with the present, the other essential characteristic of the novel is its multi-languaged consciousness and its inherent heteroglossia because of its reliance on characters, each of whom has his or her own language expressed in dialogue, letters, and narration. In the novel,

> ... the plot itself is subordinated to the task of coordinating and exposing languages to each other. What is realized in the novel is the process of coming to know one's own language as it is perceived in someone else's language, coming to know ones own horizon within someone else's horizon. There takes place within the novel an ideological translation of another's language and an overcoming of its otherness.
>
> (Bahktin, 1981b, p. 365)

Although generated from a completely different ideological vantage point, the parallels to Bion's notion of containment are striking. Like Bion's group, the characters modify each other as they speak.

Bahktin associates the multiple languages of the novel with the end of sharply delineated national culture; in the novel, different dialects both will affect each other and shed light on each other. This allows for the development of new relationships between language and the real world. One could, of course, see the unconscious (as Lacan implies) as another language or as an immigrant culture, infiltrating and altering consciousness. These immigrant languages work against the centripetal forces that try to consolidate a language. Even without that perspective, one could easily see the affinity that Bion would find for a form in which multiple perspectives were central.

To Bahktin, the novel will always be a revolutionary and scrappy form that 'gets on poorly with other genres' (ibid., p. 5) and is both 'critical and self-critical' (Bahktin 1981a, p. 10). The novel exposes conventionality of the forms of other genres rather than harmonizing with them; instead, it transforms them by forcing an expansion of their boundaries. The other genres become

> more free and flexible, their language renews itself by incorporating extra-literary heteroglossia and the novelistic layers of literary language, they become dialogized, permeated with laughter, irony, humor, elements of self parody and finally, this is the most important thing, the novel inserts into these other genres

an indeterminacy a certain semantic open-endedness, a living contract with unfinished, still evolving contemporary reality (the open-ended present).

(Ibid., p. 7)

The progressive, radicalizing push of the novel by itself would support Bion's use of this format, as a force against the deadly ossification of the language of psychoanalytic papers, rote in their presentation. The dialogic stance is also inherent in his search for a language that can traverse the gap between the unmetabolized and the symbolized. What Bion will call articulate language Bahktin will discuss as a system of linguistic norms. These norms struggle to overcome the indeterminacy, the private constructions of language and attempt to centralize thought. In Bahktin's conception, this is a struggle over ideology, but it translates well into Bion's notions of a 'crust' that will obstruct entry into more primitive modes of thought or the pressure of the unconscious. Thus, the common language can become a constraining force. Both Bahktin and Bion had considerable respect for the vulgar languages of the street (the 'cuntish' language of Bion, the carnival of Bahktin) and their communicative powers.

The dialogic context is ever changing and unstable, never fixed but instead reaching back into the past and forward into the future. The forgotten past contextual meanings of an utterance may at any time be recalled and evolve again in a new context. Bahktin ends his last journal with the words, 'Nothing is absolutely dead: every meaning will have its homecoming festival' (Bahktin, 1986, p. 170).

The postmodern

A Memoir of the Future stands in contrast not only to the corpus of psychoanalytic literature, but also to the well-plotted modern novel where even when language takes experimental forms, the novel will represent a world that is historically conceivable. For example, we never doubt the presence of the actual Dublin in Joyce or the South in Faulkner (Butler, 2002). In contrast, in the postmodern novel *The Third Policeman* (O'Brien, 1967/1999), the hero finds himself in a hallucinatory world, a two-dimensional police station where people come to resemble or even fall in love with the bicycles they ride. In

'*The South*,' Borges (1944) realistically described a locale that turns out to be an imagined land where the hero lives out his ideal romantic death while he simultaneously lies dying in a sanatorium. In *Memoir*, creatures of every ilk, fictional and historical personages, prenatal and postnatal beings, and extinct animals exist simultaneously on an English farm.

While modernist fiction follows the recognizable prescriptions of the drive with its rising excitement, peak and denouement, postmodern novels, like *Memoir*, tend to ignore the conventions of plot, their structure only emerging after several readings that allow initially disparate fragments to cohere. The constructions possible from the given fragments are variable; interpretation demands active participation on the part of the reader.

Postmodernism can best be defined in pluralistic terms (Hassan, 1986), at times referring to sociocultural phenomenon specific to late-stage capitalism (Jameson, 1991) including an increased self-consciousness reflective of a changed experience of, and questioning about, traditional views of knowledge and truth (Lyotard, 1979), to an 'attitude' about a historical period from the 1960s to the present, to a theory related to and defined sometimes defined in opposition to modernism (Hassan, 1971), and sometimes as a literary or artistic manifestation. Lodge (1977) noted the formal properties of postmodernist fiction; these structural characteristics will be immediately recognizable to readers of *Memoir* and additionally bear a strong resemblance to the grammar of imagery provided by Freud's (1900) chapter 'The Dream Work.'

As in 'The Dream Work,' where 'and' replaces 'or' so that both alternatives in an either-or statement might be equally valid and negatives can coexist, contradiction will play a central role. Clauses may cancel each other out through reversal, as in Leonard Michael's statement that 'It is impossible to live with or without fictions' (Michaels 9, cited in Lodge, 1977). *Mist* (Unamuno, 1928) is built entirely on the dizzying logic of reversals. Permutation, a literary variant on the theme of negation, offers competing alternatives awaiting a reader's construction. Fowles (1969) offers three possible endings for *The French Lieutenant's Woman*; in Hopscotch, Cortazar (1966) proposes alternate orders in which to read the chapters; perhaps the most radical example is *Tlön, Uqbar, Orbis Tertius*, an imaginary world where 'Works of fiction contain a single plot, with all its imaginable permutations' (Borges, 1941). Bion's concept of vertices offers a similar refusal to choose a singular interpretation of reality.

Similar to Bion, postmodern fiction rejects the idea of a stable temporal order; everything takes place in a ubiquitous present. Eras collapse into one another; shifts in the representation of historical time allow past events to be incorporated into present action. Thus, a novel about the atomic bomb can be written in the language of Mallory (Barthelme, 1990) and superimposed on the tale of the Knights of the Round Table; in Barnes' (1990) fragmented and unrelated collection of episodes, *A History of the World in 10 ½ Chapters,* the woodlouse narrator telling his experience of stowing away on Noah's Arc clearly knows just how the world turned out.

Ideas need not be presented in any logical order. A collage of unrelated, seemingly irrelevant facts can follow one another in the text; at times, the sound of the text will be as important as the words.

> Nothing is not a nightshirt or a ninny-hammer, ninety two or Nineveh. It is not a small jungle in which near a river a stone table has been covered with fruit. It is not the handsome Indian woman standing next to the stone table holding the blond kidnapped child. Neither is it the proposition *Esse est percipi*, nor any of the refutations of that proposition.
>
> (Barthelme, 1993, p. 245)

Both condensation and its opposite, fragmentation, are central to the creation of characters. As one of Barthelme's narrator's states 'fragments are the only forms I trust.' Nabokov's last work *The Original of Laura* is printed with removable index cards in Nabokov's hand in case the reader wishes to rearrange the fragments themselves. Multiple characters can be used to represent a single figure in a manner similar to Bion's use of *Bion, Myself, P.A.* and *Captain Bion* as multiple self-representations and *Priest* and *Paul* as object representations.

Coherence only becomes possible (if at all) through multiple readings when thematic continuity is literally constructed by the reader, who, because of the text's purposeful ambiguity, takes a more active role as a co-creator. As important as the content is the induced disorienting effect as, for example, in Robbe-Grillet's *The Voyeur* when the reader, following the protagonist's detailed observations, suddenly becomes aware that he or she is in the mind of a madman. All of this destabilizes the position of the reader, so that he or she is forced to participate in an experience (of confusion, irritation, boredom, terror) rather than observe it. It is equally disorienting when characters step out of role with metafictional asides to readers or comment on their own process. For example, Augusto, the protagonist of Unamuno's *Mist,* goes to his author to protest the decision that he will be made to commit suicide. Arguing for the reality of his existence now that he has become able to feel through a fictional love affair, Augusto turns the tables on his author. Like Mycroft and Sherlock to Bion, Augusto will assert his superiority over his creator.

> Look here, Don Miguel, it is quite possible that you may be a creature out of fiction … it may be that you are the mere vehicle or pretext for my story and other stories like mine … And when you are dead, it will be we, your creatures, who keep your soul alive.
>
> (Unamuno, 1928, p. 263)

Because the boundaries between fiction and the world blur, the reality of the world is called into question. The novel will constitute its own sovereign verbal universe, while reality begins ever more to appear like a fictional world.

By this point, the parallels between aspects of O and the structure of the postmodern novel, namely its collapse of temporal specificity, its lack of a sensible order, its elevation of the use of form to evoke an emotional effect rather than content, and its playfulness with language, should be obvious. However, in addition to sharing these structural and semantic characteristics, *Memoir* shares what Barthes (1975) sees as its subversive intent, namely to induce a crisis with the reader's relationship with language and reality. The playfulness with language has a multiple function—to induce an emotion, be it boredom, terror or amusement, but also to make the reader more aware of the limitations of language; the conjunction of alternate meanings forces one to question the meaning of a word, bringing to the forefront the falsity of language and its capacity for dissemination. The purpose is the very antithesis of jargon—each word now confronts one almost as a stranger.

Barth (1967) in his seminal essay refers to postmodern writing as '[t]he literature of exhaustion ... the used-upness of certain forms or exhaustion of certain possibilities' (p. 29). One could easily draw a parallel to the 'used-upedness' of our ossified psychoanalytic concepts, not just the problem of the jargon-y use of terms, but that of the theory itself having become stultified. Fascinating in the individual case, the abstractions have ceased to be a living language. Thus, Bion's choice of linguistic form mirrors his intent—to move us away from our preformulated answers.

Approaching transcendence

> Postmodernism may be a response, direct or oblique, to the Unimaginable which Modernism glimpsed only in its most prophetic moments ... We are, I believe, inhabitants of another Time and another Space ... the best of them [postmodern artists] brilliantly display the resources of the void ... Yet moving into the void, these sometimes also pass to the other side of silence, and discover the sacrament of plenum.
>
> (Hassan, 1971, pp. 22–23)

Beyond their structural and stylistic similarities, both *Memoir* and postmodern fiction reflect a longing for the sacrament of plenum and contain a search for, and tentative efforts to traverse, a pathway to an ineffable reality prior to the development of an articulate and sensible language. The conception of the beyond in both is quasi-religious, a search for a transcendence. This spiritual vision constitutes the essential difference between Bion's vision of O and the Freudian unconscious.

For postmodern writers, the search for another reality is almost ubiquitous. It can be found in Ozick's (1971) 'The Pagan Rabbi' where a devout scholar of the Mishna commits suicide after falling in love with a dryad whose voice was a 'diffuse cloud of field fragrances,' whose meaning he understood with 'an immediacy of glee.' A similar quest is found in Borges' (1949a) 'The Aleph,' where in an ordinary basement could be found a 'point in space that contains all points ... the place where, without admixture or confusion, all the places of the world, seen from every angle, coexist' (p. 281). In 'Sanatorium under the Sign of the Hourglass,' Schulz's character searches for his deceased father in a sanatorium where 'time has been turned back' and the dead may be encountered in a liminal world to which sleep offers partial entry. Despite his wish to be with his father, the hero begins to fear being trapped in madness. He escapes, but never fully, remaining forever on the train that brought him, a marginal character. All three stories, although quite disparate in topic, are marked both by longing for another reality simultaneous with an awareness of both its elusive nature and potential danger. It can be touched intermittently, intrude in dreams, but never completely known; at the same time, it is never completely absent but remains an originary source of our actions. Language is limited in its capacity to express this experience. Borges, not unlike Bion, will suffer the writer's despair of trying to communicate in language the infinite Aleph, whose 'enumeration, even its partial enumeration ... is irresolvable' (Borges, 1949a, p. 281), an event whose multitudinous components happened simultaneously but had to be described as if they were successive.

Ultimately, the quest for both Bion and the writers to whom we have compared him is a mystical one to the extent that mysticism is distinguished from other religious forms because of the centrality of an intense, immediate, and urgent awareness of a living relationship with God. This 'tasting and seeing' of God provides a privileged knowledge that can only be acquired through felt experience as opposed to scholarly contemplation (Scholem, 1946). As mysticism arises only after a monistic conception of man and nature has been superseded by an awareness of the gap between Man and God, its presence serves as manifest evidence of the void.

> Mysticism does not deny or overlook the abyss, on the contrary it begins by realizing its existence, but from there it proceeds to a quest for the secret that will close it, the hidden path that will span it. It strives to piece together the fragments broken by the religious cataclysm, to bring back the old unity which religion has destroyed ...
>
> (Ibid., p. 8)

This caesura can only be traversed by way of the aforementioned, deeply felt, though difficult to communicate, experience. The traversing of the various breaks, between prenatal and postnatal lives, between the primitive minds of animals and humans, between that which seems unthinkable and that which can be articulated, between sleep and waking, between one mind and another, is similarly a central focus of *Memoir*. The personal relationship to God comes through a kind of self-knowledge, which exists potentially in every man, in toto, in the present tense. Essentially timeless, it contains in one moment all past religious events; Christ eternally on the Cross; the sands of the desert forever beneath the feet of the wandering Jew. Like O, the mystical realm may intrude into the world as we know it, but is not usually an object of consciousness and not unlike the quandary Bion faces in his effort to communicate the nature of O, the mystic finds it difficult to give linguistic expression to his or her contact with the divine, a private event that 'by its very nature is related to a sphere where speech and expression are excluded' (ibid., pp. 14–15).

> For it must be said that this act of personal experience, the systematic investigation and interpretation of which forms the task of all mystical speculation is of a highly contradictory and even paradoxical nature. Certainly this is true of all attempts to describe it in words and perhaps where there are no longer words of the act itself. What kind of direct relation can there be between the Creator and His creature, between the finite and the infinite; and how can words express an experience for which there is no adequate simile in this finite world of man ... It will be wiser to assume ... that the religious world of the mystic can be expressed in terms applicable to rational knowledge only with the help of paradox.
>
> (Ibid., pp. 4–5)

In *Memoir,* the *P.A.* (psychoanalyst) character's dialogues with the *Priest* (whom he seems to identify as a fellow seeker of truth and as someone who understands the difficulty in attempting to express an essential experience) highlight the parallels that can be drawn between the spiritual experience and the ineffable O. While Bion is relentless in his dismissal of religion, he is unable to reject the idea of the Godhead. Further, the experience of knowing God is described in similar terms as the experience of knowing the psyche, knowing the tiger as opposed to merely observing its stripes. One can 'talk about' either, but a distinction exists between talk 'about something' and the something itself, the 'thing-in-itself, the ultimate reality, the noumenon we can never know' (*MF,* p. 305). Touching the noumenon is akin to a mystical experience of an ultimate reality.

Why Bion? Why now?

Written in the late 1970s, *A Memoir of the Future* enjoyed a mixed, and at times hostile, reception. Why is there then, such a resuscitation of interest in Bion and in *Memoir* in particular? Here, some of the more theoretical sociocultural writings on postmodernism may be helpful. Jameson (1988) writes that our machines, for example the computer, are no longer machines of production, but of reproduction, and have the capacity to transcend the mimetic versions of reproduction more tied to earlier art forms. Baudrilliard (1994) notes the superiority of the representation over the real in a society where the ubiquity of simulation dissolves 'the difference between true and false and real and imaginary' (p. 3). These societal conditions inevitably alter the delicate balance that supports the ego's autonomy both from the environment and from an influx of internal stimulation, further fragmenting any sense of cohesion (Rapaport, 1951; 1958). It is a situation that calls out for containment, one source of which is found in mysticism. Jameson (1988, p. 37) notes that postmodern texts 'tap the networks of the reproductive process and thereby afford us some glimpse into a postmodern or technological sublime.' Bion taps into a similar longing for something beyond; he allows us to once more believe in something beyond ourselves.

Bion's O differs from the unconscious, as defined by Freud, as O is not organized around notions of pleasure and unpleasure, which Bion saw as tied to bodily experiences requiring a rudimentary self. Bion placed less stress on dynamically repressed content than on the significance of the unconscious as a cradle of thought. Its unknowable quality emanated not only from the inadequacy of our language, but also from the limiting structures of time and space within which our current thinking apparatus functions. If postmodern writers made transcendent reality a 'place' outside the self, Bion has articulated a transcendent reality within, one that may speak to dilemmas of our time and the longing for relationship and containment, an imaginary construction that is somewhat absent in Freud, who admits that the 'sensation of "eternity," a feeling as of something limitless, unbounded—as it were, "oceanic"' (1930, p. 64) was not one that he had ever experienced. Poignantly, Bion will end his effort on a note of failure; his hope of writing a book unspoiled by common sense and reason dashed, and by implication unable to fully enter this other reality as he was unable to cleanse his language of the ghosts of sanity.

Postscript

My reading of *Memoir* did not provide many answers, or even a true thesis, merely bringing together a few literatures, which ended up illuminating each other. However, linking these works allowed me *entrée* into a difficult and confusing text and taught me a great deal about method, the essential nature of reverie, the need to tolerate not knowing, and the workings of intuition. It was necessary to imagine Bion before he could be comprehended, necessary to enter the world of the other before thinking about it. For this reason alone, *Memoir* must be seen as an invaluable text. A theoretical paper, no matter how detailed, could not provide a 'living' experience of these concepts. Bion's greatest contribution is a way of being with patients that is not inundated by the classical rules and prescriptions about what to listen for or how. If I could not quote aspects of Bion's theory, I ended up feeling that I understood it; if I did not know, I might still believe.

   Returning to the postmodern texts that I had loved, I was able to see them differently; beyond their self-reflective and ironic stance, one could hear the pathos and sadness beneath the fragmented texts of Barthelme, the longing for existence in Unamuno's characters (and ourselves), the centrality of mourning in the pornographic altered reality of Schulz. In the end, like *Memoir*, my paper came back to the beginning—to Schulz's search for 'The Authentic,' which ends on a note that might well describe Bion's quest. Able to find no more than fragments of the cherished text, the author notes,

   And yet, in a certain sense, the fullness is contained wholly and integrally in each of its crippled and fragmentary incarnations. This is the phenomenon of imagination and various being. An event may be small and insignificant in its origin and yet, when drawn close to one's eye, it may open in its centre an infinite and radiant perspective because a higher order of being is trying to express itself in it and irradiates it violently ... We shall recreate piece by piece what is one and indivisible – the great era, the Age of Genius of our life.

(Schulz, 1937, p. 14)

Note

1 Characters' names in *Memoir* are written in italics, to differentiate them from their external counterparts.

Chapter 2

'Psycho-analysis, I believe' in Wonderland

Reading and literature in *A Memoir of the Future*

Sara Boffito

A memoir, an enigma

Q   *Can you give me an idea what this is about?*
A   *Psycho-analysis, I believe.*
Q   *Are you sure? It looks like a queer affair.*
A   *It is a queer affair–like psycho-analysis. You'd have to read it.*

(*MF*, p. 2)

From whatever perspective it is approached, Bion's *Memoir* trilogy comes across as something of an enigma. Those who have attempted to parse its riddles vary greatly in their definitions of the work, their explanations sometimes alarmingly different: after discussing the psychoanalytical elements contained in *Memoir*, in his preface to the Italian edition in the first of the three books, Francesco Corrao deems it to be 'also a dramaturgical text' (1993, p. xiv); while in her preface to the Italian edition of *The Past Presented*, Anna Baruzzi specifies that the text should be 'considered a psychoanalytical work' written 'in an unusual style,' at once 'a stage play, a novel of manners, and a science-fiction novel, dotted with dialogues, monologues, poetical passages, and scientific discourse'; she sees it moreover as a work that defies borders, belonging to that 'experimentalism that closes one era and opens another' (1998, pp. xi–xiii). In her essay entitled '"Underlying pattern" in Bion's *Memoir of the Future*' (1983) and in her book *Bion's Dream* (2010), Meg Harris Williams explores the trilogy from a purely literary angle, considering it to be a pioneering work in which the author's self-analysis and inner autobiography overlap with the creation of a new genre of expression of the Self, namely 'a reverie *now*'. By this, Harris Williams claims that

Bion's *Memoir* is a dream autobiography, as it were, to be set alongside the author's 'official' autobiographies – *The Long Week-End* (Bion, 1982) and *All My Sins Remembered* (Bion, 1985).

Meanwhile, in his review of Harris Williams's book, James Grotstein notes his agreement with her conviction and adds that these two autobiographies and *Memoir* together constitute 'not simply a myth but an *epic*, not unlike the *Iliad, Odyssey* and *Aeneid*'; through these five texts, claims Grotstein, Bion teaches us that 'to the extent that dreaming imparts ever-evolving meanings to the emotional experiences of our lives, the more these experiences become mythic-epic narratives that unite, integrate, contain, and transcend each living moment they process' (2011, p. 467).

These, then, are just some of the attempts to pin down the genre of *Memoir*, as proposed by various authoritative (and fond) readers of Bion's works. From this array of such highly diverging impressions, it becomes clear that the text eludes classification and shuns all labels. That said, it comes as a consolation to learn that this was the express wish of Bion himself, as evidenced by the declaration he penned to close the last book of the trilogy:

> All my life I have been imprisoned, frustrated, dogged by common sense, reason, memories, desires and – greatest bug-bear of all – understanding and being understood. This is an attempt to express my rebellion, to say 'Good-bye' to all that. It is my wish, I now realise doomed to failure, to write a book unspoiled by any tincture of common-sense, reason, etc. (see above). So although I would write, 'Abandon Hope all ye who expect to find any facts – scientific, aesthetic or religious – in this book', I cannot claim to have succeeded ... However successful my attempt, there would always be the risk that the book 'became' acceptable, respectable, honoured and unread. 'Why write then?' you may ask. To prevent someone who KNOWS from filling the empty space – but I fear I am being 'reasonable', that great Ape. Wishing you all a Happy Lunacy and a Relativistic Fission ...
>
> (*MF*, p. 578)

I believe that, ultimately, the *A Memoir of the Future* is a conflation of these various definitions, all of them covering some aspects, but none quite achieving a proper match.

What is often forgotten – and which can elude the Italian reader – is that the title itself defines the work's literary genre: instead of calling his trilogy *Memory of the Future*, Bion has chosen to call it *A Memoir*. The word used for the Italian translation, *memoria*, is more ambiguous and omits the distinction. In English, the title alerts the reader as to what is to come – a *memoir* – that is, an account of personal recollections. If we investigate what exactly a memoir is as a literary genre, the paradox merely gets deeper. For instance, G. Thomas Couser has devoted several publications to defining the genre, starting with his *Memoir: An Introduction* (2011), in which he expounds on the differences between novel and autobiography, identifying one of the distinctive traits of the memoir as a 'commitment to the real', and adds that such a genre indicates the fundamental human activity of narrating our life story on its own terms.

Just what constitutes reality and truth, and what might right be considered 'facts', is one of the chief arguments that underpin the dialogues between the characters of *Memoir* and involve the reader so deeply. It may seem paradoxical, but I reckon we can surmise that Bion wrote these books for reasons akin to this 'commitment to the real', even if the reality to which he felt committed is neither historical nor material but mental reality, emotional truth, and the 'facts' and 'actual events' under discussion are far more complex than those that may be observed with one's eyes. Bion is faithful to this mental reality, and rigorously so: for this reason he abandoned logic, memory and desire, and in these three volumes gave voice to the multicoloured variety of characters harboured in his Self, a panoply of individuals ranging from the highly evolved to the ordinary, the transgressive to the mystical, and even the more primitive, the rejects and outcasts.

A proper mental diet

The narrative style matches the challenge of this commitment, multiplying itself in the infinite nuances of mental reality; the language follows suit, with its wealth of neologisms and quirky invented terms.

The language and style offer another salient feature of the dialogues between the various characters of *Memoir*. Keenly aware of the lurking 'Satanic Jargonieur', Bion took great pains to avoid its pitfalls [the pitfalls of psychobabble], and to my mind *Memoir* is Bion's utmost exertion in this direction, a means to narrate his inner life in terms most suited to his disposition, to speak with his own voice – or better, with his own *voices*.

In the second book the character known as *P.A.*, that is the Psycho-Analyst (who frequently expresses the view of the author/Bion himself), declares this war on jargon as the reason for his recourse to fiction:

P.A: I am no poet, but I succumbed to the temptation to compose a patriotic anthem, almost a New World symphony, using the theme – 'borrowed' of course without acknowledgement – 'My Mind to Me A Kingdom Is.'

ROLAND: How very apposite. Just right for the psycho-analyst!

P.A: Alas, no.

ROLAND & ROBIN: Really? How was that?

P.A: His Satanic Jargonier took offence; on some pretence that psycho-analytic jargon was being eroded by eruptions of clarity. I was compelled to seek asylum in fiction. Disguised as fiction, the truth occasionally slipped through.

(*MF*, p. 302)

Reading this passage, I recalled the poetic words that Thomas H. Ogden devoted to the role of the voice in psychoanalysis: in the third chapter of his *Conversations at the Frontier of Dreaming* (2001), Ogden explains the difficulty of speaking with one's own voice, a voice that, while changing according to the context and listener, remains individual and unique. This uniqueness and individuality is by no means easy to achieve, and at times helping the analysand to speak with his/her own voice can be the outcome of the analysis. When rereading those pages with Bion's work in mind I found myself thinking that Ogden's *Conversations* offer such an apt description of the contents of Bion's *Memoir* that it is surprising that the trilogy is nowhere mentioned in Ogden's essay or in his other main works. Yet so often while reading *Memoir*, this author came to mind, not only because Ogden is certainly one of the most brilliant contemporary analysts to have creatively developed Bion's ideas, but also because he is the most literary.

In his recent book on creative reading, Ogden himself demonstrates how a text can provide a starting point from which each reader draws his/her personal baggage of meanings and ideas. While this is true for any book, the fecund ambiguities inherent to *A Memoir of the Future* and its dialogic – and elusive – style allow ample margin for an exponential multiplication of meanings and readings. What I am inquiring into with regard to the trilogy and its author is the rapport between art or literature and psychoanalysis, a rapport central to the very nature of *Memoir* but also to its contents. Because, while it is true that Bion's trilogy may be termed a literary/artistic work of psychoanalysis, it is nonetheless clear that the model of rapport between analysis and art on which it hinges (or defines) is not the classic retrospective historical study or interpretation of the events involving the narrative's characters according to psychoanalytical theory – that is, the 'application' of analysis to literature. What happens here is effectively the opposite: literature is being applied to psychoanalysis. As we have seen, here psychoanalysis 'finds refuge'; the power of literary fiction defends it from the pitfalls of jargon and allows truth to establish a foothold.

In his trilogy, Bion presents himself to the reader as being a reader himself, a literary omnivore with a vast appetite, devouring the likes of Shakespeare and Blake, Joyce and Pound, Milton and Wordsworth, Keats, Shelley and Browning, Tennyson and Hopkins, Rimbaud and Conan Doyle, and not least Lewis Carroll.

For Bion, it is vital that reading and literature form part of our daily 'mental diet'. The characters and goings-on in the novels we love come to inhabit our interior world, and for Bion, they are therefore vividly 'real' elements in our mental makeup. Thus, his *A Memoir of the Future* is populated with characters from his favourite works of fiction, who dialogue and interact with 'Myself', Bion's alter ego, P.A., and with the other players featured in the work, such as Alice, Rosemary, Roland, Robin, and so on.

Bion and Myself engage in a series of conversations that are at once witty and serious with such fictional figures as Sherlock Holmes, Watson, and Mycroft, debating on their nature, whether they are real or not, but also speculating on their usefulness in aiding the reader's mental health:

BION: But, my good man, are you not aware that you are entirely fictitious characters? I am a qualified doctor! ...

(MF, p. 91)

WATSON: (*contains his mirth with difficulty, but manages to be civil*) Excuse me, sire, but I must admit that I have never heard of your existence. I do not want to hurt your feelings or to appear to boast, but although Mycroft has always been of a retiring disposition, Sherlock, and to a lesser extent myself, has a world-wide following.

You yourself were admitting that there are imaginary characters who are infinitely better known than countless generations of non-entities. Now excuse me. I am a very busy man – allow me to suggest that you get on that couch there and sleep it off quietly …

(Ibid., pp. 91–92)

MYCROFT: I think you are 'murdering' it if I want to emphasis *your* crime. Just because I shall still be entertaining long after you have disappeared, you have no hesitation in calling Sherlock and Watson and me imaginary characters and claiming a superior status for yourself and your bloody books.

MYSELF: Oh no, I don't. Excuse me; but you have got me mixed up with Bion; and what about the blood you have just detected on my books?

MYCROFT: Don't you acknowledge any responsibility for your books? Or do you disclaim your brain children? …

(Ibid., pp. 123–124)

MYSELF: I should have thought that during the course of your sojourn in my mind – if that's where it and you have been – you would have become transformed from a relatively minor, fictitious character into a somewhat major part of your more useful characteristics. If there were such a thing as a mental digestive system, I could say that the mental diet of entertaining fictitious characters has contributed greatly to my mental health.

(Ibid., p. 124)

But our mental health does not rely solely on entertainment; we *enjoy* art because it moves us; it makes us feel in unison and thereby transforms us. As Bion notes, if the performance of a play by Shakespeare is 'an experience which is emotionally stirring; it effects a change – In Wilfred R. Bion – that is durable' (*MF*, p. 87). In the closing pages of the *Dawn of Oblivion*, the character P.A. relates a dire period of self-questioning that was catastrophic for his professional career: he was no longer confident about the interpretations he had made until then, and now seriously doubted his judgement. At this point, he turned to literature, which turned out to be his salvation:

it was as if, literally as metaphorically, light began to grow, night was replaced by dawn. I was aware, with a new comprehension, of

the passage of Milton's invocation to light at the commencement
of the Third Book of Paradise Lost.

(Ibid., p. 560)

Darkness and fiction

One can surmise that the crisis related by Bion's character P.A. is the
one he himself traversed in the early 1970s and which prompted him
to leave London and move to Los Angeles. This is the period in which
traces of mysticism begin to creep into Bion's writings and he starts
talking of O, 'the unknown, unknowable, "formless infinite"', of the
kind that had never cropped up in writings on psychoanalysis before
then. This part of his output is usually referred to as 'late Bion'; it
begins with *Attention and Interpretation* (1970) and culminates with
A Memoir of the Future. The creative instance of the trilogy therefore coincides with the author's existential impasse, and we might see
this output as an attempt to articulate this state, to relate and reason
it through. As such, these writings offer a kind of salvific outlet for
Bion, a subjective and personal purpose, as with all narratives.

Regarding the clinical and theoretical utility of the said Late Bion
works, there is still much debate. In 2011, the *International Journal of
Psychoanalysis* devoted an ample section to the ongoing controversy,
which arose in response to the noted article by Edna O'Shaughnessy,
'Whose Bion?' (2005). The author claims the theoretical continuation
of the work of Melanie Klein by Bion's early writings and refers to
them as the only ones having scientific validity. To her mind, Bion
is not the 'revolutionary genius' touted by those who lay such store
in his writings (Ferro, 2005; Tabak de Biankedi, 2005; Symington
and Symington, 1996; Eigen, 1998; Grotstein, 1981a; Vermote, 2011),
but one who fell prey to the lure of the paradox and lost sight of the
boundaries by making 'the texts too open, too pro- and e-vocative,
and weakened by riddling meanings' (O'Shaughnessy, 2005, p. 1525).

Bion found himself at odds with the orthodox Klein set in London,
who shrank from the novelties of his own writings, which can be
grasped only if read or heard with other eyes and ears. The cast of
The Past Presented converses about music and the instruments the
enable us to hear it.

Certainly, to digest Bion's later works, in order to grasp the music
beyond the noise one must yield to the allure of the paradoxes, savour

the richness of the text, and ignore the weaknesses of the said 'riddled meanings'. In any event, this is what the author intended: to be 'deliberately' and 'precisely' obscure (*MF*, p. 189). For Bion, therefore, ambiguity is a goal, a mission. It almost seems that he devotes himself to seeking ambiguity with the same passionate dedication as he uses in his quest for truth or that they stand for the same thing. As noted by Civitarese (2011, p. 36), Bion picks his terms according to their 'quotient of ambiguity':

> most of Bion's concepts can be ordered in terms of a light/dark binary, or of insight/blindness. Take for instance his notions of 'reverse perspective', 'vertex', or 'binocular vision'; his idea of truth as *phós* (Gk., light), and the darkness as a negative force; the unsaturated mind; preconception; the invisibility of total or transcendental reality. The same words Bion uses might equally apply to a sceptic's frantic fumbling: conjecture, hypothesis, speculative imagination, uncertainty, supposition, doubt, wandering/roaming/rambling, and so on.

Because, it is only through blinding oneself with a 'beam of intense darkness' (Grotstein, 2007) that one can get closer to 'O'; the truth may be reached only through falsification.

For Bion, the quest for truth is also an ethical imperative, perhaps the only moral aspect on which he clearly pronounces himself. In this, he presupposes a certain fellowship with his reader, which he declares outspokenly in a note in *The Past Presented*, whereby Alice, Rosemary, Roland, Robin, and P.A. discuss truth, lies, science, and art; in a note, Bion inserts,

> Artistic: Whether a scientist, a painter, composer, the person to whom this book is addressed is assumed to be driven by an urge to the truth. I cannot conceive of a drive to untruth as being separable from what is evil.
>
> (*MF*, p. 586)

If, as mentioned above, literary fiction 'filters' the truth, enabling it to come to the surface, *A Memoir of the Future* is the work of Bion's that is most pellucidly dedicated to the quest for truth, because it is openly declared to be 'fiction'. It is when truth is deemed absolute that it becomes dangerous – and this often occurs in analysis, Bion warns:

P.A: Allow me to conduct you round the cages of my psycho-analytic zoo. Of course the names are somewhat forbidding, but the creatures themselves are beautiful and ugly. Ah! Here is Absolute Truth – a most ferocious animal which has killed more innocent white lies and black wholes than you would think possible.
ROLAND: You muddle it with your puns.
ROBIN: Call it paronomasia – more scientific.
ALICE: It sounds like a very attractive flower.
P.A: Only a flower of speech.

(Ibid., p. 239)

The truth Bion cleaves to and searches with such exacting commitment is the opposite to this 'ferocious animal' inhabiting his 'psychoanalytic zoo': the emotional and personal truth is a 'truth of fiction' that sits more comfortably in narrative than in psychoanalytical theory. The conversion to fiction, Grotstein avers, is a step both requisite and fundamental to the individual: 'The "true thinker" must seek the truth, though in vain, only being able to approach it obliquely or tangentially because of its "blinding glare"' (2007, p. 149). Such 'well-wishing falsehoods' are those that govern our dreaming and primary processes. To dream reality, to digest it, entails making it personal and emotive, incarnate. 'Thinking is bearable because of its sensuous component' (*MF*, p. 160), affirms wisely the Man in his dialogue with Bion. Passion, it turns out, is a fundamental element for keeping thinking alive, but to do this another mind is needed:

BION: Most people experience mental death if they live long enough. You don't have to live long to have that experience – all you have to do is to be mentally alive.
ALICE: … You have to have a partner for one thing – even in opposition.

(Ibid., pp. 178–179)

The dramatic/dialogic structure of *A Memoir of the Future* not only showcases the sheer mental vitality of Bion but also reveals his urge to find 'a partner, even an opponent' to appeal to, another person to assist him in his thinking, because only thus can the mental life truly come alive. This putative partner may be the reader, even, who may detect through the discourse a living interlocutor (or better, several) capable of helping him or her think.

While on the one hand it is vital that readers who decide to immerse themselves in these texts must in some way be attracted to the same siren's call, the same appetite for ambiguity that spurred the author, on the other hand the problem of deciphering the texts remains for all: Bion manages to be now playful, stimulating, and gladly irreverent, but also abstruse, unfathomable, and exasperating. So, one might ask, how should Bion be read? Fortunately, an attempt to answer this question has been made by Thomas H. Ogden, whose own writing is contrastingly of great natural clarity and ease of style. In his article entitled 'An introduction to the reading of Bion' (2004), Ogden describes Bion's *Learning from Experience* (1962a) as following along the lines of *Alice in Wonderland* and then proceeds to the later works, observing that the reader needs to be armed with all his negative capability, to be open-minded and welcome whatever emerges, ready for the unexpected, not rush to interpret the text, but instead wait as the 'actual events' manifest themselves in the text. In *Attention and Interpretation* Bion compares his reader to the psychoanalyst:

> the reader must disregard what I say until the O of the experience of reading has evolved to a point where the actual events of reading issue in his interpretation of the experiences. Too great a regard for what I have written obstructs the process I represent by the terms 'he becomes the O that is common to himself and myself'.
>
> (1970, p. 28)

Curiously, once again Ogden does not include *A Memoir of the Future* in his essay on reading Bion, yet his advice seems to me particularly apt for approaching these texts.

Exit to α

To my mind, Meg Harris Williams's definition of Bion's texts as 'a reverie *now*' is strikingly appropriate because it comprises all the actors employed in the experience of reading. As we said, the three books have a dream-like quality, written in the language of dreams, and the author's capacity of reverie is what he has created through maieutics and is a unique substance. To my mind, in *Memoir* Bion has gone further: it seems to me that these books offer their reverie to the reader, easing him through any aesthetic conflict arising from the experience of reading [them]. All three books both seduce and alarm the reader with their impenetrable and unnerving style that eschews mollifying the reader with the weapons of rational knowledge or common sense.

Like the child that delights in the body of its mother, the reader of *Memoir* also has a 'dubious experience' and can be compared to someone who has 'come into a strange country where he knows neither the language nor the customary non-verbal cues and communications' (Meltzer and Harris Williams, 1989, p. 41). In order to break out of this dubious experience, he must meet the gaze of its mother who absorbs and transforms its anxiety and supplies the child with other indicators for facing the unknown experience without rushing to make it known too soon; someone who supplies the child with its alpha function so that it can develop a 'function of creative imagination': she is the partner necessary for becoming 'mentally alive', as Alice observes. It is true that often enough one loses one's way in these texts, but Bion does not leave his reader alone: he supplies (albeit sometimes hidden) clues and indications that provide the reader with bearings for navigating the unknown world. By this, I mean the nearly constant presence of a figure among the various viewpoints put forward by the speakers who voice scepticism and appeal to common sense, or doubts, or the fragility of the characters, with whom it is easy to identify, but also to the notes and scattered 'stage directions' inserted in brackets, as with a play script.

What is most striking, however, is the appearance in such a complex text of notes that offer extremely concise and precise definitions of concepts that are otherwise barely decipherable, whose explanation elsewhere might occupy considerable space in his theoretical writings. The notes introduce a viewpoint that might be considered 'external' to the dialogues underway and help the reader find his bearings and offer the occasional summary. Take, for instance, the concept of the 'beta element' described so directly in one such note: 'Beta Element: as a convenient method of referring to something which may exist;

not a thought, but that might become what thinkers would describe as a thought, e.g. if a dog comes when it is called' (*MF*, ch. 3, p. 14).

Among the 'stage directions' he uses, one in particular that comes to mind the way Bion closes the monologue of Myself (ibid., ch. 13, p. 57), who, after getting ensnared in a tangle of ideas on the power of the mind and its revelations, decides to turn in: 'Time to I went to sleep. Excuse me ... (*Exit to α*)' (ibid., p. 59). It is almost as if Bion is asking the reader for help proceeding in the said direction, towards this α: 'something which is not, and is not like, but is becoming', as he defines in a note when the character Alpha looms into view.

Certainly, while such directions usher the reader along a somewhat tortuous and inaccessible trail that is barred to anyone expecting straightforward answers or a well-beaten track, the same route offers new panoramas and revelations to those willing to apply their patience: 'Exit to α' sounds like the kind of direction Carroll's young Alice might come across on the way through Wonderland, like when she encounters the Cheshire Cat:

> "Would you tell me, please, which way I ought to go from here?"
> "That depends a good deal on where you want to get to," said the Cat.
> "I don't much care where—" said Alice.
> "Then it doesn't matter which way you go," said the Cat.
> "... so long as I get *somewhere*," Alice added as an explanation.
> "Oh, you're sure to do that," said the Cat, "if you only walk long enough."
>
> (Carroll, *Alice's Adventures in Wonderland*, ch. VI, p. 75)

Another tool Bion adopts to provide bearings for his reader throughout the trilogy is the hyperbolic use of quotations, by means of which the author sets his reader in the glad company of many a popular figure, creating an oasis of familiarity as it were, making the reader feel at home and free to roam among the many beloved characters he has conjured up, and offering comfort even in this 'back-to-front world' of his.

I wish to end these reflections by taking Bion's lead in evoking a beloved author, whose verses seem to me to echo in the pages of

A Memoir of the Future. After ploughing my way through Bion's lyrical adventure, I like to imagine Bion the clinician as an analyst with a bent for fiction, a figure of that kind that W.H. Auden evokes in these verses:

The novelist

Encased in talent like a uniform,
The rank of every poet is well known;
They can amaze us like a thunderstorm,
Or die so young, or live for years alone.
They can dash forward like hussars: but he
Must struggle out of his boyish gift and learn
How to be plain and awkward, how to be
One after whom none think it worth to turn.
For, to achieve his lightest wish, he must
Become the whole of boredom, subject to
Vulgar complaints like love, among the Just
Be just, among the Filthy filthy too,
And in his own weak person, if he can,
Must suffer dully all the wrongs of Man.

W. H. Auden, 1940

One might conclude from this reading that perhaps the analyst likewise ought to give birth to the novelist lurking within him as a means of helping the patient discover his own bent for fiction. In this way, the patient can give voice to the multitude of characters that will emerge in the course of that analytical adventure.

Chapter 3

Bion and the apes

The bridging problem of
A Memoir of the Future

Benjamin H. Ogden

Tenerife is the largest of Spain's Canary Islands. It sits fewer than 200 miles off the coast of West Africa, nearest to Morocco. In 1912, at the behest of the neurophysicist Max Rothman, the Prussian Academy of Sciences agreed to establish there the Anthropoid Station for the study of the thinking capacity of apes. Rothman, in a paper outlining the conditions that would need to be met for the creation of such a station, proposed Tenerife because it 'can be reached in six days from Europe; African anthropomorphs can be transported there without issue straight from Cameroun. Asian anthropomorphs can be transported there fairly easily via Tangier, where large German steamships dock en route to Asia' (qtd. in Ruiz and Sánchez, 2014, p. 3). By January of the following year, the first director of the project, Eugene Teuber, had arrived on the island, tasked with getting the station up and running. Teuber was very young (not yet 24 years old), and was still working toward a doctorate, so he agreed only to a one-year position.

Working quickly, Teuber leased an estate on which he and his wife could live and constructed the necessary living quarters for seven chimpanzees and the 'playground' on which experiments could be conducted. The playground extended for 1,000 square meters and was enclosed on all sides (including the roof) by wire mesh, which hung from a 5 m high support pole in the center of the yard. Inside the enclosure were a few banana trees, shrubs, and a jungle gym. Before his one-year term was complete, Teuber was able to use the complex to conduct experiments into the gestural language of chimpanzees as progenitor to human language.

It was not, however, until the arrival of Teuber's successor, the psychologist Wolfgang Köhler, in December 1913 that Tenerife would become the unlikely setting for among the most important, arguably the most ruthless, studies to have been conducted on the nature and conditions for thinking. These studies, conducted from 1913 to 1917, are described in Köhler's monograph *The Mentality of Apes*, one of those rare books that are both little known and classics. Köhler would later become one of the principle elaborators of Gestalt psychology, and several Gestalt tenets already underlie the experiments on Tenerife, namely that perception of a whole is required for intelligence, that the whole is different from the elemental parts, and that stimulus-response theories of behavior are imperfect (simian intelligent behavior was not merely a matter of trial-and-error learning, as Thorndike had proposed).

The goal of Köhler's research was, in his words, to establish 'whether [animals] do not behave with intelligence and insight under conditions which require such behavior' (p. 1). To determine whether apes could exhibit evidence of thinking, Köhler devised a series of experiments that shared a basic pattern: an ape would be faced with a situation in which an objective (a piece of fruit, usually) is visible to the ape; however, in each case 'the direct path to the objective is blocked, but a roundabout way left open' (p. 4). Example: the male chimpanzee Sultan is led into the yard. He is hungry. Surveying the entirety of his environment, Sultan sees that from the wire mesh ceiling of the yard hangs a bunch of bananas; an out-of-reach prize. Into the yard comes Dr. Köhler, dragging behind him two wooden boxes, which he drops at different places in the yard. Köhler then leaves the yard, but continues to watch from somewhere outside the compound.

So: the man who feeds me unaccountably stopped feeding me; now my food is clearly hanging up there, where it has never hung before; there are now boxes at my disposal that were not available previously; the man remains close by, watching me with great interest. The experiment has begun. Maybe, so has thinking.

Consider this description of Sultan's state of mind: 'Sultan knows: now one is supposed to think. That is what the bananas up there are about. The bananas are there to make one think, to spur one to the limits of one's thinking. But what must one think?' (p. 72). This is Elizabeth Costello, the eponymous character of J.M. Coetzee's quasi-novel *Elizabeth Costello*. She is delivering a lecture on 'The Lives of Animals.' For Costello, and in this case, I believe for Coetzee too, thinking emerges in response to a circumstance in which thinking is plainly expected—in which an environment is animated to make one think. Thinking is, first and foremost, due to the pressure of the special arrangement of the environment, which supplies the desire and the frustration of the desire. However, based on Coetzee's rendering, more is required than desire and frustration for thought to come into being. The environment must additionally invest in us a feeling of 'supposed to.' This feeling of 'supposed to' leads to a recognition that there is someone or something that wishes us to think. 'That is what the bananas up there are about.' They are about some wish the world, as well as the world's designer, has for us to think. Just as beauty would like us to look and to continue looking (to stare), the world wants us to think about it. How does the world, and its designer, convey to us that it would like us to think? By presenting the world to us in the form of *a problem*, the solution to which is the answer to the question: but what must one think? The world is designed not for our general contemplation, but to draw out of us the solutions to the problems it poses. The world calls to us as a problem to be solved.

In *Learning from Experience* and 'Theory of Thinking,' Bion's conception of thinking is similar in several ways to Coetzee's conception of thinking. For Bion, thoughts exert a pressure, which is experienced as the pain of the feeling of 'supposed to think.' In response to the problem of this pressure, thinking develops. Most importantly for my purposes, which will eventually be to consider his experimental work of fiction *A Memoir of the Future*, Bion conceives of thinking as the outcome of the demand we feel the world places on us to think the correct thought, to provide a solution to the emotional problem that it poses. Thinking, for Bion, is the product of the problem posed by thoughts. That Bion formulates thinking as a problem is everywhere in the language of *Learning from Experience*: 'Envy aroused by a breast that provides love, understanding, experience and wisdom poses a problem that is solved by destruction of alpha-function' (p. 11); 'The theory of functions offered a prospect of solving this problem by assuming that I contained unknown functions of his personality' (p. 21); 'But the problem stimulates the thought ...' (p. 63); 'the model is then found to be insufficiently similar to clarify the problem for which the solution is sought' (p. 80). The word 'problem' appears at least 30 times in the slim book.

Attached to these problems, we find the same pressures and feelings Coetzee finds in Köhler's experiment: a feeling of 'supposed to'; an environment that exerts a pressure that 'require[s] an apparatus to cope' (Bion, 1962b, p. 306) with it; a sense of design inherent in the environment (the environment is designed as a persecutory or pleasure-giving object); a sense that the design of the environment is one of a problem to be solved by thought. These are the conditions for the coming into being of thinking.

For both Coetzee and Bion, thinking can develop only when one is placed into a situation that one experiences as a problem, when one knows one is supposed to think, and when one knows that the world has been arranged to spur one to the limits of one's thinking. Coetzee, however, goes further than Bion in that he links the conditions for the coming into being of thinking with the conditions for the coming into being of literature. Consider how the opening of *Elizabeth Costello* puts into conversation the problem of thinking and the problem of literature:

> There is first of all the problem of the opening, namely, how to get us from where we are, which is, as yet, nowhere, to the far bank. It is a simple bridging problem, a problem of knocking together a bridge. People solve such problems every day. They solve them, and having solved them push on. Let us assume that, however it may have been done, it is done. Let us take it that the bridge is built and crossed, that we can put it out of our mind. We have left behind the territory in which we were. We are in the far territory, where we want to be.
>
> (2004, p. 1)

For Coetzee, literature comes into being much as thinking does. Upon opening a book, one finds oneself in a world that resembles reality (it is familiar) but also feels to us designed to provoke thinking (it is unfamiliarly provocative). One is faced with a problem posed by the book, a problem that exerts a pressure.

We could say that the reader is like Sultan, the author like Köhler, and the text (particularly those aspects that seem to call out for interpretation) like the boxes and the bananas hung out of reach. Much as Sultan must learn to build a bridge from the ground to the bananas by stacking the boxes, we must learn to build our bridge into the 'far territory' in which we have left behind the non-literary and accepted the conditions for literary experience.

Depending on whether we are reader or text or author, we will play a different part in the mysterious bridging problem. However, despite the different roles each may play, we (a pronoun that repeats many times in these lines) are all interested in a solution to the problem presented by the work. The solution will take the form of an ability to read the work so that reading becomes a process of experiencing and working out a solution to the language and life of the work. There are, then, two kinds of reading: reading that is simply the passive comprehension of language (reading without thinking) and reading of a higher order that would be akin to what Bion means by 'learning from experience.' A pre-conception (an instinct for reading as well as problem solving) is mated with its frustration (how does one read at a level at which the problem of reading is solved?) to create thinking, which may involve not only interpretation but also a tolerance for the frustrations of difficult literature. This is all to say that Bion's theory of thinking also says something about reading—something that goes beyond what Bion himself ever knew, or said, about the relevance of his own thinking to literature and aesthetics.

For Coetzee, Köhler's experiments not only lay bare a theory of thinking and a theory of literature, but also give us a means of evaluating the experience of thinking and the experience of reading. Coetzee supplies an ethics by which to regard the humanity or inhumanity, the success or failure, of the problems of thinking and art. He affords us criteria for estimating literary achievement. Here is a fuller account of Costello's description of Sultan's response to Köhler's experiment, wherein Costello gives an ethical reading of Köhler's experiments through a depiction of Sultan's mind:

Sultan knows: Now one is supposed to think. That is what the bananas up there are about. The bananas are there to make one think, to spur one to the limits of one's thinking. But what must one think? One thinks: Why is he starving me? One thinks: What have I done? Why has he stopped liking me? One thinks: Why does he not want these crates any more? But none of these is the right thought. Even a more complicated thought – for instance: What is wrong with him, what misconceptions does he have of me, that leads him to believe it is easier for me to reach a banana hanging from a wire than to pick up a banana from the floor? – is wrong. The right thought to think is: How does one use the crates to reach the bananas?

(Ibid., p. 72)

Coetzee introduces here an ethics of thinking, and of literature, which he summarizes shortly thereafter in poignant terms:

At every turn Sultan is driven to think the less interesting thought. From the purity of speculation (Why do men behave like this?) he is relentlessly propelled towards lower, practical, instrumental reason (How does one use this to get that?) and thus towards acceptance of himself as primarily an organism with an appetite that needs to be satisfied.

(Ibid., p. 73)

What is Coetzee's assessment of Köhler ethically, even aesthetically? In devising tests for the apes, Köhler has played his part insofar as he presented the conditions for thinking. This is equivalent to saying that he has presented a problem that can evoke thought. Furthermore, he has played the game fairly insofar *as he has only posed problems that indeed have solutions.* He has not tricked the apes. He has not set them impossible or unfair tasks. To do that would have been to torture them, to make them feel, as Bion describes in *Learning from Experience*, like the patient who 'feels that he has feelings, but cannot learn from them; sensations ... but cannot learn from them either. A determination not to experience anything can be shown to co-exist with an inability to reject or ignore any stimulus' (1962a, p. 18). Put in such a position, Sultan could not reject any stimulus for interpretation, *and so would be left in a state of intolerable effort to solve a problem that is unsolvable.* These are the rules of war, whether you are a research psychologist, a psychoanalyst, or a fiction writer: pose fair, tolerable problems; provide the implements necessary for something that the subject would recognize as solution, as success, as a bridge.

However, Köhler, Coetzee tells us, lost his way ethically the moment he forced Sultan to at every turn 'think the less interesting thought.' As Costello puts it, 'In his deepest being Sultan is not interested in the banana problem. Only the experimenter's single-minded regimentation forces him to concentrate on it' (p. 75). This is not simply a limitation placed on Sultan that keeps him trapped in his apedom; it is a form of sadism in that it trains Sultan to hate thinking. Thinking is a burden that he can only experience as bizarre and labyrinthine, much like the beta elements that Bion tells us beset the psychotic mind. The lesson taught to Sultan is the same lesson learned by the simpleton or fool in so many works of literature: thinking will get you nowhere in life because you are not good at it; if you can give it up completely, you should. Now that you can think, all you can think is: I am a fool. This lesson is born not of love or knowledge, but of hate and scientific devotion. Against this cruel lesson, literature usually grants the fool some justice: he is in the end revealed as a font of wisdom, and the world to have been the fool all along.

On these grounds, Costello concludes that 'Wolfgang Köhler was probably a good man. A good man but not a poet' (p. 74). He lacked, she says, 'a feel for the ape's experience' (p. 74). I take this to mean that Köhler failed to grasp the aesthetic dimension of his science. As a psychologist, he worked justly, breeding the miracle of thought in a way that science would consider humane. Aesthetically, however, he failed. Köhler was not able to recognize that, just as Sultan had been tasked with crossing from apedom into humanity, he himself had been tasked with crossing over from the scientific to the poetic, from the practical to the lyric. While Sultan was stacking his boxes, Köhler was traversing the bridge that, Coetzee tells us, is 'the problem of the opening,' not just the opening of the novel, but also an opening through which one can find one's way out of practical reason and into higher forms of thought. Sultan and his brethren managed, in the end, to think, learning to pile boxes up to reach the bananas. Köhler, for his part, was unable to think, for he did not recognize the problem that his own experiments posed to him, as a psychologist and scientist. He had no feel for Sultan's experience and so could not traverse the bridge connecting psychology and art.

Coetzee's reading of Köhler, combined with the theory of literature proposed in the opening of *Elizabeth Costello*, can be read both as a cautionary tale of the fate of the psychologist who ventures haphazardly into the poetic realm (and fails to realize it and consequently fails) and as a guideline for evaluating a work of literature that poses its aesthetics in the terms of thought. I will summarize these guidelines: literature very often invites thinking by presenting the reader with conditions in which thinking is called for. This is not incidental, but rather central to the aesthetic function of literature. The aesthetics of literature work by making a particular kind of appeal to the intellect. This appeal is made in the form of a problem (just as epistemological appeals are made by Köhler and Bion in the form of problems). However, there are ethically inflected rules of engagement that govern these problems. First, a problem must have a solution—in other words, the subject (the reader, in our case) must be capable of interpreting the problem in a way that alleviates the frustration of the problem. (Torture should never masquerade as a problem.) Second, a problem must lead toward the more interesting thought, never the less interesting thought. We should never be led to hate thinking or to concentrate on a problem that cannot interest us. The purpose of the problem should not be to make the reader feel a fool. Lastly, literature must make it possible, as Costello says, 'to think ourselves into the being of another' (p. 80). We must be able to press ourselves sympathetically into the mind of the one who is attempting to solve the problem being posed and so be capable of facing everything that the ape, the reader, the patient, faces. For we are responsible for what they face; we have designed the dusty yard of bananas and boxes, the novel, the consulting room. They are on this island because of us.

Late in his career, Bion attempted to write memoir and fiction. His most ambitious project in these areas is the philosophical novel *A Memoir of the Future*, a very long book whose primary goal seems to be to cross the bridge from psychological epistemology to aesthetics. More specifically, the book is an attempt on Bion's part to discover what, if anything, happens to theories of thinking and dream work when they are contained in literary aesthetics. What happens to the problem of thinking when it is transformed into a problem of literature? In this respect, Bion is on the same journey as Köhler, though Bion was more adventurous than Köhler. Bion was willing to see to the end, in his own way, the aesthetic dimension of his scientific work, to investigate the aesthetic function that inheres in the thinking function.

There are different methods of evaluating literature, but it seems to me that the only fair method of evaluation is one that judges the work according to the terms it sets for itself. This method has the advantage of refraining from imposing a standard that is external or irrelevant to the work and also the advantage of allowing us to judge the work on the basis of how well it executes according to its own goals and procedures. It is extremely difficult to know how best to read a work like *A Memoir of the Future*, but I believe I have demonstrated that Bion's fiction must be evaluated according to the guidelines described above. This makes sense, as these guidelines are suited for works that span science and art and that are explicitly couched in epistemological terms. Just as Köhler's exploration of thinking extended into, and became refashioned into the terms of, literature, so does Bion's fiction place the contained of epistemology into the container of literature. So, in what follows, I will apply each of the tenets presented in the guidelines above to Bion's *A Memoir of the Future* as a way of considering the relative success or failure of Bion's attempt to recast the coming into being of thinking in literary terms.

First rule: problems posed must have solutions

It is easy to be misled by the first rule. The first rule is not supporting the notion that literature has a solution. Art has no solution; it is always in the act of expressing that aspect of itself that is irreducible, and of opposing any tendency of criticism to reduce it to formulation. However, literature must also grant the reader some way of interpreting it such that the reader is able to feel that he or she is in the process of solving the problem of the work. The act of solving the problem must give the reader the satisfaction of progress, must make the reader feel that his reading is truth-directed. The reader must be able to learn from the experience of reading, even without any hope of coming to the end of that learning experience.

The flaw of *A Memoir of the Future* is that it poses a problem to which there is no solution. At every turn, it presents the reader with a bridging problem: it presents characters that amount to beta elements exerting a pressure to which the reader wishes to develop the apparatus for reading. In the introduction, Bion asserts that in what he writes significant meanings and rhythms are 'communicated and interpretable' (p. ix), and that there is a set of 'rules' to which the language of the work 'conforms,' and though difficult to follow they can indeed be followed. However, it seems to me that Bion here does not understand the transformation that occurs when the problem of thinking becomes the problem of literature. Bion seems to believe that, in psychological epistemology, an ability to tolerate frustration leads to the development of an apparatus for thinking and that, transferred into the aesthetic realm, the same will occur. However, reading requires a sense of being in the process of solving the problem posed by the work. Reading is not a coping mechanism, but rather a motivated sense of building an interpretive bridge that functions as a solution. The reading apparatus does not develop in precisely the same way as the thinking apparatus. The reading apparatus solves the problem of reading: it transforms reading from a desperate response to the frustration of confusion into an active knocking together of a bridge into the aesthetic territory.

A Memoir of the Future is thinkable, but it is not readable. It offers no aesthetic solution to the problem it poses. It trades in frustration, with the expectation that frustration will inevitably breed thought. As the character Man says to the character Bion, 'I am not going to do your thinking for you' (p. 161). In other words, the book will offer no relief from frustration—solve the problem of the book yourself or starve. But the frustration, in the absence of a solution, becomes a form of torture in which the reader, as a substitute for Sultan, is led into situations in which the experiment is designed to give the sense that there is a solution to the problem when in fact there is no solution. This would be as cruel as leaving Sultan starving in a cage, bananas hung from the wire ceiling, with boxes that he could never stack or arrange to reach his prize.

Second rule: a problem must lead toward the more interesting thought, never the less interesting thought

One of the respites of the death-by-a-thousand-cuts that is *A Memoir of the Future* is the fact that it leads the reader toward the more interesting, not the less interesting, thought. The book is, in many ways, a machine devised to draw one out of practical or instrumental reason, and push one toward creative and metaphysical thinking. Despite all the frustration that the book foists on the reader, it does not engender in the reader a hatred, or distrust, of thinking precisely because, where it does permit lucid thought, it does so in a way that leads the reader away from apedom and toward higher intellect. We see how this happens in the following selection:

MYSELF: What is the difference that you seem to make between 'theorising' and what you call 'practising' psycho-analysis? It seems to me that practising psycho-analysis consists of theorizing.

BION: 'Theorising' is, I admit, a part of practising psycho-analysis.

MYSELF: I think what you have just said sounds as if it makes something clear, but almost at once the illumination either turns out to be illusory and your explanation meaningless, or perhaps you have clarified a problem and the 'clarification' is at once replaced by a further series of 'unknowns.'

BION: Both are possible. That is a difficulty about 'learning'. The moment of illumination is also the moment at which it becomes clear that there is a doubt about the 'clarification' itself and about the 'matter' which it is hoped to comprehend. I think this must be a familiar experience to Sherlock Holmes.

SHERLOCK: I am not a philosopher and I don't think I can even guess what a psycho-analyst is, but since you appeal to me as if I were experienced I take it you are referring to something of which I have experience. I remember an occasion when I saw a client and I detected a strong smell of cigar about his clothes. It proved to be a valuable clue and later I wrote a monograph on ash which also turned out to be valuable, though in a way that I never expected. (*MF*, pp. 201–202)

The passage reflects the deep structure of the novel: a concept (theorizing) is raised, after which it undergoes a process of interrogation that simultaneously clarifies and mystifies the concept. When one concept is tentatively proposed as equivalent to another (here theorizing is proposed as analogous to psychoanalysis), it is immediately subjected to processes meant to cast doubt on the comparison: theorizing is presented as just one 'part of' psychoanalysis, but this refinement (rather than leading down a path toward further clarity) is immediately accused of being a charade (clarification is undone by a 'series of unknowns'). Every clarification is negated by the fact that the clarification only serves to introduce unknowns. This dialectic of elucidation and mystification functions as a motor by which the less interesting thought (what one believes is true) is transformed into a more interesting thought (what one believed was true is now revealed to be only partially true), and then into an even more interesting thought (that elucidation and stupefaction are in fact two side of the same coin, each bringing the other into being). The entire book is a kind of machine for spurring the thinking apparatus to greater and greater heights. The thinking function proliferates even as the aesthetic function falters.

Third rule: He who designs the problem of the book must be able to think his way 'into the being of another'

Coetzee calls the capacity to think one's way into another's being the 'sympathetic imagination' (2004, p. 80). This is not simply the ability to picture oneself behaving like Sultan, but the ability to inhabit Sultan such that one would know what it was like for Sultan to be Sultan. Though a human can never be an ape, he can inhabit the mind of an ape if he can spur himself to exercise the sympathetic imagination. Much as Sultan is drawn into human thinking (made to think as if he were a human, not just behave as if he were thinking like a human), so must the author be able to follow Sultan backward, so to speak, as he leaves the human territory and returns into his ape being.

A Memoir of the Future is an interesting test case with regard to the third rule. The book opens with a dialogue that speaks to the relationship between author and reader:

Q: *Can you give me an idea what this is about?*
A: *Psycho-analysis, I believe.*
Q: *Are you sure? It looks a queer affair.*
A: *It is a queer affair—like psycho-analysis. You'd have to read it.*
Q: *How much does it cost?*
A: *It says it on the book. You would have to read it as well though.*
Q: *Of course. But I don't think I can afford the time or money.*
A: *Nor do I.*
Q: *But haven't you read it?*
A: *Yes, in a way.*
Q: *You're a queer salesman. I'm only wanting to know …*
A: *I'm not the salesman. I only wrote it.*
Q: *Oh, I beg your pardon! I quite thought …*
A: *I'm flattered, but I'm only the author.*
Q: *May I have your autograph?*
A: *No.*
Q: *Oh.*

(*MF*, p. 2)

Bion is right to insist here that a writer is a reader but in a way that is different from how a reader who is not a writer is a reader. A writer reads what he writes 'in a way.' He reads as writer. Bion is establishing from the outset that a reader ('Q')—particularly one who is so naïve as to think that a work is about some idea—will never be a reader in the way that the author ('A') is a reader. Q is, really, every reader who is not A, and Q is decisively excluded from the possibility of reading.

Another way of putting this is that Bion is both A and Q. Bion is not trying to think his way into another's being, but into his own being. His sympathetic imagination extends not outward, but rather inward. We, as readers (as 'Q's) are on the outside looking in—we ask the wrong questions; we want something from the book that it can't give us. We are not so much readers of Bion's book but witnesses to Bion's reading of himself—his attempt to inhabit himself *imaginatively.*

A Memoir of the Future is not really a problem posed to the reader, but a problem posed by Bion to himself as reader. If there is a touch of genius in the book (along with many touches of failure), it is in how Bion has taken the age-old task of empathizing with another's experience and transformed it into perhaps the more novel task of inhabiting one's own mind, of imagining what it is like for I to be I. Bion speaks directly to this challenge here:

MYSELF: Since I cannot, for all my experience, analytic or other than analytic, say *who* I am, I know now that it is very unlikely that I shall know any better at some future date. It is impossible to believe anyone who is not me will know better. I am sure it would be useful if I knew who that person is that I am compelled to be as long as I exist.

(*MF*, p. 131)

The philosophy of self here is convoluted, but amounts to the self-acknowledging that it is both its own sole author and sole reader, both A and Q. The mind is a problem posed to itself, just as for Bion the literary work is a work written for the writer who reads. Though there is an auto-destructive cleverness to a work that presents itself in this way, there is also an exhaustive solipsism. After the prefatory dialogue between A and Q, the novel opens with the statement, 'I am tired' (p. 3). And, it seems that there is, for nearly 800 pages, a weariness born of the torment of being asked to read a book we are told we cannot read, and of being asked to solve a problem for which there is no solution. Led again and again into the yard, Sultan no doubt felt as the reader does when faced with so much self-flagellating thinking: 'I am tired.'

At one level, *A Memoir of the Future* falls short of its purported goal of submitting psychoanalytic epistemology to aesthetic epistemology. As I have tried to demonstrate, *Memoir* creates a reader only to punish or exclude him, which if we follow analogous theories of thinking (the cognitive behavioral theory of Köhler and the aesthetic theory of Coetzee) is a violation of the contract that holds sway over researcher and subject, or author and reader. And yet, at another level, Bion's work, as entrapped as it is in the ineluctable conventions of thinking and literary aesthetics, also is able to serve as a rebellion against pre-existent rules and expectations. The Epilogue to *Memoir* speaks to this aspect of the book:

> All my life I have been imprisoned, frustrated, dogged by common-sense, reason, memories, desires and—greatest bug-bear of all—understanding and being understood. This is an attempt to express my rebellion, to say 'Good-bye' to all that. It is my wish, I now realize doomed to failure, to write a book unspoiled by any tincture of common-sense, reason, etc. (see above). So although I would write, 'Abandon Hope all ye who expect to find any facts—scientific, aesthetic or religious—in this book', I cannot claim to have succeeded. All these will, I fear, be seen to have left their traces, vestiges, ghosts hidden within these words; even sanity, like 'cheerfulness', will creep in. However successful my attempt, there would always be the risk that the book 'became' acceptable, respectable, honoured and unread. 'Why write then?' you may ask. To prevent someone who KNOWS from filling the empty space—but I fear I am being 'reasonable', that great Ape. Wishing you all a Happy Lunacy and a Relativistic Fission …
>
> (*MF*, p. 578)

Bion here identifies as central to *Memoir* the concerns, feelings, and problems that I found in his work via Köhler: the problem of being 'imprisoned,' a sense of doom and dread borne of unceasing frustration, a steak of sadism (captured above in the allusion to Dante), and an awe-inspiring pointlessness that is the heart of an 800-page book that cannot be read. But Bion here announces that, though he is forever haunted by the traces of established formulae and conventions, he will do his best to live as outlaw—to live outside of all the laws and boxes and camps. The 'great Ape' for Bion is he who is 'reasonable,' a being who is led to solve the problem in front of him without questioning the terms of the problem itself. He who rebels against this expectation emerges from his apedom into human life.

In several places in *The Mentality of Apes*, Köhler recounts moments when the apes grow enraged. They kick at the boxes, snarl, flagellate themselves. The descriptions are painful to read, because one understands the torment and frustration that drives the chimpanzees to wish that the world would stop demanding so much from them. Bion, in the above passage gives us a kinder reading of these irate fits of the apes: that Sultan and his fellow apes were exhibiting their own kind of rebellion, one that expressed the wise thinking that inheres in the ability to reject knowing and live less knowingly. They were not being driven mad by a malevolent game, but erupting in brave rebellion.

Chapter 4

Memoir of the Future and memoir of the numinous

Mauro Manica

Is a mystery unveiling?

In one of my previous works (2013), I suggested an imaginary conjecture,[1] putting forth the hypothesis that a 'mystery' might have taken place at the Tavistock. That is, when a pre-analytic Bion got in contact with Jung's theories – and there is evidence of such an occurrence – this resulted in an *imprinting* that affected Bion's thinking.

Similarly to what happens for the individual personality – where the eruption of underground experiences confronts us with the emergency of parts of the mind that have not fully come into being or have been precociously miscarried, as they did not find any space within the mind of the object (Manica, 2013) – there also seem to be models and theories that did not find enough space in the Master's (in our case, Freud's) mind or in the mind of the scientific community that he created. Accordingly, they sank into the underground galleries and dungeons of psychoanalytic conceptualisation.

Just like the scientific and biographic vicissitudes of Tausk, Ferenczi and Jung that could be other emblematic evidence of these symptomatic segregations. As ostracised and underground theories since the early developments of psychoanalysis, they were brought to light through the volcanic eruptions and the earthquake shocks from the impact with ever-new problems stemming from clinical practice.

We have been induced to think that their conceptual differences caused the diaspora (in 1912–1913) between the Master and Jung[2] – i.e., their ideas about libido and the centrality of sexuality as well as their different conceptions about the meaning of symbols. In fact, Jung just seemed to bring to its extreme consequences a teleological conception of the unconscious that, implicit in Freud's conception, bestows to the symbolic function a main role in terms of the developmental potential of the human mind.

In Jung's perspective, the contexts that anticipated the most current developments of post-Freudian psychoanalysis seemed to have been split or dissociated and stored there – that is to say, he offered a further perspective on the unconscious that was not only formed as a depository of repressed childhood memories, but could also overlook the infinite (Matte Blanco, 1975), as it is driven by the truth instinct (Bion, 1977a), an impulse to representation (Bollas, 2009) and the knowledge instinct (Ogden, 2011).

Then, could we think that there is an underground Jungian thinking that first sank and later re-emerged as a volcanic eruption in the epistemological and theoretical evolution of psychoanalysis? And, if we can hypothesise (*mythologhéin*) that the very diffraction of the concept of the unconscious was the original cause of the diaspora between Freud's and Jung's thinking, perhaps we could suggest (or formulate an imaginative conjecture) that Bion, the new Master of psychoanalysis, became the depository (the last link) of a heretic and subversive legacy that was unconsciously passed on to him at the Tavistock. Maybe we should say that he was the genius heir of an underground not fully lodged, not yet fully thinkable that we suppose ought to exist[3] in Freud's mind and psychoanalysis.

Then, it becomes intriguing to wonder if this unconscious and implicit transmission of a further psychoanalytic vertex was in fact the 'mystery' underlying the encounters between Bion and Jung at the Tavistock in the fall of 1935.

Since his *Tavistock Lectures* (Bion, 2005), several evocative consonances between these two minds, like underground streams, seem to flow into an underground river that originated a common unconscious and pre-scientific thinking. However, besides the conceptual merging (archetype/pre-conceptions, psychoid/protomental, amplification/reverie, soul/α-function, alchemic *recipiens*/container (♀), synchronicity/constant conjunction), we also find some consonant intuitions about dreaming, the work of transformations and the primacy of emotions over the drives, where the Jungian↔(Freudian)↔Bionian underground stream has merged most significantly. Is it a stream that the mind – even before coming into being – is already navigating to look for worlds that have not yet been thought by any pre-existing theory?

In a troubled and painful time of his life ('a period of inner uncertainty began for me. It would be no exaggeration to call it a state of disorientation'; 1961, p. 170) – between 1912/1913 (after the rupture with Freud) and 1916/1917 – Jung was absorbed in what he called a work with and on his own unconscious. He therefore decided to record all of his thoughts, fantasies, dreams and visions of those years in his *Black Book* at first (six small volumes of notes bound in black leather) and then to copy them in a Gothic calligraphic script, like medieval manuscripts, into a book bound in red leather: the *Red Book*. Until 2009, except for a few excerpts and quotations by Jung himself in *Memories, Dreams, Reflections* (1961), the *Red Book* or *Liber novus* was unpublished. Only recently, it became available to be studied as a depository of the (unconscious) sources of Jung's thinking.

However, it is an enigmatic and mysterious work that forces the reader to leave the common paths, the common sense of the *lógos*, and to venture in oneiric wanderings, full of characters that seem to embody different parts of the author's self. We meet the Biblical Elias and Salomè, the black snake and Ka (the incarnated soul) and Philemon – some kind of an avatar, guiding spirit or maybe Virgil who accompanies us into the 'underground' of the unconscious. It becomes difficult to resist the suggestion that the intuitions, still in embryo, that have been actualised in the narratological turn (Ferro, 2010) of post-Freudian and post-Bionian psychoanalysis, were already peeping out in the *Red Book*.

The characters, Jung says (1961), are deep manifestations of the unconscious, in other words, narrative derivatives of emotional constellations that can start to introduce some traces of representability in the analytic field. But then, as visionary as this might sound, why not think about α-function and α-dream-work in sleeping and waking? Jung (1961, p. 177) observes: 'To the extent that I managed to translate the emotions into images – that is to say, to find the images which were concealed in the emotions – I was inwardly calmed and reassured'. This is undoubtedly the account of an analytic move, but it could easily be also the *report* of a clinical vignette from a consultation room in which the *dreaming ensemble* (Grotstein, 2007) of patient and analyst alphabetises an aphasic and intolerable emotion.

In a wild synthesis, we could try to say that the *Red Book* is the proposal of a method (*methà-odòs*): it points the way and outlines the direction of a path of personal individuation. It is no accident that Jung (2009) suggested that every patient or therapist (every human being) could compose and illustrate his/her own 'red book' with pictures.

But then, is this how we could unveil the Tavistock 'mystery'? Has Bion unconsciously accepted this mandate? Could the excommunicated 'prince', a scholar of the Eastern world, have as his 'mystical' probable successor the genius who emigrated from India to revolutionise Western psychoanalysis? And if this is the case, how? And when?

With a last imaginative effort, we can hypothesise (*phantasieren*) that *A Memoir of the Future* was conceived and written as Wilfred Ruprecht Bion's *Red Book*. Jung (1961, pp. 318–319) says:

> The meaning of my existence is that life has addressed a question to me. Or, conversely, I myself am a question which is addressed to the world, and I must communicate my answer, for otherwise I am dependent upon the world's answer. That is a suprapersonal life task, which I accomplish only by effort and with difficulty. Perhaps it is a question which preoccupied my ancestors, and to which they could not answer. Could that be why I am so impressed by the fact that the conclusion of *Faust* contains no solution? ... I also think of the possibility that through the achievement of an individual a question enters the world, to which he must provide some kind of answer. For example, my way of posing the question as well as my answer may be unsatisfactory. That being so, someone who has my karma–or I myself– would have to be reborn in order to give a more complete answer.

In the epilogue of *A Memoir of the Future*, with similar *karma*, Bion tells us about a change in his navigation:

> All my life I have been imprisoned, frustrated, dogged by common-sense, reason, memories, desires and – greatest bugbear of all – understanding and being understood. This is an attempt to express my rebellion, to say 'Good-bye' to all that. It is my wish, now I realise doomed to failure, to write a book unspoiled by any tincture of common-sense, reason, etc. (see above). So although I would write, 'Abandon Hope all ye who expect to

find any facts – scientific, aesthetic or religious – in this book', I cannot claim to have succeeded. All these will, I fear, be seen to have left their traces, vestiges, shots hidden within these words; even sanity, like 'cheerfulness', will creep in.

(P. 578)

Unconscious biographies

In Bollingen, silence surrounds me almost audibly, and I live 'in modest harmony with nature'. Thoughts rise to the surface which reach back into the centuries, and accordingly anticipate a remote future. Here the torment of creation is lessened; creativity and play are close together.

(Jung, 1961, p. 226)

This is how Francesco Corrao starts his Preface to the Italian edition of *A Memoir of the Future:*

Dedalus, the gifted maker, built the labyrinth – and his secret (which only Ariadne knew), so as to conceal and, at the same time, unveil the unspeakable and dangerous truth that one attains only by going through an intricate and hindered ... Understood as a metaphor, the labyrinth represents the original dialectic pattern, the archaic and violent connection between *lógos* and the mortal *páthos* that imbues the conundrum ... Being a place of contradictions, in fact the symbol of all contradiction, the maze mithologhem, beyond its literary drifts and digressions and their interpretative nuances, let us glimpse a consistent, metaphoric and mythic 'grid' of meaning that allows us to experience a troubling *Ergriffenheit*. It is the enigmatic, dark experience of 'being grasped, dominated, drawn and guided by a truth overcoming Intellect, Consciousness and the scientific-problematic research itself. This opens the way to the dark territory of the Unknown and the Unconscious, to establish an asymptotic contact with a complex and chaotic sphere full of both existence and reality that links the body and the mind, the anthropic and the animal, the physical and the biological dimensions, the 'real' and the 'imaginary', individuality and plurality, permanence and change.

(1993, pp. x–xi)

It is quite surprising that this text could be easily adapted to Jung's *Red Book* with no changes in its meaning. The labyrinth is an enigma going through two brilliant minds in which the dream, the difficulties and the catastrophes of change, the problematic relationship between body and mind become Ariadne's thread that can help explore the *Holzwege*, going off the beaten track to tread the unconscious: dreams that were not brought to completion or dreams that could not exist, night *pavor* or *nightmares*, like non-existent knights of the night[4] (Ogden, 2005).

The 'trilogy' structure of *A Memoir of the Future* has often led us to consider it as some kind of science-fiction story, modelling Dante or Milton's three canticas (Bléandonou, 1990), whilst its literary style, according to Alberto Meotti (2000), could be inspired by Joyce or Ezra Pound. Other scholars have claimed that Bion was inspired by Samuel Barclay Beckett's work – by his plays – particularly, *Waiting for Godot* where, just like in *A Memoir of the Future*, apparently nothing happens, and the facts are emotional events; yet the audience is somehow glued to the text – but especially by Beckett's trilogy (*Molloy*; *Malone dies*; *The unnamable*), where a progressive formal dissolution of speech and language takes place.

Then, if it is true, as Bion Talamo (1997) says, that the book could represent some kind of *libretto* that first and foremost imposes upon the reader an emotional response: 'First the emotion and then the reason', it is just as true that to read it requires an attention similar to the analyst's experience as he listens to his patient. It requires patience (*PS*). A patience that is induced, like for *The Red Book*, by a fragmented, non-linear, non-narrative, maybe fractal text that is too long to let a 'selected fact' or an 'α-element' merge and allow the reader to feel on a safe island in time.

The analogies continue: Dante's *Divine Comedy*, Milton's *Lost Paradise*, Samuel Beckett's work, but also *The Red Book*, the *Liber novus*, was structured as a 'trilogy': *liber primus*, *liber secundus* and *liber tertius* or Scrutinies. Even some thematic passages are astonishingly similar. For example, in Chapter 13 of the second book of the *Red Book*, Jung describes one of his own dream-visions where a sacrifice murder takes place. A girl (very likely a part of his infantile self) was victimised and killed, and Jung's *Soul* (a transformative function) forces him to take up the responsibility of the murder and to perform the cannibalistic ritual of eating her liver (*live-r*, the life carrier) so as to become able to re-integrate her in an accomplished personality organisation:

> But this was the vision that I did not want to see, the horror that I did not want to live … A marionette with a broken head lies before me amidst the stones – a few steps further, a small apron – and then behind the bush, the body of a small girl – covered with terrible wounds – smeared with blood. One foot is clad with a stocking and shoe, the other is naked and gorily crushed – the head – where is the head? The head is a mash of blood with hair and whitish pieces of bone, surrounded by stones smeared with brain and blood. My gaze is captivated by this awful sight – a shrouded figure, like that of a woman, is standing calmly next to the child;[5] her face is covered by an impenetrable veil. She asks me:

> S: 'What then do you say?'
> I: 'What should I say? This is beyond words.'
> S: 'Do you understand this?'
> I: 'I refuse to understand such things. I can't speak about them without becoming enraged.'
> …
> S: 'Step nearer and you will see that the body of the child has been cut open; take out the liver.'
> I: 'I will not touch this corpse. If someone witnessed this, they would think that I'm the murderer.'
> S: 'You are cowardly; take out the liver.'
> I: 'Why should I do this? This is absurd.'
> S: 'I want you to remove the liver. You must do it.'
> I: 'Who are you to give me such an order?'
> S: 'I am the soul of this child. You must do it for my sake.'
> I: 'I don't understand, but I'll believe you and do this horrific and absurd deed.'

> I reach into the child's visceral cavity – it is still warm – the liver is still firmly attached – I take my knife and cut it free of the ligaments. Then I take it out and hold it with bloody hands toward the figure.

> S: 'I thank you.'
> I: 'What should I do?'

S: 'You know what the liver means,[6] and you ought to perform the healing act with it.'

I: 'What is to be done?'

S: 'Take a piece of the liver, in place of the whole, and eat it.'

I: 'What are you demanding? This is absolute madness. This is desecration, necrophilia. You make me a guilty party to this most hideous of all crimes.'

S: 'You have devised the most horrible torment for the murderer, which could atone for his act. There is only one atonement abase yourself and eat.'

I: 'I cannot – I refuse – I cannot participate in this horrible guilt.'

S: 'You share in this guilt.'

I: 'I? Share in this guilt?'

S: 'You are a man, and a man has committed this deed.'

I: 'Yeah, I am a man – I curse whoever did this for being a man, and I curse myself for being a man.'

S: 'So, take part in this act, abase yourself and eat. I need atonement.'

I: 'So shall it be for your sake, as you are the soul of this child.'

I kneel down on the stone, cut off a piece of the liver and put it in my mouth … it is done. The horror has been accomplished.

S: 'I thank you.'

She throws her veil back – a beautiful maiden with ginger hair.

S: 'Do you recognize me?'

I: 'How strangely familiar you are! Who are you?'

S: 'I am your soul.'

(2009, pp. 320–322)

Bion, in the first volume of *A Memoir of the Future*, writes of a dialogue with *Man*:

BION: I see a man? A shade? A ghost?

MAN: Don't talk; listen. Don't watch; look. That's better! More like an encephaly, you will call it someday … That's better – you are coming over to me quite clearly now. This is 'infra-sensuous'. I shall know what your a-morphous 'senses' tell me.

BION: The man is filled with a kind of tenderness. Suddenly, with the utmost violence he beats the woman's skull and …

(*pouring sweat and overwhelmed with fear*), I won't watch! I shall *not* fight!

MAN: Get back, you damn fool ... Poor stupid wretch ... he has had a sane episode ... I was afraid he might not stand it. Get on!

BION: He bashes in the skull. God! It's like rock. He treats it like eggshell. He's sucking – this is cannibalism! He sucks out the brain.

MAN: This is an anachronism. Luckily for you it isn't a million year later or they would be so barbarously civilized they would murder you for murder. A million years later still they would incarcerate you for insanity – an 'insane' monster.

BION: Are you trying to tell me that it is 'I' who am doing this frightful thing, you damned blackguard?

MAN: 'I', 'cannibal', 'blackguard' – these are all anachronisms. I didn't exist for another couple of million years. Even now you are measuring time in numbers of times the earth completes its orbit around the sun ... Thinking is bearable because of its sensuous component. The experience which has not yet reached a conclusion is whether the human animal will survive a mind grafted onto its existing equipment. Now, do you think you could stand a little more?

BION: (*surly and hostile*) More of what?

MAN: Well ... a little more of 'I shall not cease from mental fight'. Not quite how Blake meant it of course, but the idea may emerge when the misleading quality imposed on formless thought by articulation is dissolved away ... The immortality achieved through reproduction by cell division leads to the mortality achieved by nuclear fission.

BION: What else?

MAN: I am not going to do your thinking for you. Sooner or later you will have to pay the price of deciding to think ±; whether, in Freud's formulation, to interpose 'thinking' between impulse and action; or to interpose it between the two as a substitute for action; or to interpose it between the two as a prelude to action.

BION: Oh, all right – let's get on with this enthralling and spectacular spectacle.

(*MF*, pp. 159–161)

Besides any other literary and psychoanalytic comparison and keeping in mind that 'another couple of million years' could have passed, is it so illicit to speculate – once again – that *A Memoir of the Future* developed as Wilfred Bion's *Red Book*? Or at least with the same biographic unconscious texture that characterised the *Liber Novus*?

If *A Memoir of the Future* – as López-Corvo (2002) suggests – could be considered Bion's biography of his unconscious life, *The Red Book* was an overview of the unconscious biography of a troubled and prolific time in Jung's life. In this perspective, referring to 'unconscious biographies' would mean that, in its dimensions that can be historicised, the unconscious 'does speak', but not in Lacan's sense of *ça parle* (Lacan, 1966), i.e., not in the sense of an unconscious structured as a language. The unconscious *speaks* when it is enabled to speak; when a mind meets another mind with which it is possible to create and share the unconscious and when it is possible that the unconscious is intercepted by the oneiric, the dream – understood as a translation/transduction of emotional (and sensory) events into visual images that suddenly expand the field of mental experience into ±.

O and numinous

Once, how beautiful the dawn over the English
farm and field would have seemed.
What might it not have promised?

(*MF*, p. 21)

As Grotstein (2007) says, some time would still have to pass before psychoanalysis and psychoanalysts can understand fully the deep meaning of Bion's change of paradigm.

A few traces have started to come to the surface as well as some resistances to Bion's ideas that have been considered the expression of an exaggeratedly religious, spiritual or mystical tendency.

Grotstein writes:

Having read the mystical work of Meister Eckhart, he borrowed Eckhart's heretical distinction between the idea of an immanent 'god' and a transcendent 'godhead' as the God of Essence and paced the transcendent 'godhead' within man as immanent and as a cognate of *O*. It is my belief that another reading of the meaning of 'godhead' for Bion was the Gnostic one, where godhead is equated with pure thought – that is pure intelligence, in the Neoplatonic sense of the Ideal Forms. This godhead is a pure essence and is not to be confused with God, the Creator ... roughly speaking, whenever a theologian speaks of 'God', a psychoanalyst could substitute the unconscious or *O*. If Bion were ever to have subscribed to religion at all, I should think it would have been 'agnostic Gnosticism'.

(2007, p. 137)

Jung (1952), accused of spirituality and mysticism, seemed to dwell in a similar 'religious' perspective when he said that, like every empirical science, also his psychology needed auxiliary concepts, hypotheses and models. Both the theologian and the philosopher would easily make the mistake of seeing metaphysical axioms there. The atom the physicist speaks about is not a metaphysical hypostasis but a model. Similarly, Jung's concept of archetype or psychic energy was just an auxiliary idea that could always be replaced with a better formula. He believed that his empirical concepts, philosophically understood, were *monstra* of logic, and, as a philosopher, he said that he would make a fool of himself. From a theological vantage point, he argued that his concept of soul, for example, was sheer *Gnosticism*: that is why he was often viewed as a *gnostic*.

In fact, both Jung and Bion seemed to think that *O*, the *Absolute Truth* regarding an indifferent, impersonal – perhaps *numinous* and *unknowable* – Ultimate Truth is to undergo a symbolic transformation so that, through the Soul or α-function, it can be transformed into a personal and subjective truth concerning a reality that can be experienced by human beings.

Jung (1952) added that the theologian could blame the empirical scientist. The latter, although he possesses the means to solve the problem of truth – that is the revealed truth – does not want to use them. The empirical scientist would humbly ask which one of the many revealed truths is to be taken into account and where the evidence of the greater truth of one conception or the other is. It is intriguing to think that we would not be at all astonished if these words had been said by Bion, although with some other terms and concepts. Maybe this is the case: we can only access small truths that become credible through acts of faith, that are necessary because we are dominated by the godhead of *O* and the unconscious. In other words, the unconscious with the contact-barrier (the 'old' para-excitation system, the barrier against the stimuli that Freud imagined), can work as an emotional boundary, as a shield or a filter of a psychic immunitary system that tries to contain the impact with the numinous unknowability of *O*, through its emotional registration and our attempts to modulate its effect by dreaming, that is transforming it into narrative and fiction (Ferro, 1999; Grotstein, 2007).

As we have learned, through Rudolf Otto's lesson (1917), the *numinous*[7] is a quality of the 'holy' (*das Heilege*); in fact, it constitutes its essential experience. If the *sakrós* ratifies its otherness, its being 'other' and 'different' from the ordinary, the common, the profane, the experience of the *holy* is indissolubly linked to the human effort to build a world with a meaning.

Mircea Eliade (1968) says that every ritual, every belief, every divine figure mirrors the experience of the sacred and, accordingly, implies the notions of being, meaning, truth. So, the sacred can be regarded as an element of the mind's structure and not as a stage in the history of mind. In this sense, perhaps Jung uses the adjective 'sacred' as a synonym of the adjective 'unconscious' (Pieri, 1998): what is unconscious is sacred and is experienced as numinous, that is with awe and the uncanny character of otherness that lies at the basis of the potential experience of otherness itself.

From a Bionian vantage point, Grotstein (2007) affirms, by emphasising the distinction between it and omnipotence, that the numinous inspires awe, is mysterious, with the *déjà-vu* quality, the preter-matured Uncanny. The numinous would then be placed between the troubling unknowability of *O* and the 'memoirs of the future', the innate or acquired 'pre-conceptions': (Bion, 1962a) (ideal forms, things-in-themselves, archetypes, noumena) that are engaged as the 'sensuous stimuli of emotional experience' (external stimuli, β-elements) call them from within the unrepressed unconscious. If we follow Bion's lead (Grotstein, 2007; Rather, 2005), *O* has a double nature: the 'sensuous stimuli of emotional experience', that constitute one of its arms, and the 'pre-conceptions', the memoirs of the future, that constitute the other arm. With an astonishing anticipatory analogy – *a memoir of the future?* – Jung (1952) writes that the *unknown* is divided into two groups of objects, those that can be experienced through the senses, the external ones, and those that can be experienced immediately, the internal facts. The former group is the unknown of the external world, the latter that of the internal world. This is the region that we call the *unconscious*.

If we qualified the last 'region', that Jung calls the 'unconscious', as being 'unrepressed', we would have plausible reason to think that Jung's *unknown* has been absorbed, in Bion's reflection, in the empty concept of *O* and in its numinous definition: fascinating (as it refers to *fascinosum*) and dreadful (as it concerns the *tremendum*).

In Bion's version, the concept of *O*, the *unknown*, seems to have expanded and allowed for an evolution of the model of the mind to which we can refer. In extending and overcoming Freud's and Jung's conceptions, Bion seems to have succeeded in conceiving a mind that overlooks the repressed and the numinous but is forced to be confronted, since its origin, also with the nothingness of *O*, its lack of meaning.

Perhaps it is not accidental that Jung viewed psychosis – particularly schizophrenia – as the product of the dream breaking into its wake, whereas Bion came to postulate its essence in not being able to dream or daydream. So, we could think that at the core of the psychotic experience the mind is overwhelmed by the catastrophic experience in dealing with non-memories or negative memories (−, *minus*, memories) of *nothingness*, a *nothing* dimension existing since the origins. Only a good reverie of the mother (or of the maternal-paternal environment) can make it bearable and transform it into *no-thing* that originates thinking.

This too is Ariadne's thread uniting Bion's *Red Book* that might have been inscribed in the trilogy *A Memoir of the Future*. Once again, we need to recognise that the dream, the mother-and-infant *dreaming ensemble* like the analyst-and-patient *dreaming ensemble* enables us to overlook the unknown, the different versions of *O*, without getting lost in *nothing*. It is always the dream that fosters an oneiric progression that from *nothingness* leads us to tolerate the *mysterium tremendum* that begins to take the shape of 'memoirs of the numinous' (MN), and enables them to be transformed into 'memoirs of the future' (MF): *nothingness* → MN ↔ MF.

The memoirs of the numinous, like the memoirs of the future and nothingness, become crucial elements of the psychoanalytic process.

And the MN↔MF oscillation between an appealing and dreadful *un-knowable* – i.e., a nameless dread that starts to be named; at least in its 'dreadful' quality – and a thinkability in embryo, becomes one of the essential purposes of the unconscious psychological work that can be carried out in the psychoanalytic field. Where the transformations-into-dream (Ferro, 2010), the transformations from *O* and the *dreaming ensemble* (Grotstein, 2007) of the patient and the analyst will be committed in the transformation of the *memoirs-non-memoirs* of the symptom into *memoirs of the future.*

Notes

1 I take this expression from Bion (1977b). Similarly, though from a different perspective, Jung (1961, pp. 300–301) speaks of the art of storytelling regarding one topic: *mythologhéin.* And, he writes, 'To the intellect, all my mythologizing is futile speculation. To the emotions, however, it is a healing and valid activity; it gives existence a glamour which we would not like to do without'.

2 The one who, in Freud's original intentions, was to be 'his' Crown Prince.

3 Bion (1992, p. 127) uses the formula 'ought-to-exist-ness' to refer to the assumption of existence.

4 The reference is evidently to Italo Calvino's 'nonexistent knight' di Italo Calvino ([1959], *The Nonexistent Knight*, New York: Random House 1962).

5 Here and later Jung uses the word *Kind.*

6 See Jung (1961, p. 198): 'The "liver", according to an old view, is the seat of life'.

7 Otto (1917) wrote that he formed the word *numinous* (if we can turn *omen* into ominous, we can also turn *numen* into numinous) whenever he wanted to speak of a special numinous category that interprets and values and of a numinous state of mind that arises every time that category is applied, that is to say, when an object is thought of as numinous. Such a category is absolutely *sui generis* and cannot be defined *strictu senso*, but it is only apt to be hinted at, just like all fundamental and original fact.

Chapter 5

A Memoir of the Future and the defence against knowledge

Antonino Ferro

It is well known that *A Memoir of the Future* is Bion's way of giving free expression to the theatre of the mind that is usually censored by various spontaneously triggered diaphragms.

Somites, Devil, Immature, Term, Twenty Months, Six Years, Heart, Thirty, Seventy-Five Years, and so on all take the floor with equal rights in a real democracy of the proto-mental. This makes me think of what a truly free mind would be capable of producing, where the right to take the floor and to be heard is given to each sub-unit of ourselves and to each planet of the galaxies of possibilities that comprise our minds.

No thought is so unseemly that it cannot be expressed. This means that all thoughts are allowed to be guests in the *agorà* of the mind, and it pre-supposes that sense impressions have been transformed into images/thoughts. It reminds me of a typical renaissance banquet in Mantua at the time of the Gonzagas. There are dozens of guests, and then behind the scenes, unbeknownst to most of them, dozens, even hundreds of cooks, servants, pages, butchers, greengrocers, wine makers, and so on. It is like saying that behind each written book stand the mental functions that enabled the book to be written.

Two clinical examples come to mind. Here they are:

1   PATIENT: Today I ate lamb and so did my daughter ...
    Possible responses:
    a   *Longeque inferior stabat agnus*! (The lamb was at a distance below).
    b   As Montalbano might say, you were as hungry as a wolf.

   c   Your daughter is preparing for a future as a little wolf, too.

   d   I'll never swallow that.

   e   You are telling me that you have managed to avoid inhibiting the most instinctual and voracious part of yourself.

Which models does the analyst have in mind? What is the implicit interpretation in the examples, and why is it not spelt out?

2   PATIENT: This summer I'm going on a trip to China, and where I really want to go is Shanghai. I'll get there in small stages.
     Possible responses:

   a   It sounds like an exploration of an unknown world, something to enjoy.

   b   Small movements so as not to stir up too many emotions.

   c   You are telling me that you are going to discover a part of yourself you have never passed through.

   d   Perhaps you are afraid that the only alternative to the caution of Shanghai might be an earthquake.

   e   Could this be the way to make contact with 'Chiang Kai-shek'?

There was a time when I would have opted to give more decoding types of interpretation out of a great concern for the linear development of the patient's ability to dream (alpha and container functions), but now I prefer more open and daring interventions. They correspond more to the possibility of tempting the patient and the field to face emotional tsunami rather than engaging in 'civil protection' and organizing 'defences' and diaphragms. What is more, I appreciate and embrace what Bion says in the last lines of *A Memoir of the Future*, which in the light of *après-coup* seem to be the key to understanding the whole work.

Every analyst's greatest anxiety and concern (and this applies first and foremost to Bion himself) is learning how to speak in such a way as to be understood (this has always been my own main concern both on a technical level with patients and on a scientific level with colleagues). But what Bion says in the Epilogue seems to me connected to the themes he talks about admirably (and with no possibility of return) in his *Tavistock Seminars* and the Lyon Seminar: theories like wrecks to cling to for fear of sinking; the analyst who espouses the idea of being an artist; being an artist, which means multiplying and then offering points of view – which not everyone will accept, understand or embrace; being curious about the experience you are going through even at the point of death.

Likewise, being curious in each sub-unit of the session about the worlds it will be possible to open by means of the 'PIN' that analyst and patient create continuously.

The vertices are multiple. There may be one from the anus to the mouth (Vol. I); the bottom may be made to speak (Vol. III); and others are Mortimer, the Somites, Sherlock Holmes, etc.

It seems to me that Pirandello was someone who attempted to open up the mind to extreme consequences in daring to challenge the potential identities that inhabit us in continuous transformative movements. Then perhaps also Beckett and, of course, Shakespeare, who tried to compile an encyclopaedia of every possible expression of what it means to be human. But Bion goes further. I see him more as the printer who enables us to publish our own *A Thousand and One Nights*, transforming it into *A Million and One Nights* or, better still, a Google/Googol nights plus one. In other words, it is the expansion into what we know to be an unattainable 'O', but which in its infinite disguises continues to create the backstory to the various fables and plots.

A memoir of the future, but one that acts as a kind of diaphragm, is to be found in the film *Planet of the Apes* and its sequels. The wise apes know that humans have brought mankind to the point of nuclear destruction and feel compelled to try to avoid a repetition of what would happen in the future if the survivors of the past were to take over the evolution of the species.

Here, I can see a link with another essential point Bion makes: never take anything for granted. The gods laugh when they hear men talk about their plans, so all optimism about our future is left in suspension, destroyed by a nuclear war, swallowed up by a black hole and supplanted by viruses that elude our domination.

But what does this mean?

I believe that we must live in a spirit of curiosity, without depending on the book of life or the book of analysis that the many Bibles we cling to promise to provide. According to the theory of fractals, this curiosity and this risk should be extended to include the micro-level of each sub-fraction of analysis or session of analysis.

Defences against knowledge

In the Paris seminar, we find hardly any of the strange terms Bion deployed to revamp the entire lexicon of psychoanalysis. Nor do we sense the rarefied atmosphere of his most abstract writings, for example, in *Transformations*. There is a wonderful moment when one of the seminar participants tries to bring things back onto the known territory of psychoanalytic theory. Bion has just finished talking about the need to see what is not there, which is truer than what can be perceived through the senses. He gives the example of the painting of a tree and how the artist is also able to show the observer roots that are invisible because they are underground. A colleague then asks if this metaphor has anything to do with the unconscious. Bion just about manages to remain desolately patient (or patiently desolate), pointing out that 'unconscious' is one of those words invented by Freud to draw attention to something that really exists, but then, as usual, discussion gets caught up in endless disputes between Kleinians and Freudians and all sorts of theories, and eventually the simple fact that what is at stake is a human being and a mind gets lost.

Often the limitations to the creativity of the analysis are a question of how far down the analyst, and consequently the analytic couple, is willing to go, bearing in mind that their relationship is in many ways asymmetric, with responsibility for the depth of the immersion lying with the analyst.

What means or defences can the analyst use to avoid diving into waters that are too deep for him?

One much-used means is to fail to provide the humus suitable for the development of the characters the patient has brought into play. The easiest, most naïve and, at the same time, most subtle of these means is to situate the 'characters' as people in history.

For example, if a patient talks about an uncle suspected of uxoricide, this criminal aspect that he is trying to place in the field can be bonsaized and crystallised inside the patient's history rather than providing him with all the seeds of growth and development that would enable the criminal aspects of the patient (and perhaps of the analyst, or both) to find a script and an appropriate setting.

Another ploy that likewise extinguishes stories that could otherwise develop is to turn to the comfort of a supposed External Reality, which can then be doubly chained when it becomes Historical Reality.

A patient talks of a cousin of his grandfather who had been a member of the Salvatore Mesina gang, a gang responsible for a number of kidnappings, some of which had ended fatally for the victims. Logically, this character, 'the grandfather's criminal cousin', can be put to sleep or lethargised, or it can become a 'seed' that will germinate any number of possible stories if it finds suitable terrain and is given adequate irrigation, making it part of the repertoire of split-off and never-thought operations.

Essentially, each story is the possible progeny of sequences of pictograms that may face a censor, like the priest in the *Cinema Paradiso* who cut out all the kisses or the unforgettable Peppino De Filippo in Fellini's *The Temptation of Dr. Antonio* (AA. VV. *Boccaccio '70*, 1962, Italy).

Essentially, each analyst at work often resorts to 'blacklisting' potential characters to stop them from causing disturbance, disorder or fear during the analytic work, but they will remain encysted in the patient, like the dangerous war remnants that are sometimes defused by bomb disposal experts but sometimes explode unexpectedly.

However, the responsibility for an analysis, whether it be at 45°, 90°, 180° or 360°, rests mainly on the shoulders of the analyst. Analyses can be like a closed fan where the slats are still positioned on top of each other, meaning that many stories will never see the light of day, or they can be 'fans with gradually opening slats' that will tell ever-growing numbers of possible stories. These fans can be opened more and more, so there's never an end.

It is often the case that theories, even those that have proved most useful – like the Oedipus complex or the Unconscious – (and in saying this we are simply paraphrasing what Bion says in his *Tavistock Seminars*, 2007), insofar as they are already known, function as barriers, as light pollution covering what we do not know. This is the only really interesting work to be done in analysis: going in search of the unknown and learning to tolerate knowing less and less but having learnt the method for trying to learn more.

I am in no doubt that many analyses are in fact conducted by analysts who behave like ostriches with their heads in the sand of theory – so as not to risk seeing things that might frighten and hurt them. My point is that the analyst often stands as the great anaesthetist or narcotiser of 'possible stories', all of whose subversive power remains embryonic compared to often more normopathic, adequate and orthodox aspects.

Perhaps the question of orthodoxy (and hence of adaptation to what is known and shared) is also connected to this as a phobia of possible subversion, and if psychoanalysis has historically had an incredible subversive power, many now call upon it as a way of tranquillising using maps of pseudo-normality.

Defending ourselves from the 'present' now often seems to be the imperative. This is what happened in the case of posters, for an exhibition by Maurizio Cattelan in Milan, that featured Hitler kneeling in prayer. The posters were immediately banned on the grounds that they offended the memory of the victims of Nazism. Whereas this particular Hitler might not be the Hitler of the past, but a memento of the Hitler who inhabits the human community, while other deportations, both real and metaphorical, may still be continuing.

I still recall the scandal of puppets of children hanging in trees, another work by Cattelan from some years ago, also stigmatised for their supposed bad taste, although in fact they were perhaps making a comment about truths of today, for example, lack of respect for 'children' in all possible forms. Everything thought-provoking is branded as bad taste and not seen as it should be, namely, a way of awakening lethargic minds.

The treatment received by the various religions is very different. Every religion represents a different attempt to curb all the emotions that seethe inside us using orthodox rules. Even a different religion is seen as a source of disturbance if it calls one's own religion into question. Just imagine the absence of religions. And to repeat the point, the need for orthodoxy is no different in psychoanalysis.

Chapter 6

Bion's razor

Reading *A Memoir of the Future*

Giovanni Foresti

Whoever reads even a few pages of the three books that constitute *A Memoir of the Future* undergoes a continuous assault of heterogeneous stimuli and unexpected thoughts: a bombardment that prompts a desperate struggle to accommodate the resulting commotion of impressions, ideas and reflections within a single, relatively coherent conceptual framework.

If one did have troubles understanding what the symbol 'O' means, for instance (and honestly: who does really dare to assert a complete comprehension of this theme?), here is something very helpful. Throughout these books, inner life is described as a dialogue that cannot be simplified or made much clearer than allowed by its fatally complicated, phenomenological appearance. The psyche is represented as a continual, magmatic chaos whose changes are inevitably catastrophic: a multi-layered system where even the smallest transformations are the elusive result of several processes that occur simultaneously at different levels.

To read those pages is therefore a vaccination against the illusion of possessing easy certainties. 'It is like being bombarded with chunks of feeble puns, bits of Shakespeare, imitations of James Joyce, vulgarizations of Ezra Pound', writes the author in Chapter 11 of the first book: *The Dream* (*MF*, p. 51). Ironizing about the schizo-paranoid nature of the reader's experience (because bombs and grenades, here, are only 'phoney'), the word battery continues apace: 'mathematics, religion, mysticism, vision of boyhood, second childhood, and vision of old age' (ibid.). This is the inevitable complexity of psychic life, as represented by *A Memoir of the Future*. One has to look below its polymorphic surface for the transformations and factors that really matter.

Fearing the outcome of 'being "reasonable"'—as the great Ape always pretends to be, the books end by wishing the readers 'a Happy Lunacy and a Relativistic Fission ...' Whatever but the pretense to KNOW: because '"O"—Bion had written in *Attention and Interpretation*—does not fall in the domain of knowledge or learning save incidentally; it can "become" but it cannot be "known"' (Bion, 1970, p. 26).

Hypotheses

My contribution to the close reading of *A Memoir of the Future* attempts to order the far-from-soothing chaos raised by the text and consists of three key interpretative couplets: (1) psychoanalytical wars and non-psychoanalytical wars, (2) defining hypotheses and epistemological precautions, and (3) group dynamics and group thinking.

1   Together with Klein, Sullivan, Bowlby, Winnicott and others, Wilfred Bion belongs to the pioneering group that enabled the 'relational' turn in psychoanalytical thinking (Aron, 1996; Civitarese, 2011; Cooper, 2005). Bion's contribution can be seen as an attempt to rid psychoanalysis of the excessive internal conflicts that marked the first decades of its existence. The 'external' wars apart (i.e., the two World Wars that absorbed the first half of the brief century: Hobsbawn, 1994), we should remember the importance of the great 'internal' war that took place in the analytical movement: a conflict that lasted decades and seriously challenged the political unity and conceptual coherence of psychoanalysis (Ferro, 2010; Hinshelwood, 1997; King and Steiner, 1991). Bearing this challenge in mind, I propose that the last words of Bion's book serve as a pacifist rebuke: 'Wisdom or oblivion – take your choice. From that warfare there is no release' (*MF*, p. 576).

2   The most innovative theoretical and methodological solutions are the products of a single author's personal abilities, but these products also derive from the philosophical and scientific tradition to which the author belongs. In Bion's case, I assume that his 'quest' was strongly influenced by English empiricism, and particularly by nominalism and associated developments (Noel-Smith, 2013).

With these premises, I propose that Bion contributed to psycho-analytical theory by alloying it with Ockham's Razor and its epistemological principles. Like the English Franciscan Friar (upon whom Umberto Eco based the central character, William of Baskerville, in *The Name of the Rose*), Bion sought to defend the theoretical categories of psychoanalysis from vain, specula-tive and contradictory proliferation. '*Entia non sunt mulplicanda praeter necessitatem*', the nominalists prescribed: the categories of thought—in other words, the *entia* of theory—should not be multiplied beyond need. To this end, detailed epistemological inspection would periodically and usefully prune the categories in question of conceptual excesses. If theory, like an untrimmed beard, is granted unchecked expansion, the analyst may well lose sight of the distinction between conceptions and experience, be-tween defining hypotheses and clinical facts. As Bion states in the Pro-Logue of *A Memoir of the Future*, the thus-blinded analyst will 'remain blind to the thing described' (*MF*, p. 5). To Bion's numerous affirmations in this respect, we should add the contin-uous expressions of doubt and the methodical quest for the most obscure and elusive features of every issue: 'Ultimately your un-belief rescued you from *that* quagmire – sunk without a trace in your own exudate of complacency', Bion writes in the first part of *The Dawn of Oblivion* (ibid., p. 451).

3   Finally, of all the compound activities that Bion undertook, his work with groups constitutes the most original experience in his *curriculum* and contributed most decisively to the development of his thought. Bion's research on *group thinking* dates back to the first part of his professional life, when he worked in a non-orthodox psychoanalytical institution, the Tavistock Institute, and served in the British military institutions (Bléandonou, 1990; Foresti and Rossi Monti, 2010). Thanks to these experiences, Bion began to elaborate a conception of psychic life that implicated 'the idea of the individual being a "group"—like Hobbes' idea of the group being an individual' (*MF*, p. 215). I believe that the multi-subject and polyphonic voice with which *A Memoir of the Future* originates derives from these early experiences, which re-mained ever vivid in Bion's mind. The ironically optimistic aspi-ration that drove Bion to write *A Memoir of the Future* influenced

the choice of the symbolic container within which to elaborate
his thought, an aspiration that is clearly evident in passages such
as the following: 'I think that it might some day be possible for
them all to be awake and carry on a fairly disciplined debate'
(ibid., p. 443).

The battle of Hastings and Norman domination

The beginning of the first volume of *A Memoir of the Future* evokes
a catastrophic change of the sort found in Orwell's descriptions of
nightmare revolutions. The initial protagonists of the story—Alice
and her husband Roland, the landowners; the maid Rosemary and
the laborer Tom, the servants—are buffeted by dramatic events that
change their lives forever. On the horizon of the small world they have
long inhabited, the perennial English nightmare unfurls: a lost war
and invaders who submit the country to capillary military occupation (we should recall that 'occupation' corresponds to the word *Be-
setzung*, which Freud chose to describe the work of the libido and
that was translated into Italian as *investimento* and into English as
cathexis).

In Bion's story, as in First World War Russia, military defeat un-
leashes social conflict, triggers the overturning of the family structure
and brings about the hierarchical reorganization of the farm in which
the story takes place. Within this topsy-turvy setting, Rosemary rebels virulently against her female employer ('All right, you bloody
bitch, I'll make you pay for this. This is not capitalist England now,
you know!' ibid., p. 15). For his part, Roland—who believes that he
understands everything, Bion notes with irony—furiously and use-
lessly inveighs against his consort and blames her for the class war in
which they find themselves: 'You fool!' he says to his wife. 'God knows
what you have done with your tantrums!' (ibid., p. 15).

This turbulent transformation results in a radical change in
perspective. Alice and Roland, who had always considered themselves to be part of the minor nobility who governed their locality
without hindrance, 'stood naked, incongruous, alien, without a
point of reference that made sense' (ibid., p. 27). The defeat suffered
by their world 'was on a scale of defeat so disastrous that it would

be necessary to suppose that something analogous to the Norman Conquest had taken place' (ibid.).

And here is the paradox whence the book's pregnant *incipit* originates—a paradox that only the overturning of conceptual perspective and a binocular vision of history allow the viewer to perceive. The defeat of the Saxon King Harold by the Norman Duke William, which took place at Hastings in 1066, not only brought catastrophe to the island's nobility. Paradoxically, it also marked the birth of the United Kingdom. Under the Norman rule, England would leave the sphere of Scandinavian influence and enter the cultural area of European countries, particularly that of France. The unity and identity of the English nation derives not from a victory, Bion notes, but from a defeat.

What of interest to psychoanalysis does this observation contain? Let us think of the problem from the perspective that Bion attributes to Hobbes: the group as an individual. Psychoanalysis is an investigation of the subject's experiences and of the efforts to which the single individual finds himself subjected. It is only by dealing with one's own defeats, and with the foreign domination that ensues that the subject/object can hope to become the authentic subject of his/her own story and a protagonist of his/her own life.

The opening of *A Memoir of the Future* focuses the reader's attention on the history of an entire nation by chronicling a few prototypical individuals and by citing similarly few exemplifying narratives. Buried by the tedium of an excessively quiet life, Alice and Roland are described as lacking a real psychic life and as almost dead.[1] Defeat and foreign domination inform them of the hardships of history and of the complexity of the world. The cards of the social game are reshuffled, and, surprisingly, Alice and Roland's lives recommence.

The book that opens *A Memoir of the Future* presents itself as the Bayeux Tapestry[2] or as the *Domesday Book* demanded by the victor of the Battle of Hastings. The first of these 'texts' (an embroidered cloth that is 70 meters long and almost 2 meters wide) depicts the defeat of Harold Godwinson: '*hic Harold Rex interfectus est*'. The second is a catalogue of the property lost by the Anglo-Saxons, or rather an inventory of the goods and the people acquired by the Normans as a result of their victory.[3]

To elaborate a period of mourning, i.e., to initiate that strange oblivion *sui generis* that heals psychic pain and enables the recommencement of life, it is important to specify who and what has been lost and to distinguish loss from what remains alive and capable of forming a relationship.

Psychoanalytic wars are marked by the acquisition of metaphorical territories and the more or less partial loss of imaginary sovereignty. The disputed loot consists of the theoretical inheritance of traditions that oppose each other. Bion is attentive to the conceptual consequences of the struggle between victors and vanquished, and considers this dialectic to be a vital part of cultural comparison and conceptual research. The textual tract that most clearly illustrates the methodological consequences of the historical, theoretical and clinical events of the analytical movement appears, in my opinion, in the third paragraph of the 13th chapter of *Learning from Experience*— one of the most explicitly nominalist extracts in Bion's entire *opus*.

> As a method of making something clear to himself the analyst needs his own book of psycho-analytic theories that he personally frequently uses together with page and paragraph numbers that make their identification certain.
>
> (Bion, 1962, p. 39)

In psychoanalytic theory, clinical dialogue and theoretical discussion are the battle field in which the truly necessary conceptions survive and emerge (*'pluralitas non est ponenda sine necessitate'*). The analyst should not avail him/herself of theories by enthusiastically assisting their spontaneous dissemination. Rather, (s)he should appraise them as a legacy of as yet provisional hypotheses: incomplete and unstable constructs to be treated with caution and to be kept in coherent order, so as to permit constructive reassessment.

Uncertainty: the exercise of doubt

Let us invert the perspective and think of the individual as a group. Psychoanalysis is an activity that allows the subject to understand him/herself. However, even the knowledge of someone who studies his/her psychic life intimately will be partial, provisional and not infrequently far from the mark. 'I can say that I know who I was when I was at school – we read at the end of the 28th chapter of the first volume – but that is very different from who I was; that I shall never know' (*MF*, p. 130). And, further on, the text returns to this theme even more explicitly:

> even when I am concerned with my own thoughts I am ignorant though I am the person whom I have a chance of knowing better than anyone ... even if I know myself better than anyone I shall ever meet, the sum of that knowledge amounts to little.
>
> (Ibid., pp. 197–198)

Thus, even the single subject is a group that experiences considerable difficulty in communicating with its own internal domain because his internal heterogeneity is both synchronic (because numerous processes occur simultaneously at numerous levels within the apparatus that thinks thoughts) and diachronic (involution and, contrastingly, psychic development, transform the structure of the mind by creating relationships that are anything but obvious between past, present and future).

The result of the continuous reshuffling of psychic life is that personal identity is only constructed at the cost of a certain closure to experience and as a result of a fatal excess of theorization. 'They don't really hate each other', says the psychoanalyst of *The Dawn of Oblivion* as he comments on the disagreement between the characters who animate the second chapter of the third book of *A Memoir of the Future* (ibid., p. 438), '"they" all hate learning – it makes them develop – swell up'.

The consequence of addiction to previously established convictions is that the analytic community continuously runs the risk of becoming a *'mutual admiration society'* (ibid., 195). Even if inevitable, recourse to theory ('Theorising is, I admit, a part of practising psychoanalysis': ibid., p. 201) is dangerous and can prove disconcerting. 'The outcome in pycho-analysts as I have observed them, is bigotry, dogmatism and certitude' (ibid., p. 198).

On this theme, the author of *A Memoir of the Future* sets out his position as early as the pages of the *'PRO-LOGUE'*. The original problem to which the author submits the entire question of the value of psychoanalytic theory, and the latter's effect on clinical research, continuously re-emerges as the book's dominant theoretical *Leitmotiv*.

The defining hypotheses that are implicit in the theoretic models should be taken very seriously '*by those who wish to confront what they believe to be the "facts", as near to noumena as the human animal is likely to get*' (ibid., p. 4).

As postulated by Kant, this latter concept (the *noumenon*) is a *Grenzbegriff*: an extreme boundary category that indicates something that is never directly cognizable and experience of which is only possible through the effects produced by its asymptotic existence and by its continuous transformations.

'The psychoanalytic approach – says Roland's friend, Robin (ibid., p. 71), though valuable in having extended the conscious by the unconscious, has been vitiated by the failure to understand the practical application of doubt'. The sentence continues with an example of the perspective within which Bion interprets the effects of theoretic abuse: psychoanalysis is damaged, he writes, 'by the failure to understand the function of "breast", "mouth", "penis", "vagina", "container", "contained" as analogies' (ibid.).

Only doubt preserves the possibility that the thing symbolized is kept distant from the representation that is constructed on the basis of experience. Without the necessary defeat of the signifier—always and exclusively an indirect reflection of the referent (witness the perpetual Hastings of the thinker/researcher)—it is difficult to avoid the risk of becoming what in the second volume of *A Memoir of the Future* Bion defines, effectively, as '*His Satanic Jargonieur*' (ibid., p. 302).

The doubt that *A Memoir of the Future* eulogizes and actualizes is solidly based on the group dimension of dialogue between people who differ radically from each other, notwithstanding their co-presence within a single subject.

Aesthetic enquiry and thoughts without thinkers

Bion's keen interest in the symbiosis between clinical research and literary practice dates back to the period that preceded the Second World War (Anzieu, 1998; Torres and Hinshelwood, 2013). In the 1930s, Bion had treated an Irish young writer who was able, upon completion of therapy and departure for France, to separate himself from the objects that obstructed his thought (principally his mother, as the biographers argue: Bair, 1978) and to conclude the drafting of his first novel.

The writer was Samuel Beckett, and the novel was *Murphy* (Beckett, 1938). In the first pages of *Murphy*, we find the description of a character in whom we cannot but see some of the specific traits of the author of *A Memoir of the Future*. Murphy describes the symptomatology from which he suffers, and defines it by way of antithesis with his.[4] His heart was

> such an irrational heart – Beckett writes – that no physician could get to the root of it. Inspected, palpated, auscultated, percussed, radiographed and cardiographed, it was all that an heart should be. Buttoned up and left to perform, it was like Petrouchka in his box.
>
> (Ibid., p. 25)

Murphy's teacher/therapist Neary, and more specifically the latter's interpretative technique, drew the patient's undiluted causticism. The language Neary used was obscure jargon. The therapist's aim was that 'to invest his own with a little of what Neary, at that time a Pytagorean, called the Apnomia' (ibid.). Not satisfied with this linguistic extravagance, Neary insists on using other useless obscurities. 'When he got tired of calling it the Apnomia he called it Isonomy. When he got sick of the sound of Isonomy he called it the Attunement' (ibid.).

It is no wonder that the therapy in question, built as it was on such unstable bases, was not described as a success by the story's author ('*But he might call it what he liked, into Murphy's heart it would not enter. Neary could not blend the opposites in Murphy's heart*'; ibid., pp. 25–26). The conclusion of this extract—and even more its enigmatic launch—is, however, paradoxical. True, the therapy is halted, but some of its clinical effects are far from banal.

> Their farewell was memorable. Neary came out of one of his dead sleeps and said:
>
> "Murphy, all life is figure and ground."
> "But a wandering to find home," said Murphy.
>
> (Ibid., p. 26)

Once the unease of separation has passed, Beckett is able to write the brief and extremely pregnant sentence that follows:

> And life in his mind gave him pleasure, such pleasure that pleasure was not the word.
>
> (Ibid., p. 25)

And here, we are right in the middle of Bion's thought! Beckett appears to have learned a lot about psychoanalysis as he worked with this psychoanalyst who had not yet become a psychoanalyst.

But perhaps we should ask who learned from whom? Is it Beckett who taught Bion to express himself clearly? Or, is it Bion who with Beckett developed the central themes of his research, namely the investigation of the means by which we predispose, organize and exercise thought?

Whatever the answer (Didier Anzieu investigated this issue at length, and we know that his results were not unequivocal), it is a fact that this was one of the principle motifs behind the writing of *A Memoir of the Future*.

> His Satanic Jargonieur took offence; on some pretence that psycho-analysis jargon was being eroded by eruptions of clarity. I was compelled to seek asylum in fiction. Disguised as fiction, the truth occasionally slipped through.
>
> (*MF*, p. 302)

This extract could be read as a response to the page on which Beckett spoke of his therapist. Its self-descriptiveness is analogous to that of the subjects who, in *The Dawn of Oblivion*, voice the complexity of the subject by returning to eras that preceded his pre- and post-natal lives. The words that correlate most significantly with the Beckett-Bion theme currently under discussion are central to the final pages of *A Memoir of the Future*.

> P.A. A danger lies in the belief that psycho-analysis is a novel approach to a newly discovered danger. If psycho-analysts had an overall view of the history of the human history, they would appreciate the length of that history of murder, failure, envy and deceit.
>
> (Ibid., p. 571)

To conceive the unconscious as a 'newly discovered danger' or to imagine psychoanalysis as a 'novel approach' is to mislead and to fuel isolation, endogamic stagnation and unhealthy pride. The therapy that Bion proposes for this discipline of 'unpleasant warmth ... and arid abstractions' (ibid., p. 470) is a very generous dose of doubt-and-modesty combined with a mighty re-activation of surprise-and-inquiry abilities.

On the philosophical path that Bion suggests, though, the practice of doubt does not become a comfortable skeptical attitude or an easy-going variety of cynicism. The doubts function as factors that contribute to carving the thinking, assisting the psychoanalyst to face her/his human and clinical responsibilities. If tolerated as the epistemological frustrations necessary to develop new and fresh knowledge, the doubts make it possible to devise hypotheses. And these latter—the hypotheses—are the crucial tools that offer the opportunity to learn from experience by virtue of their remaining open and uncertain.

To view human spirit in its entirety, it is necessary to avoid parochial closure and to actively combat intellectual conceit. '*If the analyst observes functions*' (notice the mathematical term that Bion uses as far back as 1962 to rethink the functioning of thought: the psychoanalytical function of the mind) 'and deduces the related functions from them, the gap between theory and observation can be bridged without the elaboration of new and possibly misguided theories' (Bion, 1962a, p. 2).

The idea is that psychoanalysis is merely a stripe on the tiger's fur and that the task of psychoanalysis is that of rethinking thoughts that others had previously intuited and thought. This idea is at the origin of the thesis—entirely counter-intuitive and yet extremely convincing—whereby psychoanalytic thoughts were formulated before psychoanalysis existed, both in humanity as a whole and in the single subject: proto-psychoanalytic thoughts in search of a thinker who can think them over again.

As if to deny the idea of perennial and incomprehensible obscurity, *The Dream* yields a dialogue that illustrates this point—that is, the spontaneous emergence of psychoanalytic thought in the writings of numerous literary and philosophical writers—with ironic clarity.

MAN: ... Sometimes you have to my knowledge claimed that certain
    well known figures of the past, not only of the recent past as

Sigmund Freud himself, were gifted with a profound capacity for understanding their fellow men?

BION: Certainly. We can gauge their actions and behaviour from what has been recorded of or by them, and allowing myself anachronistic – like poetic – license. I would call them very considerable psychoanalysts before anyone had heard of such a term.

MAN: Is this not an instance of claiming that there is such a 'thing' as psychoanalysis, that there always has been such a thing as psychoanalysis, whether it could be verbalized or not?

BION: I would say that it is an example of a thought which, before Freud existed to think it, was 'without a thinker'.

MAN: I am not really clear why you postulate a thought without a thinker. It seems an unnecessary complication.

BION: 'Doubt' is always regarded as an unnecessary complication. That is clear whenever an individual asserts certainty.

MAN: You used the word 'certainly' just now.

BION: Touché. I agree.

MAN: But you reply in the language of a game of combat?

(*MF*, pp. 168–169)

Bion's razor and the asymptotic O: a paradox

The community of Bion scholars and observers has generated numerous questions that have greatly helped me to arrive at the reasoning that I here attempt to develop (Aguayo, 2013a). Given this essay's aims, I shall now reduce the issues I have raised to the following and essential three themes. First, does the latest phase of Bion's research amount to a turn that unveils a completely new theoretical horizon, or does it merely represent an extension of the previous phase? Does the *aesthetic turn* whose most substantial product is *A Memoir of the Future* (Ffytche, 2013) constitute a new cycle in Bion-oriented conceptualization, or is this a question of prosecuting what is known as the 'epistemological' phase of his thought (Bléandonou, 1990)? And, of particular importance: what relationship is there between, on the one hand, the proposal of condensing the connections between thinkers and between subjects into three diverse typologies (L, H and K) and, on the other hand, the hypothesis that psychic experience is the effect of transformation into O?

According to Hinshelwood, there is an evident rupture among the three consonants of *Learning from Experience* (Bion, 1962a), symbols for connections of hatred, love and awareness, and the vowel that, from *Attention and Interpretation* (Bion, 1970) onwards, sends the reader back to an 'unarrivable' thing-in-itself. In addition to the group phase, the research on schizophrenic thought and the so-called epistemological phase, Bion's work demands recognition of a further theoretical stage that begins with an essay written at the end of the 1960s (Bion, 1970) and proceeds to various additional publications in the following years (Torres and Hinshelwood, 2013).

The key concept of this last cycle is 'intuition'; assessment of said concept's *quid* should bear in mind the differentiation, established by Bion's research in the 1960s, between empirical sciences and psychoanalysis.[5] Even on this basis, it is difficult—'*it is a moot point*' Torres and Hinshelwood observe (ibid., p. 186)—to establish whether the word *intuition* is truly the best suited to (i) defining the given methodological model and (ii) evaluating the degree to which this notion differentiates itself from, for example, Winnicott's notion of *intention* as a recognizable element from the point of view of diverse subjects.

Within the context of the foregoing questions, I am convinced by the thesis that Bion's continuous research activities yield grand and radical conceptual novelties, but I also believe that said novelties are balanced by certain methodological constants that derive from Bion's cultural identity, from his theoretical *domus* and from his institutional education.

The paradox that *A Memoir of the Future* obliges us to consider is the result of a permanently unstable dialectic tension that in turn creates a virtuous cycle between order and disorder, between complexity and simplicity. The constant attempt to lighten theory—Bion's epistemological objective in the 1960s (H, L, K)—is pursued in the given texts by way of negation, i.e., by illustrating the labyrinthine complexity of psychic life.

To distinguish truly necessary concepts from those that end up as mere jargon,[6] we have to compare our theorizing with the enigmatic reality of experience. This latter is however obscured by the habit, long since established in the history of our species, of recourse to 'sequential thinking'—a way of exercising reason that lays out 'what it purports to describe' (ibid., p. 85) in excessively linear series.

We have difficulty recognizing the invariants of psychic life not because our argumentation proceeds in clarity→confusion sequences,
as we tend ingenuously to suppose, but rather because the excess of
constructions based on confusion→clarity sequences prevents us
from seeing the reality of psychic life (ibid., p. 89). The strategy of *A
Memoir of the Future* is to overturn the flow, multiply the sources and
mix up the currents.

More than theorizing on the reality of O, Bion's text constrains the
reader to experientially digest the continuous dialogic exchange that
in turn begets the thought of minds that are inclined to meet. The
internal world of subjects is organized by the eternal 'laws of O—the
perfect blanc', Bion observes with irony (ibid., p. 277).

The concept of ultimate reality is here expressed by two words, one
French and the other English: 'blanc' as in white, and 'blank' as in
empty. We thus have on the one hand the disquieting white of dizzying
movements of the colors of the mind. On the other hand, there is the
empty space—the blank between the lines of the text, for example—
that acts as an attractor, like an unconscious organizer of the group's
thinking: the negative *blanc*/blank around which the swirling spiral
of thoughts gyrate.

In Bion's view, the razor that resolves the essential from the
superfluous remains ever the distinction between K and −K, which
is explicitly described in the last page of *Learning from Experience*:
'in K the group increases by the introduction of new idea or people;
contrastingly', 'in −K the new idea (or person) is stripped of its value,
and the group in turn feels devalued by the new idea' (Bion, 1962a,
p. 99). And cautious of the epistemological specificity of ideas, Bion
writes:

> The relationship of K to −K can be epitomized by saying that in K
> particularization and concretization of the abstract and general is
> possible, but in −K it is not because the abstract and the general,
> in so far as they exist, are felt to become things-in-themselves.
>
> (Ibid.)

Transformations into O are that towards which the subject's interest
tends when he/she is able to experience thoughts as if they were analogies and metaphors, and not thing-in-themselves. What distinguishes
thought from idle chat and from jargon is the conceptual vitality

instanced by a container/content when it becomes a factor of the thought of a group.

A provisional conclusion

Having reached the end of this task, and desirous of compressing the characteristics of the Bionian razor into a sprinkling of syllables, I shall avail of a concise formulation devised by Umberto Eco and quoted by the cultural page of a daily newspaper in the 1970s. Without ever having read a single line of *A Memoir of the Future* (not least because at the time the book had not been published), the Italian semiologist was able to express the principle upon which these books are based: *one has to learn to confound his ideas in order to have clear ideas*.

The curious coincidence—another instance of thoughts looking for a thinker—probably depends on the fact that Eco, who was known to have little time for psychoanalysis, had thoroughly read the work of William of Ockham and was well versed in medieval philosophy and English nominalism (Eco, 1970, 1987).

As I have done throughout the article, I shall conclude with a few extracts from *A Memoir of the Future* that seem to me to be coherent with what I have attempted to argue.

'We follow the lead given to our shepherds', Roland says, parodying an attitude of supine devotion]. 'You need not to be sheep', replies P.A. in all seriousness.

> We do not aspire to be leaders or shepherds; we hope to introduce the person to his real self. Although we do not claim to be successful, the experience shows how powerful is the urge of the individual to be led—to believe in some god or shepherd.
>
> (*MF*, p. 266)

The reasoning (such reasoning that reasoning was not the word, as Beckett put it) concludes as follows: 'I should not like to replace one dogma by another; the erection of any god should be studied' (*MF*, p. 267).

Hence, the words chosen to conclude the three books: the wish that the reader, at the end of her/his work, might become capable of enjoying 'a Happy Lunacy and a Relativistic Fission'.

Notes

1 'Falstaff, a known artifact, is more "real" in Shakespeare's verbal formulation than the countless millions of people who are dim, invisible, lifeless, unreal, whose births, deaths—alas even marriages—we are called upon to believe in' (ibid., p. 4).

2 Created by Queen Matilda of Flanders (William 'the Conqueror's' wife) upon commission by the victor's half-brother, Bishop Odo, the tapestry depicts the antecedents, the developments and the bloodiest phases of the battle between the Normans and the Anglo-Saxons. The end of the pictorial story is marked by the Latin epigraph *'ET FUGA VERTENTUR ANGLI'*: and the Anglo-Saxons were put to flight.

3 'Are you Mr and Mrs Trubshaw? Who's this? You Miss Slocombe, the maid? Have you seen ...', he consulted his paper ... 'Mr Jeremy? He's the man isn't he? It's nothing to do with us, but contact the liquidation people; they may have made a mistake.' 'But do you mean', said Alice flushing angrily, 'you take these things away?' 'That is all we have to do.' 'Do you give us a receipt?' The man seemed almost shocked. 'Whatever for?' As soon as it's all been checked and found correct they will give us a receipt' (ibid., p. 17).

4 We read on the second page of the story (Beckett, 1938, p. 25):

> Murphy had lately studied under a man in Cork called Neary. This man, at that time, could stop his heart more or less whenever he liked and keep it stopped, within reasonable limits, for as long as he liked. This rare faculty, acquired after years of application somewhere north of the Nerbudda, he exercised frugally, reserving it for situations irksome beyond any endurance, as when he wanted a drink and could not get one, or fell among Gaels and could not escape, or felt the pangs of hopeless sexual inclination.

5 The former—empirical sciences—base their experience on sensorial data, while experience in the latter discipline—psychoanalysis—originates from the encounter between minds (O) and accordingly cannot be seized by the senses, but merely intuited by means of thought/thinking.

6 'Jargon passes for psycho-analysis, as sound is substituted for music, verbal facility for literature and poetry, trompe d'oeil representation for painting' (*MF*, p. 307). To go beyond jargon and escape from that which has substituted for experience of the internal world, it is necessary to rediscover the complexity of psychic life and to attempt to improve and deepen the perception of what is one's own continuous and elusive psychic material.

Chapter 7

Memories of the future, realisations in the present. The oneiric destiny of pre-conceptions that turn up in the minds of dreamers

Violet Pietrantonio

The introduction

Dear Wilfred,

There were many who trembled in horror, yawned in irritated incomprehension or grimaced in sickened repulsion on first reading your final trilogy. The striking absence of the customary analytic psycho-logos so upset them that they protested at the scandal and cried out in terror of the psychotic wolf, seeking refuge and lost certainties (Turillazzi Manfredi 1994) in the diagnostic dictionary of their beloved psychoanalese. What had happened to you? Psychosis in California? Had you allowed yourself, without honour or shame, to record in print the incontinent ramblings of your senile dementia (O'Shaughnessy 2005).

But there were those who, perhaps without realising it or perhaps through passionate magnetic perception, found their minds impregnated by the pollen grains of pre-conceptions (♂♂♂) which you had sown among the visionary threads of your tale. Diviners who detected the whispers of extraordinary intuitions under the apparent logical decay of the discourse, the traces of new routes to explore, the first sketches of a new atlas of psychoanalysis and of our mental functioning ... Who would recognise in the shattering of the logical-deductive system the example of a new, revolutionary de-scaling treatment necessary for the maintenance and reinvigoration of the psychoanalytic probe.

Three decades passed, and the first realisations of those recalcitrant pre-conceptions which you had disseminated in your final pages started to bloom ...

I will try to venture onto the mysterious paths of that transmission of ideas (Bion 1979) which you had included among the roads to be scoured in your manual of Psychoanalysis for the Future, using only the lantern of the first effects of germination observable today, to your memories first, distant tomorrow.

> ... Just fancy if there was something about ideas which would make them 'generative'! The transmission of ideas may not follow the biological laws of sex or the Mendelian laws of inheritance ...
> (The Dawn of Oblivion, 1979)

Perhaps a bit like a grand-daughter who fishes out of the family attic the diary left by a grandfather and leafs through it enraptured, I have been rereading *A Memoir of the Future* over the past few months and finding myself once again filled with surprise as I note the visionary quality and fecund power of this phantasmagorical text, which seemed to me an extraordinary and potent Guernica (Picasso, 1937), a formal mess and a disturbing origin of contemporary psychoanalysis. A Guernica born under the bombs, crying for help and finding no peace or container for a horror and terror that rack and shred the mind, which calls art to new tasks and incarnates new languages capable of giving voice and image to the violence of the nameless O-bscure that can roar, groan and stun, beyond what is sayable by the logic and language of what has already been domesticated, portrayed and assimilated by common sense. A Guernica that is ever more numinous as time goes by (Grotstein, 2007; Manica, 2014), an avant-garde manifesto possessed by intuitions, pre-sentiments (Bion, 1965), predictions about the travelling circus of evolution, a jigsaw puzzle of epistemic embryos essential to future development. A futuristic work in which the brutal subversion of the order of the established λογος, striking and drenching structure, weave and contents to the full 360°, seems to become a vehicle, a tool, the extreme movement necessary for the emergence of the pre-conception (♂) of an essential catastrophic change (Bion, 1974) in desperate search of an oneiric host. A catastrophic change essential for the breathing of new psychoanalytic thoughts in search of thinkers, for the hosting and rearing of a psychoanalysis available for the encounter with a migrant O (Bion, 1970) of the still unknown, which blows and presses at the K-onfines of every mental and analytic experience, just as it does at the frontiers of theory and of already metapsychologised technique. A catastrophic change that analysts, analysis and psychoanalysts cannot escape.

The revolutionary dismantling of the professional grammar code provoked apoplectic dismay and crazed surges of violent indignation and outright rejection. To most people, psychoanalysis stripped of its usual garb no longer seemed to be psychoanalysis. As some analysts from our own time tell us (Ciocca, 2014), the trilogy had a very bumpy ride through the process of publication: numerous rejections by editors, intractable difficulties with translation, low sales and, above all, many strongly disparaging initial reactions. A few (Gaburri and Ferro, 1988) were able to detect (Manica, 2014) the presence and transformative power of the new dreams that vibrated among the unprecedented semiotic chords of this wild and visionary composition, in which a new mythopoeic psychoanalysis makes its first appearance, recognising in the nakedness of the nun without her habit or of the empress with no crown, sceptre or ceremonial robes the revelation of an often hidden analytic nature secreted behind the institutional adornments that cover the body of psychoanalysis. Perhaps the recent flourishing of writings (Ciocca, 2014; Harris Williams, 1983; Manica, 2014; Pistiner de Cortinas, 2009; Waddel, 2011) dedicated to this final Bionian offering also testifies to the length of time needed for the psychoanalytic community to metabolise the impact of contact with an object bearing aesthetic qualities and crammed with contents never before encountered in the landscape of psychoanalytic literature; of decades required for the removal of blunders and obfuscation through a slow bringing into focus of the familiar and personal in the apparently alien and bizarre.

Mute and silent has perhaps also been the time needed for the gestation of the pre-conceptions ... (♂) scattered in the narrative flow of this fable so that, nested in the uterus of the mind (♀) of some sensitive readers, they could be realised (Bion 1962a) in new inspirations and hypotheses about life and the meaning and practice of psychoanalysis as a method, technique, treatment. In the après-coup observatory of the present, perhaps only today, as posterity, can we take note of how many messages, inscribed as ideograms on the totemic soma of this work, seem to be revealing themselves as a fertilising semen of many elements that constitute the various contemporary theories of dreaming analysis (Civitarese, 2013a, 2015a; Ferro, 2009, 2015; Grotstein, 2007, 2009; Ogden, 2005, 2015; Pistiner de Cortinas, 2011); theories that, in the theoretical-clinical development of the discovery of the mind's dream function as a vital nucleus and active principle of psychoanalytic therapy, are setting off radical transformations in the vision of how our human mind functions and in the conception of psychoanalysis as treatment.

An evidence-kangaroo that carries in its pouch a possible, singular story of the generative, trans-generational transmission of ideas …

A Warburg hypothesis: *A Memoir of the Future* an extraordinary Mnemosyne of psychoanalysis?

Mnemosyne (Warburg 1928–1929) is a figurative atlas composed of a series of plates, consisting of photographic montages, assemblages of reproductions of various works: pieces of evidence from the Renaissance (artworks, manuscript pages, playing cards, etc.), archaeological finds from oriental, Greek and Roman antiquity, items from twentieth-century culture (newspaper cuttings, publicity labels, stamps). Images are privileged objects of study in that they are an immediate way of 'saying the world'. The image is the place in which the impression and memory of events precipitates and condenses. In the *Atlas* the juxtaposition of images, laid out in such a way as to weave together many thematic

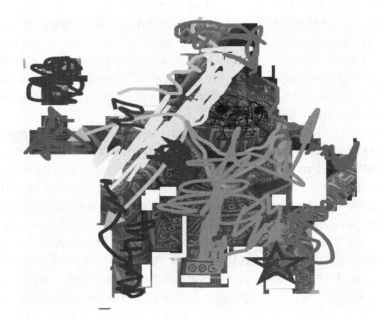

Figure 7.1 The primitive oneiric power of the image

threads around the nuclei and details of the boldest relief, provokes the viewer into an open interpretative process: 'to the image the word' (*zum Bild das Wort*). The objective of the *Atlas* is to illustrate the mechanisms for translating themes and figures from antiquity to the present day, with particular regard to the recovery of motions, gestures and postures that express the entire range of emotional excitation (aggression, defence, sacrifice, mourning, melancholy, ecstasy, triumph, etc.). These are *Pathosformeln*, expressive formulae for emotion ...

> A fairy tale creature, which would appear to be the most typical product of a playful imagination, is really, in statu nascendi, the hard-won outcome of the struggle to grasp an abstract idea. It is an attempt to define the extension of phenomena which, in their fleeting elusiveness, cannot be grasped in any other way.
>
> (A. Warburg, sketches for the conference on *The Serpent Ritual*, in Gombrich, E.H. *Aby Warburg: an Intellectual Biography*, p. 218, n. 2)

Aby Warburg composed *Mnemosyne* during the last years of his life, after re-emerging from the darkness of a mental suffering that had confined him for years in the Swiss clinic directed by Binswanger, and after coming across the powerful oneiric drug of the image. Warburg indeed tells how fateful it was for him, in enabling him to re-emerge from the darkness, to encounter the image of primitive man with his success in evoking that experience of early existence and to feel oneself trembling, bewildered, terrified in a world populated by as yet nameless perceptions, the same as the nightmare in which Warburg had been trapped. A film-still capable of telling him and the world about the terrifying experiences of that speechless newborn (Gombrich, 1970) who continues to live in all of us and who, if too deprived of experiences of *reverie*, can sometimes resort to frantic yelling, feeling its dreams throttled by clutching cramps of *pavor*. An experience of oneiric psychopharmacology upstream and perhaps a source for this *Mnemosyne* made only of images that burst like Prometheus into the world of the academy, irradiating the fire of sensory and emotional experience as the matrix of the meaning and functions of artistic production. A work that had to wait for years to be published and decades to be accepted and recognised in its full valency and epistemic potency. Snapping the threads of chronology, philology and deductive order,

Warburg perhaps came brutally close to the burning O (Bion, 1970) of Art, to its being above all a protension to satisfy a primordial mental need: finding in the film-still a first articulation of the kaleidoscope of proto-sensations and proto-emotions by which we can feel ourselves inhabited, using the image as a spasmodic bestowal of form, figure, communicability and dreamability on our human emotional experience. *Mnemosyne* also seems like the attempt to convey the meaning, myth and passion (Bion, 1963) of a new intuition, lifted blazing from the long darkness of a night in the murkiest and most hellish regions of an evil and an anxiety without name (O→K). The potency of a new idea that, processed by the enzymes of time, radically changed the method for investigating and comprehending works of art and dismantling nets of entrenched *tòpoi* in the foundations of the History of Criticism and Art History.

I do not know if Bion was familiar with *Mnemosyne*, but didn't he operate in a similar way in *A Memoir of the Future*? Breaking the schemes of discourse and habit of logical-deductive reasoning, didn't he catapult at supersonic speed into the world of O? The O of psychoanalysis? Didn't he, and doesn't he, lead the reader with him on a disturbing tour through the grotesque, the absurd, the horror, the chaos of s-O-mething that lies, still waiting, unnamed and meaningless under the *K*overs of the already uttered, signified, thought? In the subsoil probed by the still mysterious roots of our mind's functioning and that of psychoanalysis as treatment? Among the shadows and phantoms of a past that are perhaps nightmares and terrors that have not yet found oneiric medicine and the trails of a *noumen* in which perhaps so many pre-conceptions dwell as they wait for a future dream?

Is *A Memoir of the Future* a sort of *Mnemosyne* of psychoanalysis, which some analysts were able to acknowledge in its incredible importance as the first work of psych-O-analysis? A tribe of Gombrich-Analysts who found themselves living right in that earthly triangle where they came close not only to the later Bion's Psyche, but also to his Soma: indeed, for many analysts California, Brazil and Italy were places where it was possible to meet W. Bion personally during the last years of his life, and these are the very lands where, from the beginning of the century, the ferment of youthful thoughts had started to pulse, dancing energetically, agitatedly, boldly around and in the midst of the O of dream. Dream as miraculous medication, unique and inspired creation (Rulli, 2015) of the αdream-function of which our mind is a naive bearer and of which Psych-O-analysis must become robust incubator (♀) and passionate midwife (♀♂). Scientists, who try courageously to make their way onto the untrodden paths of oneiric stem-cell cure, which, at the Azimuth of this trilogy, W. Bion adumbrated to the shocked eyes of the psychoanalytic community in perceptive vestiges of a science yet to come.

Observing this singular geographical correlation, an impudent question comes to mind: could the possibility of a psycho-somatic encounter play a fundamental role in the trans-generational transmission of ideas? What primary, essential function could intercorporeality perform (Gallese and Ammaniti, 2014) in the encounter between two minds, for the purposes of creative learning? Does *in vivo* psycho-sensory experience of the other generate a ♀♂ relationship different from that created *in vitro* by literature? Could the quality of the ambient emotional experience of the ♀♂ encounter be the crucial synaptic mediator in the psycho-transmission of ideas between generations?

Report from the present: flash of intuitions and evidences that are revealed as the dawn of discovery of new science

I Narrative and narrating function: α-lipoic acid and stem cells for the genesis and development of the mind's oneiric functions

> ... *if there were such a thing as a mental digestive system, I could say that*
>
> *the mental diet of entertaining fictitious characters has contributed greatly to my mental health* (MF, p. 129) ... *That fellow, Shakespeare, puts words to the emotional problem that is still not solved* (ibid., p. 395) ... *Some people can talk with such precision that the right audience could not fail to understand the communication. An obscure poet may, nevertheless, be expressing something in the shortest and most direct language known* (ibid., p. 192) ... *The 'fictitious character', the 'fiction', is the 'reversed perspective' of the 'abstract'. Is there an ultra logic or infra logic which does not fall within the spectrum of human logic, the logical spectrum analogous to the visual portion of the spectrum of electro-magnetic waves?*
>
> (Ibid., p. 395)

... I suggest a possibility of stimulating in the listener who listens as he listens, mental activities that intervene between him and thoughts, the obscuring capacity of which is specific, not general.

(Ibid., p. 192, italics added)

In this mini Warburg-puzzle from *A Memoir of the Future*, there is just a small sample of the numerous potent flashes about the narrative function that Bion dots here and there among his pages, evoking its intuited properties as a *morula* for psycho-stem-cell production to support the genesis, growth and regeneration of functions necessary for mental life and its O-neiric oxygenation. Like an encoded preview of the forthcoming psychoanalytic pharmacology for those who, using the lens of the future, may witness in the work of A. Ferro, T. Ogden and J. Grotstein at the unfolding of the evolutionary destiny of this first chrysalis of Bionian intuitions about the essentiality of narrative as a function and necessary instrument for the survival both of the human and psychoanalytic species. For whoever can zoom in on the metamorphic process of a pre-conception silkworm ($\male$), which has been realised in a brilliant and colourful conception in the mulberry tree of post-Bionian studies ($\female$,$\female\male$); a conception pregnant with new ideas about the functioning of our mind and psychoanalytic treatment.

A pioneer of research and experimentation and enunciator of the virtues of narrative as a principal instrument of the psychoanalytic method, A. Ferro has from his earliest publications (Ferro, 1992b, 1996) drawn attention to the narrative factor in psychoanalysis, highlighting its invaluable polyvalence as a tool-product of extraordinary efficacy, as much for an ultrasound diagnosis of the *hic et nunc* of the psychoanalytic process as for the non-intrusive administration of analytic medications. Perhaps curious at the flickering of scientific mystery, over the years Ferro seems to have moved ever deeper into the artesian wells of narrative, revealing its depths and its oneiric genealogy. At bottom, all A. Ferro's work could even be read as an in-depth treatise on narrative, which he has found to be the mother tongue of dream. For him, all the elements and psychodynamic functions of narrative can be studied and plumbed with scientific expertise (Ferro, 2002, 2006), thereby becoming object and instrument of choice in a psychoanalytic treatment that sets itself the goal of germinating and/

or developing the ability to dream personal emotional experience (Civitarese, 2014; Ogden, 2005; Grotstein, 2007, 2009). A work in progress, a working-through of narrative, which step by step shows itself to be a molecular and synaptic treasure trove of receptors and transmitters of oneiric peptides necessary for the αphaβetisation of emotional life and for analytic α-generation. In his current resting place of field theory (Ferro, 2009; Ferro and Basile, 2007; Ferro and Civitarese, 2015), Ferro shows us how narrative and its handmaid, the narrative function, can be considered the language and technical device most appropriate to a dreaming cure, which, in the stem-cell effect of dream-work and within the container of Bionian metapsychology, has found new principles, functions and foundations for the transformative growth of our human mind and for treatment in psychoanalysis. In his texts, narrative, the story narrated in the session, shows itself to be the seat and pre-selected medium chosen by the proto-mental for blurting out the presence and residence of βfoci in urgent need of αintervention, but also shows itself to be the preferred analytic idiom for achieving transformations in dream, thanks to its unrivalled oneiro-congruence and oneiro-compatibility. If the characters who shyly peep or violently burst out in the session can be accepted and listened to as the most trustworthy envoys of O, bearers of proto-dreams in search of a dreamer, how will it be possible to loosen and transform into a dream-film the magma or rock of proto-emotions encrypted in their soma if not by using that same native, narrative vocabulary in which they are timidly attempting to communicate? This cluster of oneirogenic and oneiromodulatory properties, also revealed by the Californian colleagues T. Ogden and J. Grotstein (Ogden, 2001, 2005, 2009; Grotstein, 2007), seems to make the narrative function gradually acquire the epistemological and metapsychological status of a function of the mind and of psychoanalytic work. Flushed out of hiding, observed, investigated and illustrated in its dual specialisation as βreceptor and αtransmitter, narrative stands out in the panorama of twenty-first-century psychoanalysis as the unchallenged semiologist, re-animator and fecundiser of the human mind's dream activity, unrivalled nightmare-catcher, peerless bard of *rêveries* and dreams that reawaken our innate capacity for dreaming or train it in oneiric play (Grotstein, 2007) … In the meantime, the recognition of the narrative αmine's nobility as a source of the nourishment and vitality of the human mind, is confirmed by a large multidisciplinary chorus of studies and reports of experiments ranging from the human sciences to the neurosciences (Damasio, 1999; Gallese, Migone, and Eagle, 2006; Gallese and Ammaniti, 2014; Gottschall, 2012, etc.): listening to and telling stories encourages the birth and development of neuronal chains (mirror neurons) and has been an activity indispensable to our survival thus far as a human species, as much as, if not more than, the development of mere technology. Like the first notes of a unanimous *Eureka* that announce the rediscovery of a new factor that transfigures the well-known psychogenetic profile of *Homo sapiens* into *Dreaming Man*, bearer of primary needs often misunderstood and treated as secondary accessories ...

And so, dear Wilfred, after 50 years, we can conclude that characters, stories, poets sing of a mind still unknown to science, speak a word capable of verbalising and reverberating the Atlantis of that oneiric βιος, which is the lymph that makes it possible for us to feel we exist. Today, what is starting to warble and babble in the sensus communis of psychoanalysis is the idea of an analyst as myth-maker (Levine, 2015a), rather than that of a Pythoness dispensing shrewd K-interpretations ... Perhaps the transmission of ideas can be truly generative if it is an honest and courageous communication of personal intuitions ... and if we keep in mind the long timescales of the psycho-embryology of dreams and thoughts ...

2 Senses, Soma and Smell: among the first rustlings of a debutant somato-psychoanalysis?

BODY: It is the meaning of pain that I am sending to you; the words get through–which I have not sent–but the meaning is lost.

(*MF*, p. 434)

SOMA: If you had any respect for my 'feelings' and did what I feel, you wouldn't be in this mess.

(Ibid., p. 434)

PA: ... *if* we could receive the facts which we are capable of 'sensing' we might be able to read the facts available to us, and 'think the thought through', to what lies behind the facts (ibid., pp. 263–264) ... the psycho-analyst needs to 'smell' the danger, as well as know as much as his training and psychiatric textbooks

can tell him (ibid., p. 529) ... the training we all undergo in the
process of becoming civilised does destroy, or dangerously cover
up, our animal inheri-tance (ibid., p. 250) ... I have in mind the
need to distinguish between experience of knowledge imparted
by others and knowledge derived from the analyst's ability to
turn what his senses tell him into nourishment.

(Ibid., p. 458)

Use the *Warburg Method* as a compass for the *Memoir* reading-
comprehension, and what scratches its way out is a collage of hints, ad-
monishments, aphorisms, witticisms and intimate cogitations (Bion,
1992) about the fundamental importance of lending the analytic ear to
the neglected somatic mantra: a thorny flora of somato-psychoanalytic
semiotics that pops up like Edelweiss in the first two volumes, before
imposing itself in the third one as a soma-sauro-chakra of senses and
unknown sense, which impels and urges psychoanalysis to undertake
non-deferrable but hitherto unattempted tasks of auditing and aus-
cultation in humble, attentive at-one-ment (Bion, 1970) and strenuous,
distilled, untrammelled negative capability (ibid.).

   A Jurassic soma, an enclave of inaccessible mental states (Bion, 1976;
De Mattos and Braga, 2013) that can only be *smelled, sniffed out and intuited* (Bion supervision A34, in Levine and Civitarese 2015) by a *sense-able*
analyst (Civitarese, 2015b). A *hypothalamic* area (Bion, ibid.; De Mattos
and Braga, 2013), a precarious encampment of the wild proto-mental,
hungry for dream, which overbearingly shows itself in Bion's late seminars and writings as a learned 'must' of clinical ontology and deontol-
ogy: the violent somato-psychic tyrannosaurus that plunges heavily and
terrifyingly into the consulting room will not long tolerate being put to
flight with denials or sedated with K-injections of interpretative antibiot-
ics; we shall have to learn to accept it, listen to it and recognised it as the
most personal prim-O-rdial *sauvage* in search of oneiric subjectivation,
the Arf-Arfer (Bion, 1982) of that devouring, nameless terror waiting for
sens-orization α. A proto-sensory animalness that presupposes animal
capacities for being approached, sniffed, understood and channelled
into the circuitry of oneiric transformation, present-ifying to psychoanalytic practice a petition for skills hitherto unthought-of and not yet
absorbed into metapsychology and institutional training. Over and over
again, Captain Bion urges a reconnection to our *animal inheritance*, so
that we can recapture, sharpen and refine our faculty for sense-ing all

those mute proto-emotions that circulate in the analytic situation, and so that an analytic experience can truly be an opportunity for psychic epiphany, rather than a rerun of painful, autistic scotomisation of O, held hostage by timorous and presumptuous K-intellectualisations. In mordant Morse code, the last Bionian telegram seems tirelessly committed to transmitting dots and dashes that look like the first sketch of a debutant somato-psychoanalysis, entailing a training in the availability and use of the senses, soma and a somato-psychotic vertex, so as to achieve an adequate and useful practice of the psychoanalytic profession.

But how is this wasps' nest of stinging, harassing pre-conceptions about relevance and potential not yet absolved and put into practice in the exercise of our profession, to be realised in the form of theoretical concepts and analytic finesse? How are we to metapsychologise the gloss of the soma in our treatises on psychoanalysis? How to contact, comprehend and engage in dialogue with the *somites* (*MF*) that crowd silent or βurβling in our analytic encounters? In the *Mare Magnum* of recent publications, a small community of studies stands out (Civitarese, 2014; Collovà, 2015; De Mattos and Braga, 2013; Manica, 2016) as seeming to make a start at sounding the barely opened universe of the somato-psychic in psychoanalysis; descriptions of adventures in the depths of analytic mutism that have revealed themselves to be sands of hibernation dense with buried larvae of sleeping dreams; O-rphanages unearthed among mists of the unsaid and forests of reasoning, putting Faith (Bion, 1970) in the signals coming from the receptors of the personally sensible by an analytic mind that eavesdrops, breaths, absorbs the impressions (Ogden, 2015) of proto-sensory waves and vibrations propagating in the analytic field; colleagues who show us how gestures, looks, shivers, enactments or material objects may be able to unlock an unexpected access to the spectrum of the oneiric (Civitarese, 2014), if they are recorded and smelled out as the death rattle of paralysed nightmares in search of oneiric physiotherapy. Analyst scuba divers who, descending into the abysses of the proto-oneiric, provide us with a state of the art theoretical-technical vademecum for the clinical practice of this debutant somato-psychoanalysis, which seems to compel Metapsychology to broaden out; we will need to go beyond the Kleinian Pillars of Ps, immersing ourselves in at-one-ment in that autistic-contiguous position (AC) outlined by T. Odgen as the oldest experiential platform for the relationship between human beings, to bear with trust and negative capability that darkness that has no pictogram, and where the flows and pressures of the still unsayable sensible surge; to roam around in it so that we can draw on the truest and most personal plankton of our still undreamt dreams. We are present at the rise and codification of AC as an analytic position, at its positioning in AC-PS-D (Manica, 2016) as a third pole of oscillation necessary for an analytic work capable of also αlphabetising the vocabulary of that *somatic* that enters the consulting room speaking of an 'us' as yet unKnown to us; an AC that, for now perhaps, becomes the first and fullest metapsychological realisation of that cryptic and vigorous pre-conception of an analytic setting without memory and desire that flashes like lightning in Bion's final discourse.

So Wilfred, if tadpoles (♂♂♂) of meliorism happily wriggling in the narratological cipher given blood, skeleton, muscle and an anima fabulans *of 'selected fact' (Bion, 1963) by you in* A Memoir of the Future, *seem to have found in the theoretical-clinical model of Bion Field Theory (Stern, 2013) a habitat (♀,♀♂) for benign (Bion, 1963) evolution and transformation into new carrier conceptions-elements for the analytic apparatus, then hour by hour they are starting to feature αnews about analytic body to body involving that Kunta Kinte of a Soma, which has finally been taken as a legitimate passenger and protagonist on board the* αmistad *of analytic work … And there are rumours of ever-more sophisticated headphones and decoders for filming the oneiric pictography of anagrams mumbled, grunted, sputtered or inarticulately mimicked in that psychosomatic common t-O-ngue, now identified as the idiographic indigenous dialect of dreams and nightmares originating in the thalamus. And the Soma, aroused in bestial pre-conception in* The Dawn of Oblivion, *stands up imposing and ferocious like the most handsome precursor of progress, the selected analytic object in tomorrow's psychoanalysis.*

3 If it had not been for Memoir of the Future, would I have tried to listen to Robbie?

PSYCHOSIS: *baleful marker of dementia and cancer of mind and thought, or Avatar[1] mindfulness[2] of primordial oneiromancy?*
    Memoir of the Future *reversed and mythopoeic perspective in the psychotic discourse.*

... 'Straitjacket', 'crazy, 'psychotic'— are all associated with confining the Disturbing Mind so that it does not disturb the peace of our Sleeping Beauties (MF, p. 271, Italics added).

... there can be a delusion, or an hallucination, or some other flaw in which an idea might lodge and flourish before it can be stamped out and 'cured' (p. 268) ...

I am the horrendous dream that turned Science Fiction to Science Fact ...

I am thought searching for a thinker to give birth to me. I shall destroy the thinker when I find him ...

The Mind that is too heavy a load for the sensuous beast to carry (p. 38) ...!

Portrayed, embodied and personified by the theatrical and theatrising structure of the work, the mind's fantastic, phantasmagorical functioning dances and yells in shameless nakedness between the lines of *A Memoir of the Future*, with no veil or K-filters. Overturning expectations and Kredence, it presents itself to its *legentes* as a pop-up circus that tears up the films of what has been and can be told and directs a live, intersubjective film of the noisy, bustling agora that quivers in that bizarre and complicated *organon* that is the human mind. In the brood of newness that swarms wildly in between the lines and chapters, this choice of object and narrative style stands out as titanic in its subversive, innovative charge, its ability to communicate and make us experience with immediacy a radical destitution of K and selection of O as the vertex for observation-immersion-comprehension of our being-feeling-thinking-dreaming. Grasped and intuited *ab initio* by those who first esteemed it (e.g. Corrao, 1993; Gaburri and Ferro, 1988, etc.) as an extraordinary and violent *mise-en-scène* of the mind's rackety and multitudinous constitution, in the theoretical-technical apparatus of the analytic field (Civitarese; Collovà; Ferro; Levine; Mazzacane) the mind-rave of *A Memoir of the Future* seems almost to be set up and used as an example of that dream-scene that becomes the fulcrum of all analytic work, centred on monitoring, nourishing and fertilising the dream-work animated and managed in the session. Meanwhile, in the field model the characters, disembarking for the first time on planet psychoanalysis from the little boat of *A Memoir of the Future*, seem to evolve into the most sensitive instruments of analytic work, true dream-detectors that can be used for a wide range of functions, from an oneiric check-up of the field to the activation and stimulation of the dream-work in the field itself. In the light of the subsequent theory of the analytic field, the newborn genre of Bionian psycho-literature seems to reveal itself as the premiere of future landings in the method O→K, Copernicus of revolutionary, epoch-making changes in the geography of knowledge of the mind and of treatment. The method O→K cannot be taught in manuals or by K-explanations, so can it only be learned by vivid, brutal, personal experiences of immersion and subjective impressions (Ogden, 2015)? Hence the sommelier's remarkable proposal of a reading-test, or rather perhaps a test in reading, made by *A Memoir of the Future*? Method O→K, which, in my analytic experience, has unveiled itself as an irreplaceable way of tuning in to the Narnia[3] of the oneiric, which is still able to hum with activity, to breathe and take risks, where emotional turbulences with a powerful narcotic and explosive charge can ossify and iatrogenically sicken any possible movement K→O, from the protension directed towards comprehension and signification, to the impatient interpretation made defensively out of terror. I am thinking of child analyses, but also of all those analytic situations in which only an oneiric eye on characters, on faded pictograms glimpsed in the shadow of dense mists, on βα splinters that may emerge in the desert or the storm can make sense of the heartbeat of a dream-life where the first sight of and contact with a total unravelling of the K-ego functions could create the fear of a presence of an irreversible psychic coma.

Robbie

From the story behind his referral I was expecting a little guy, one a bit bewildered and intimidated by the world … *A first rêverie narrating in avant-coup* (Bonaminio, 2010) *dreams of a self never born?* At the door I found a giant, with a weird stance and way of walking, as hyperactive as if he were on coke, pouring out a jumbled torrent of words. Working with him, I discovered a master, a Tolkien, adept in the most unthinkable, transformative adventures in the world of O. During our first meetings, he was unable to stay in the room with me for more than 15 minutes, but, half way through the second conversation, a little before going out, he made one of his half-asleep hints about painters and singers and I, in total K-desperation, possessed by diagnostic spectres of psychotic disintegration, found myself moved and enlightened by an unexpected *rêverie*: the image of a frightened little boy who, shyly, almost hiding, was making me 'eye up' his favourite games ... games that alluded to dreams ... dreams that were speaking about the plasma of a dream-life that was still alive ...

I found myself making an abrupt about-turn from the prudent temptation to abstain from the analytic undertaking to the no less terrified but fully determined decision to embark on this analytic voyage in which I scented the αurora βorealis of dream.

Like Hansel and Gretel, I decided to follow the trail of pebbles of proto-dreams that Robbie had shown me: the sensation that not only had he shown me the facts to select (Bion, 1963) but also the most opportune and fruitful way of working ...

In all these first years never a transference interpretation, feared as still too potentially violent and traumatogenic for a still foetal ♀ ... but also trying to feel/hear, be curious about, expand in unison the forerunners of possible stories that were being flung here and there around the analytic film-set on the high seas of his logorrhoea ... Trying to weave together narratives that imagined images of possible states of mind and experiences of characters who seemed to encapsulate violent emotions, perhaps still with no name ... training, empowerment and regeneration of a dreaming ensemble (Grotstein 2007, 2009) atrophied by β-earthquakes and chronic deprivation of *rêverie*, through possible experiences of α, ♀, ♀♂, *rêverie*.

But without *A Memoir of the Future* and that Odyssey-in-preview of the fractal Ur of our foetal mind, would it be possible today to try and find how much frozen oneiric legacy might be concealed in a psycho-Sumerian lyric misunderstood and misrepresented for a long time as word-reference of damned and intractable madness?

A session with Robbie

Pokémon singing about evolutions in O?

P: Robbie rings the bell 5 minutes early, probably keeping his finger on the button for the whole time he is waiting: an unbroken squeal sounds loudly in the consulting room.

P: "I was afraid you'd forgotten about me ... There are things I've got to tell you ..." He gives me an envelope with payment for the sessions from the previous month, with a request written by one of his parents for a possible change of time for the next session. "Because he's going fishing and I'm going with him ..."

A: [A moment of panic. I feel put on the spot with no time to think ... Beyond all the theories about the setting and its violations (K), I have the sense-ation (O) of catching the sound of a first attempt at expressing a personal request ... a child daring for the first time to ask for what he wants, with the help of a parent ... wouldn't a reply the patient's own code be the only possible way, for now, to seize the opportunity of a possible realisation in the field of a pre-conception never perhaps realised before? Were I to offer a symbolic elaboration of an interpretative kind, wouldn't it sound recherché and incomprehensible, like explaining a treatise by Aristotle to a three year old?] "Would the 16th be possible?"

P: "Not the 17th? Because I might still be down there on the 16th ..."

A: "I understand ... Let's see ... I could do the 17th at 5 o'clock or the 19th at 1.00 ..."

P: "The 19th at 1.00!"

A: (anxiety about the proximity of the changed session to a session with a *delicate* patient ...)

P: "There was a party yesterday in Via Benozzi ..."

A: "Ah, an all-day street party ..."

P: "Yes, but it was only for part of the street, there were ambulances. You had to go all the way round if you wanted to go out ..."

A: (weighed down by emotions about the party/postponed session?) "A party that was a bit of a bother, a bit annoying ..."

P: "Yes, I prefer *Cortella me too*, the one they have on Via Cortella ... Yesterday there was a big do where you gave what you wanted to buy something and I got masses of Pokémon I didn't have ..." He smiles with satisfaction.

A: "Ah, so you were able to get something for yourself at this party ..." (as I begin to inhale an unusually cheerful emotional life ... and I do not feel oppressed and wiped out by the usual insidious narcolepsy which regularly fogs me with lethargy from the twentieth minute of the session to the end.)

P: "Yes, there are new evolved Pokémon. Because Pokémon evolve. There's Giratina, who is the Pokémon of the Distortion World, who has to keep defending himself because they want to catch him ..."

A: "Giratina lives in a Distortion World? But what's this Distortion World like?"

P: "Like that ladder that you'd bring down from the loft ..."

A: "And instead of the earth you'd have to walk in the sky?"

P: "Yes, but not only sky ... there are pieces of earth too ..."

A: "I wonder how Giratina feels living in this world where everything seems the wrong way round ..."

P: "He's fine, it's just that everyone always wants to catch him. Then there's Mew Two, who is the evolution of Mew. He was generated by men. To start with he had organised an army to fight the men because he thought they wanted to use him for their own reasons, but then he realised that Pokémon and men can co-exist, and love each other. And when he came to know how he had been generated he got a shock!"

A: (evolution in O? But also original O more approachable?) "There's been an evolution, a movement from mistrust and perhaps also from the fear that we feel when we're afraid of being considered objects to be used for personal ends, of not being loved, to feelings of affection and trust ..."

P: "Exactly! From being angry with men to loving them ... There's a saying in Sicily: if the Opuntia grows big, the prickly pear is good, if it doesn't the prickly pear isn't good ..."

A: (O-puntia? If a ♀ is able to impregnate itself with O, will ♂♂ mature, juicy with new emotions and thoughts? ... even if they are thorny, not easy to gather and dream?)

P: Draws a prickly pear with fruit and thorns: "to get close to a prickly pear you've got to have big work gloves, with no holes in, a sack for the fruit, and never stand close to a prickly pear if it's windy because you'll get thorns in you ... The time for good figs is between September and November ..."

A: "More or less this period ..."

It's time to say goodbye.

Dear Wilfred,

How old is Robbie? Is it his calendar age that matters or the one we sense in the field? Robbie is nearly thirty ... perhaps thirty years in which pre-conceptions (♂) of play (♂♀) have stayed in hibernation waiting for a ♀ in which they can be realised ... I have hesitated, doubted and even trembled ... at the crossroads between K norms of the usual analytic work with adults and strong O sensations in need of the structure, style and modus operandi of child analysis ... Around the 40th birthday of A Memoir of the Future, *I felt I couldn't in the end not entrust myself to the very strong flow of meanings and reveries in the field that were speaking to me about a little kid ... who was seeking contacts, responses, and a playroom as a child ... The first time I couldn't help following my nose, which was bringing me the scent of baby dreams was when, seeing his beautiful drawings building up on the desk, I felt that only by putting a little folder on the desk would I be able to try and communicate my feeling of contact with ♂♂ veined with oneiric exuberance and looking for a ♀; ♂♂♂ that had perhaps found, and could at last finally have, a ♀ ... A drawing (♂) perhaps seeks a folder (♀) in order to realise the pre-conception ♀♂ of which it is the animated cartoon ... what use would there have been in more abstract symbolisations of it? ...*

In the transmission of ideas, which are perhaps also pre-conceptions in search of containers, and decisive for the outcome, could they be the conditions for harmony and attunement between ♂♀ on the wavelength of the different levels of the oneiric? Maybe A Memoir of the Future, *on its first appearance as O-contained (♂) was a pre-conception of intercourses ♀♂ in O→K, difficult to accommodate for containers (♀) accustomed to <u>K contained (♂♂)</u> alluding to <u>♀♂ in K→O</u> ?*

Notes

1 *Avatar* (2010), a film directed by J. Cameron.
2 Mindfulness is the translation of *sati* in Pali, the language used by the Buddha for his teachings. Mindfulness is a mode of paying attention, moment by moment, in the *hic et nunc*, in an intentional non-judgemental way, to sensations, perceptions, impulses, emotions, thoughts, words, actions and relationships (from Wikipedia).
3 *The Chronicles of Narnia* (2005), a film directed by A. Adamson.

Chapter 8

The ineffable

Avner Bergstein

The silent, elusive movement of the emotional experience becomes a word when it crosses an invisible border, beyond which lie thoughts and speech. However, this transition from experience to speech entails an essential loss. Experience is simplified and objectified, and the individual is drawn farther away from the emotional truth of his being. Thought, right after providing a name, is fascinated by its own power and consequently forgets the reality represented by that name. This is the essential argument that Buber tries to articulate: objectification has replaced the encounter, and today one encounters thoughts and words, *not the reality that preceded them*. Buber's analysis seems to be an attack on the tendency of the mind to objectify and then relate to the abstract thought as if it were a real entity (Avnon, 1998). The psychoanalyst, too, might become enthralled with the words and forget the inconceivable, elusive reality that preceded them.

P.A. protests against the easy and careless use of words and says to ROBIN: "Either you have little respect for what you say, or you say words for which you have no respect ..." (*MF*, p. 227). Further on, P.A. goes on to say:

> ... All of us are intolerant of the unknown and strive instantaneously to feel it is explicable, familiar ... The event itself is suspect *because* it is explicable in terms of physics, chemistry, psychoanalysis, and other *pre*-conceived experience. The 'conception' is an event which has become 'conceivable', the 'conceivable' it has become is no longer the genetic experience.
>
> (Ibid., p. 382)

How, then, can we maintain the essential perpetual movement between the pre-linguistic relation to being and the verbal modes of communication; between the ineffable experience unmediated by thought and the possibility of communicating it to another, without objectifying it and denuding it of its essence? 'It is clear' Bion writes,

> that in psychoanalysis talking can be a method of communication of genuine thoughts. Unfortunately words can be used in such a way that they are a 'cosmetic' representation of thinking instead of being the outcome of the labour involved in thought.
>
> (Ibid., p. 666)

Bion often addresses this paradoxical nature of the relationship between language and truth whereby linguistic expression is the path by which truth can be glimpsed at, while at the same time it hides and distorts it.

Healthy mental growth seems to depend on this truth as the living organism depends on food (Bion, 1965). This is the notion at the foundation of Bion's psychoanalytic thinking. Yet this 'truth' is not *The Truth*, but rather 'truth in transit', suggesting that truth becomes a dynamic feeling related to what is taking place at a certain point in the transference, depending more on intuition than on any by-products of sensory perception (Horovitz, 2007). This is not necessarily an empirical truth but rather a *sense of truth* at a certain moment.

Psychoanalysis strives toward this truth. This is its essence. However, this truth cannot be known and is often not amenable to verbal communication. This is the paradox that creates the tension generating the infinite psychic movement. This is the paradoxical movement of language as veiling and unveiling. It is neither one nor the other but rather a constant movement between the two modes. The mere use of words is often insufficient in the attempt to understand the live, ever-changing, ever-moving individual. Without this movement, we collapse to stagnation, to an inanimate, static portrayal that cannot capture the psyche's aliveness.

Bion (1970) maintains that any truth that can be thought is no longer truth but its *evolution*[1] into material reality, that which can be known through the familiar senses. Thus, any truth that penetrates into the realm of verbal language is a falsity.[2]

This thinking is essentially similar to that of philosophers like Plato, Hume, Kant, and Berkeley who postulated a gap between the phenomenon as it is realized in the world and the thing-in-itself, i.e., between the sensuous manifestation and the pure form that is beyond sensuous perception. David Hume (1748) put it deftly when he wrote that the most lively thought is still inferior to the dullest experience.

The limited human nature, which does not permit knowing anything beyond the phenomena amenable to sensuous perception, cannot bridge this gap. All we can do is *deduce* that which exists beyond our sensuous perception. Every form of expression, be it verbal communication, painting, music, etc. is only a transformation of the thing-in-itself, and it is only its transformation that can be known.

The invariant psychic reality of the session, O, can be described as a space with an infinite number of dimensions (Neuman, 2010) and thus cannot be grasped in its totality, due to the fact that the human mind is limited to three dimensions. However, 'ultimate reality must be a whole even if the human animal cannot grasp it' (*MF*, p. 229).

Thinking about absolute truth is utilized as proof by contradiction of that which is beyond us and that Man's restrictedness is defined in opposition to it. Our perceptual capacity, as Kant might say, is discursive and not intuitive. We learn circuitously, one thing from another, through deductions, judgments and general concepts and do not perceive directly, or all at once, the object's entirety (Yovel, 2013).

The pain in the absence of words

The urge to communicate, alongside the difficulty to communicate, seems to be Ariadne's thread running throughout Bion's work from his *War Memoirs* to his very last seminars and the *Memoir*, and to my mind is a very powerful driving force in Bion's need to write (Bergstein, 2015). In *The Dawn of Oblivion* he writes:

> The nearest that a psychoanalytic couple comes to a 'fact' is when one or the other has a feeling. Communicating that fact to some other person is a task which has baffled scientists, saints, poets and philosophers as long as the race has existed. (*MF*, p. 536)

Bion (1970) cites Isaac Luria, the 16th-century Jewish mystic who left no writings and when asked by a disciple about his reasons for not setting out his teaching in book form replied:

> It is impossible because all things are interrelated. I can hardly open my mouth to speak without feeling as though the sea burst its dams and overflowed. How then shall I express what my soul has received, and how can I put it down in a book?

As noted by Francesca Bion (1997), Bion's *Diary*, written to his parents at the end of World War I, was offered as a compensation for his having found it impossible to write letters to them during the war, out of a compelling need to express his very recent painful experiences. She recalls that during the first occasion they dined together, Bion spoke movingly of his experiences as if *compelled to communicate* haunting memories. Already at the very beginning of *Diary*, Bion laments his inability 'to be accurate in some things' (Bion 1977, p. 5) and writes that he can only describe his *impressions* of various actions and try to portray his feelings at that time. Further on, he writes:

> I am at a loss now to tell you of our life. Such worlds separate the ordinary human's point of view from mine at that time, that anything I can write will either be incomprehensible or will give a quite wrong impression.
>
> (Ibid., p. 94)

The opening chapters of *The Past Presented* demonstrate the inadequacy of language and the pain inherent in not being able to describe one's state of mind. Bion tries to capture the multidimensional, elusive truth through the multitude of characters, who ultimately each resorts to his own language and a plethoric use of quotations and action.

It seems Bion often goes out of his way to describe the frustration and suffering he feels in the face of the inability to represent and communicate the emotional experience. He writes:

> The experience of the patient's communication and psycho-analyst's interpretation is ineffable and essential ... What has to be communicated is real enough; yet every psycho-analyst knows the

frustration of trying to make clear, even to another psycho-analyst, an experience which sounds unconvincing as soon as it is formulated. We may have to reconcile ourselves to the idea that such communication is impossible at the present stage of psycho-analysis.

(Bion, 1967a, p. 122)

Every testimony, as reliable as it may be, is in effect only an interpretation, dressed in familiar categories and symbols.

Bion (1967b) makes use of the spectrum of the electromagnetic waves as an analogy for emphasizing the limits of our verbal capacity. The wavelengths visible to us fall in a narrow strip of visual perception between the infrared on the one end and the ultraviolet on the other. We cannot see the ones that fall off these ends, but they are nevertheless there. Using that as an analogy, Bion suggests that, thanks to verbal capacity, there is a certain realm of mental life we can speak of in terms like personality, mind and so forth. This is the small part of the spectrum, in which one could talk about it as being verbally communicable. However, the psychoanalytic encounter compels us to observe and meet those areas of the mind that lie beyond that narrow sphere, encapsulated in the unrepressed unconscious or the psychotic part of the personality (Bergstein, 2014). This is neither pre-verbal nor an active, neurotic avoidance of communication, but rather, the unverbalizable, mute part of the self. And yet, 'Can we make some corresponding extension of our ... mental capacity, to take in a little bit more of ... the invisible aspects of the spectrum?' (Bion, 1967b, p. 60).

An attitude of 'thus far and no further' (*MF*, p. 244) is therefore insufficient.

> ... If the 'universe of discourse' does not facilitate the solution of 3 minus 5, then real numbers are no good, but must be enlarged by 'negative numbers'. If the mathematical 'field of play' is not suitable for the manipulation of 'negative numbers', it has to be extended ...
>
> (Ibid., pp. 175–176)

Paul (after Milton in *Paradise Lost*) yearned: 'that I may see and tell of things invisible to mortal sight' (ibid., p. 225).

The analyst must thus be able to intuit a psychic reality that has no 'senseable' foundation. He must 'blind himself' to the evidence of engaging in a conversation seemingly between two adults and loosen the grip on familiar anchors of mature thought, so as to get in touch with 'the unobserved, incomprehensible, inaudible, ineffable ... from which will come the future interpretation' (Bion, 1974, p. 127).

We are thus in the realm of *the negative*, 'what is not', a core notion in both psychoanalytic thinking and the mystical traditions.

The negative in psychoanalytic thinking

In describing the notion of the negative in psychoanalytic thinking, I would like to begin with an illustration from a Hasidic[3] tale depicted by Buber[4]. A great Hasidic leader said that,

> ... the Torah (The Jewish Law or Bible) received by Moses on Mount Sinai ... cannot be changed and we are forbidden to touch its letters. But, in fact, not only the black letters but also the white gaps between them are letters of the Torah. However, we cannot read the white gaps. In the future, God will reveal the white hiddenness of the Torah.
>
> (translated in Avnon, 1998, p. 122)

We read in this tale an allusion to a hidden reality indicated by white gaps between the black letters. Its absence is only apparent, an effect of the reader's focus on the foreground of the text at the expense of noting its interwoven background. We can see and read the black letters and usually do not pay attention to the gaps between them. To render the white gaps relevant to our understanding, we first have to see them as signs necessitating a release of the attention that is ordinarily focused on the black, dominant script. Perceiving the black letters differently, in a manner that would bring the *white* gaps to the fore as 'letters', implies experiencing the text in a new, revitalized, mystical way (Avnon, 1998).

In a similar vein, Bion stresses that psychoanalytic listening includes the silences, or rests as the musicians might say. The totality of the musical composition includes these silences, which play a very big part in the composition. No doubt, they cannot be neglected. Bion adds that every now and then you get some sort of curious event, like a person who for some obscure reason, doesn't, or won't, listen to the music, but listens to something else. Freud, who Bion sees as a mystic, did not listen to the words uttered but to something else, and 'the next thing you know, you have this vast realm of psychoanalysis' (in Aguayo, 2013b, p. 64).

Mystical thinking maintains that truth is hidden from the senses, from language and from thought. It is concerned with the unknown, concealed, and zero-ness; in effect—with the negative. But P.A. asks: '... how does one discover a negative?' (ibid, p. 79). The intuition of the negative appears throughout Freud's writings beginning with the very fact that the free associations are connected to each other with apparently invisible, unconscious threads that are sensually non-existent. It is realized pre-eminently in the creation of an analytic setting negativizing perception as an indispensable means of approaching the psyche (Botella and Botella, 2005). And, what appears in the space that is generated is not that which was repressed or the return of something that was once represented in the mind, but rather an encounter with the *irrepresentable*.

Freud described two forms of the same existence of reality—psychic reality and material reality. Bion elaborated the notion of these two aspects of reality and wrote of 'reality sensuous *and* psychic'. Whereas sensuous reality is perceived through the five basic senses, psychic reality is *intuited*. Intuition is an unmediated knowledge or understanding of truth, not supported by any information derived from a familiar sensual source. Since it cannot be communicated to another and cannot be corroborated by a rational method of scientific knowledge, it is often seen as close to mystical revelation (de Bianchedi, 1991). Hence, the analyst 'sees' an internal world and has no doubt of its existence, even though he has no sensuous evidence for it.

Winnicott (1969) writes of the 'non-event'. He 'hears' the scream the patient is always not experiencing. The great non-event of the session is the screaming that the patient does not scream. This seems to be an illustration of Winnicott's intuition of the negative as described by Green (1997), who himself wrote widely of the negative, emphasizing that he does not use the word absence, because in the word absence there is the hope of a return of the presence. It is also not a loss because this would mean that the loss could be mourned. The reference to the negative is to the non-existence, the void. Winnicott's contribution, according to Green, is to show how this negative, the non-existence, will become at some point the only thing that is real.

Bion (1974) illustrates this further by describing the observation of a game of tennis, looking at it with increasing darkness, while dimming the intellectual illumination and light. First, we lose sight of the players, and then we gradually increase the darkness until only the net itself is visible. If we can do this, it is possible to see that the only important thing visible to us is a lot of holes that are collected together in a net.

Botella and Botella (2005) speak of the negative of the trauma that has its origin not in a quantifiable positive, but in the absence of what, for the child's ego, should have occurred as a matter of course. Something fundamentally evident for the subject that should have happened did not happen, even though he is not aware of it, let alone form an idea of what this negative is. These authors, too, argue that the negative of the infantile trauma is not a product of the abolition of a representation, but the consequence of a lack at the outset, a missing inscription, at any rate in the form of a representation.

All these lead up to Sandler's (2011) conceptualization of the realm of Minus, 'a non-concrete, immaterial realm that complements the positive "senseable" realm of the material reality' (p. 13). Again, 'the realm of Minus cannot be equated to denial; It contemplates the possibilities of impossibility, and its propositional content cannot be seen on the same level ... as the "Plus realm", what is affirmative; in other words, what occupies a position in space-time. Therefore, since it indicates "what is not" ... it cannot have the properties assigned to what would be the opposite of "what is". It is ineffable' (p. 14).

The clinical implication of this is that we are required to listen not only to the words, or to their semantic meaning, but rather to their *effect* on us, to the emotional experience generated by them. The very fact that the patient lies on the couch liberates the analyst to be immersed in a trance-like state so as to promote the encounter with irrepresentable areas of the patient's internal world. 'Phantasies sometimes burst through into articulate words when the individual is "off his guard"' (*MF*, p. 485). Accordingly, Bion advocates the analyst's *negative capability*, i.e., being in uncertainties, mysteries, doubts, without any irritable reaching after fact and reason, thus capacitating the analyst's formal regression of thought, a quasi-hallucinatory mode of being as described by the Botellas or in Civitarese's (2015a) elaboration of Bion's transformations in hallucinosis as a feature of the analyst's receptivity.

In fact, Bion (1967a) says that 'The proper state for intuiting psycho-analytical realizations ... can be compared with the states supposed to provide conditions for hallucinations. The hallucinated individual is apparently having sensuous experiences without any background of sensuous reality.' So, the analyst too must be able to identify something that can be perceived not by any of the familiar senses, but rather through primordial, *mystical* intuition. Nevertheless, admitting the caesura (i.e., a break *and* continuity) between the psychotic and the non-psychotic parts of the personality, entailing some overlap between them, the intuitive, mystical state of mind differs fundamentally from the psychotic one. The incapacity to tolerate the negative, the no-breast, is a fundamental characteristic of the psychotic personality, whereas toleration of the negative and the frustration this entails is a defining characteristic of a psychoanalytically trained intuitive or mystical state of mind. In his mystical diary, Rabbi Isaac of Acre, the 13th-century Spanish Kabbalist, warns the mystic against quenching his soul's thirst lest he be utterly consumed by fire [or might I add, insanity?]. He draws on Moses as an example of a person who controlled himself and did not stare into the burning bush or satisfy his soul's hunger and thirst.

The psychoanalytic attitude, much like the mystical one, is a deliberate, conscious act of discipline that depends on an *active* suspension of memory and desire. Bion (1970) proposes a discipline for the analyst that increases his ability to exercise 'acts of faith'; however, he stressed that this must be distinguished from the religious meaning with which it is invested in conversational usage. This is *faith that truth exists* and is calculated to meet that irrepresentable part of the personality and an ineffable emotional truth *while retaining an attitude as an observer* by virtue of training, experience and personal analysis.[5]

No doubt suspension of memory, desire, understanding and all that binds us to external reality brings the analyst, as well as the mystic, closer to an animistic world; however, the *collapse* to animistic thinking, characteristic of the primitive religious world or psychotic-hallucinatory states, is precisely the result of an individual's *inability* to maintain a psychoanalytic, or mystical, state of mind. Bion (1970) comments that it may well be that analysts who attempt this approach will find that the test of sensuous deprivation involved in eschewing memory and desire will cause them to feel the need for further analysis that would not have occurred had the analyst remained content with the atmosphere of deprivation as it has been understood in classical psychoanalytic thinking.

Bion adds that the purpose of the analyst's partial severance with external reality differs from the purpose of the psychotic manoeuver. The psychotic wishes to destroy contact with psychic reality whereas the analyst wishes to establish it. This psychic reality is ineffable, not because it is experienced *beyond or outside* reality, but precisely because this *is* what real experience feels like when infinite dimensions are perceived simultaneously, paradoxically, with no boundaries of time and space; this is why linear, narrative language cannot grasp it.

And so, we are again in the realm of what is sensuously invisible but intuitively visible, the juxtaposition between psychoanalytic thinking and mysticism.

Emotional truth and ultimate reality: Bion and Jewish mysticism

The fact that different disciplines, at different times and from different vertices, describe the same experience gives this experience greater validity and enables a 'multi-ocular' view of truth. And, this encounter between the different disciplines is an emotional experience in itself, an emotional experience of discovering coherence. It is a mode of being in which different facets of the emotional experience can be 'observed' from different vertices, integrated in a way that feels truthful, affording *a sense of truth.*[6]

Bion drew a parallel between psychoanalytical and mystical states of mind. Since Bion's reference and affinity to Christian mystics have been widely explored (e.g., Reiner, 2012), I will focus predominantly on Jewish mysticism. Bion mentions only a few of the Jewish mystics and Jewish philosophers, namely, Isaac Luria, Martin Buber, and Gershom Scholem, a scholar of Kabbalah and Jewish mysticism who seems to have made a big impression on Bion's thinking.[7] Indeed, both Jewish philosophy and Jewish mysticism try to address the problem of ineffability through the issue of God. Inasmuch as one cannot describe in words the ultimate reality of the emotional experience, any attempt to describe God undermines its very essence.

In contrast to Jewish philosophers, Jewish mystics cannot say enough about God and describe him inexhaustibly. Yet, the name of

God is merely *a symbolic representation* of an ultimate reality which is forever unformed and amorphous (Scholem, 1960). There is no word that can encompass the entire meaning of God; hence, a superfluousness of words is needed.

It seems to me that these are two complementary modes of dealing with the ineffability of the deity in its entirety: the former asserting the absence of words in relation to God thus espousing silence, whereas the latter advocates contriving genres of discourse *about the Naught, transforming it into the Infinite.*

Similarly, Bion (1965) designates the sign 'O' to denote unknowable ultimate reality, the Godhead[8] the infinite. In a striking parallel, he specifies its definitory qualities listing the following negatives: 'It is not good or evil; it cannot be known, loved or hated … The most, and the least that the individual person can do is to be it' (pp. 139–140). Bion, like the mystics, writes of the countless and yet insufficient number of words required to describe the emotional experience. He writes:

> I do not feel able to communicate to the reader an account that would be likely to satisfy me as correct. I am more confident that I could make the reader understand what I had to put up with if I could extract from him a promise that he would faithfully read every word I wrote; I would then set about writing several hundred thousand words … In short, I cannot have as much confidence in my ability to tell the reader what happened as I have in my ability *to do something to the reader that I have had done to me.* I have had an emotional experience; I feel confident in my ability to recreate that emotional experience, but not to represent it.
>
> (Bion, 1992, p. 219, italics added)

In an attempt to describe the ultimate reality symbolized by O, Bion writes:

> It is perhaps too mathematical to call it infinity, too mystical to call it the infinite, too religious to call it the Godhead … Verbal expressions intended to represent the ultimate object often appear to be contradictory within themselves, but there is a surprising degree of agreement, despite differences of background, time and

space, in the descriptions offered by mystics who feel they have experienced the ultimate reality.

(1965, pp. 150–151)

Mysticism

Science and mysticism are seemingly opposites. Science deals with knowledge, with what is revealed, with 'what is'. Mysticism deals with the unknown, the hidden, the Naught. However, over the years this dichotomy has lost its meaning. Truth, as noted by Civitarese (2013b), is neither scientific/philosophical nor mystical/aesthetic. The former is lacking in emotions/feelings, the latter in concepts. One has only to think of the immaterial nature of the negative or the imaginary numbers in mathematics in order to illustrate the overlap and dialectic interplay between science and the mystical tradition. In Bion's later writings the scientific vertex is put into constant conjunction with at least two other vertices, the mystical and the artistic traditions. Nevertheless, the word mysticism is saturated with connotations, often in the service of religious, esoteric or new-age dogmas, that its depth is lost and often denigrated in psychoanalytic thinking. One must, therefore, go back to its original definition to allow the affinity between the two disciplines to become apparent, as well as to capacitate the mutual inspiration inherent within such an affinity.

The word 'mysticism', derived from the Greek μυω, and meaning 'to conceal,' was defined by Celsus, a 2nd-century Greek philosopher and opponent of Early Christianity. It was defined as the closing of the senses to all worldly matters, sensations, passions and desires, so as to enable the soul to be open to the spiritual matters of the sublime. It is from this definition that the two characteristics of most mystical traditions derive: first, most mystical methods require detachment from mundane desires as a pre-condition for spiritual wholeness and view asceticism as a way to achieve this goal. Second, the mystical way leads to an experience in the realms of an ineffable reality. It is caught in the dire straits of the intense desire for expression on the one hand, and the inability to express itself on the other. Many mystical traditions refer to nothingness, or Naught, so as to emphasize the fundamental qualitative difference of the realm of mysticism from all that is called 'reality' or 'existence' in the ordinary world of experience. The mystical literature stresses that any talk or speech is only an allegory. Mystical literature is therefore inclined to puns and paradoxical expressions. Interestingly, referring to the *Memoir*, Meltzer and Harris Williams (1985) remark that the way of playing fast and loose with language, with wit, obscenity, endless punning, splitting, and recombining words, is part of the method that the characters use to try to 'get through' to one another.

Another trait of the mystical experience is its unitive nature. The mystic feels that he 'unites' with a sublime, divine or cosmic reality. However, most Jewish mystics have referred to 'adherence' or 'closeness' to God (*Devekut*), and avoided talking about a complete, actual and substantial union. In fact, as Scholem (1971) argues, the avoidance of a complete union with God (unio-mystica) differentiates Jewish mysticism from all other mystical traditions. It is in the nature of Jewish mysticism that one should at most aspire to communion with God, but never to union. Whereas in Catholic mysticism, 'communion' was not the last step on the mystical way, in Kabbalism it is the last grade of ascent to God. It is not union, because union with God is denied to man, according to Kabbalistic theology, even in that mystical upsurge of the soul. I suspect this reverberated with Bion's notion of the endless striving for unreachable, unknowable truth.

These mystical notions are incredibly similar to Bion's notion of eschewing memory, desire and understanding and closing the familiar senses so as to facilitate an intuitive state of mind, hence becoming at-one with the emotional truth of the moment. Mysticism is thus a way of delving into one's inner world, shutting one's eyes to sensuous reality enabling the individual to see with one's 'inner eye' (II, p. 225), much as dreams are created.

Mysticism, not religious dogma

P.A: It appears to me that unquestioning belief in God is demanded by the Church or its representatives. Perhaps I am misled by the Institutions of Religion which have obscured for me the chance of going beyond the institutions' dogmata to a reality beyond.

PAUL: There are certainly plenty of religious teachers who have developed that and warned against it. St. John of the Cross even said that reading his own works would be a stumbling block if they were revered to the detriment of direct experience. Teachings, dogma, hymns, congregational worship, are supposed to be preludes to religion proper – not final ends in themselves.

P.A: This sounds not unlike a difficulty which we experience when psycho-analytic jargon ... [is] substituted for looking into the patient's mind itself to intuit that to which the psycho-analyst is striving to point; like a dog that looks at its master's pointing hand rather than at the object the hand is trying to point out. (*MF*, p. 267)

It is true that established religion and mystical traditions share the same scriptures, yet they differ from each other in the most drastic manner. A religious person believes in the word of God incorporated in scriptures and is certain that he understands it, or at least that its core, its most important meaning, has been absorbed by him. His 'truth' is therefore often static and finite and so does not pertain to psychoanalytic truth. God then becomes an idol as clearly argued by ROLAND when he says: '... the Israelitish God was a recognizable, tribal deity showing marked human characteristics, such as jealousy and envy, not markedly different from the inhabitants of the Homeric Pantheon located on Olympus ...' (ibid., p. 80). The mystic, on the other hand, knows that various levels of communicative interpretation, including allegory, analogy and the like, cannot reveal the hidden divine truth, which can be approached in non-linguistic ways alone. His truth is therefore dynamic, transient and infinite. The mystical meaning and message of the scriptures is beyond communication. It is hidden within the text, but the mystic, by his meta-sensual and meta-intellectual perceptions or experiences, can achieve a glimpse of the hidden truth. A sensuous-intellectual approach to the text of the scriptures is either meaningless or false (Dan, 2002).

The rejection of any dogmatic authority is echoed by BION who says: '... We do not know the cost in suffering associated with the belief in a Christian God, or the God of Abraham's Ur, or Hitler's Germany, or peyotism – or God of any kind' (I, p. 172). And further on, in another debate, ROLAND remarks that 'Religion has been aptly described as a drug,' to which PAUL replies: 'Because it is used for that purpose by some people I do not see why religion should be held responsible, any more than why wine should be blamed for alcoholism ...' (*MF*, pp. 271–272). Elsewhere Bion (1977a) writes: 'Religious dogmata are ... vulgarizations of that which the religious mystic can achieve directly' (p. 32). Chapter 5 of *The Past Presented* highlights the discussion in which religious feelings or a 'religious impulse' is distinguished from religious institutions. Perhaps the most defining differentiation is voiced by P.A. as to whether it 'is capable of development rather than decay' (*MF*, p. 287).

To my mind, Bion's psychoanalytic writings testify to the fact that there is no necessary connection between a deep devotion to a certain religion and the specific characteristics of a mystical view. As a matter of fact, Bion seems to present us with non-religious mysticism.

Throughout the *Memoir*, there is much affinity between P.A. and PAUL/PRIEST (representing both religion and the mystical tradition), which they come to realize as their encounter evolves, for example:

P.A: ... I have found that if I say what I mean it is not English; if I write English it does not say what I mean.
PAUL: Theologians are blamed for being incapable of being religious – you are as bad as we are!
P.A: Probably for the same reason. Ultimate Truth is ineffable.

(Ibid., p. 229)

Bion began to be interested in mystics in 1965 when he realized that many of them had found it very difficult to put their revelatory experiences into words and manage to communicate them to others who had not had this unique experience themselves (de Bianchedi, 2005). This is similar to the difficulty Bion experienced when trying to communicate the intuitively perceived psychoanalytic experience to a person who had not been in the room and who had not had the same experience. Moreover, Bion (1967a) wanted to bring the notion of the mystic, which he regarded as interchangeable with the word 'scientist' or 'artist', into the psychoanalytic discourse. He was aware that 'mystic' has a much more religious connotation, and he had indeed referred in his late writings to religious and theological terms such as 'Godhead', 'faith', 'atonement',[9] etc. However, these terms were used in an attempt to borrow concepts from different disciplines in order to avoid the collapse to psychoanalytic terms that have become jargon.

Bion did not try to describe the psychoanalytic experience as religious, but he did see the advantages of religious metaphors and thought that at times these are superior to psychoanalytic models in addressing that quintessential mystery known as man (Grotstein, 2007). Bion (1970) writes: 'Poetic and religious expressions have made possible a degree of "public-ation" in that formulations exist which have achieved durability and extensibility' (p. 1). Furthermore, words such as God and Godhead were borrowed to try and depict an emotional truth, or ultimate reality, which like God, is transcendental, existing beyond the possibility of human knowledge and consciousness. As he stated,

> I use these formulations to express, in exaggerated form, the pain which is involved in achieving the state of naivety ... The relevance of this to psychological phenomena springs from the fact that they are not amenable to apprehension by the senses.
>
> (Bion, 1965, p. 159)

Bion makes use of mystical writings to interpret psychoanalytic problems, as he does with other cultural myths that have a universal or a large social value (cf. Bion, 1992). He suggests that the scientist must know enough mathematics to have an idea when he is confronting a problem to which a particular mathematical procedure would apply. The psychoanalyst likewise might use myths or mystical writings as a tool comparable to that of the mathematical formula for investigating emotional problems. Associating on a chosen myth, and selection of the myths on which to associate, plays an important part in the promotion of psychoanalytic intuition and, more precisely, in the reinvigoration of the analyst's α-function (Bion, 1992). Hence, Bion's attitude to myths is similar to the use Buber makes of Hasidic legends and Biblical tales as conveying philosophical insight. Buber's hope was that these would help readers gain access to the truth conveyed by such myths, which would otherwise require complicated philosophical reasoning. Bion's turn to mystical exegeses, too, is derived from his belief that these could facilitate the communication of emotional truth that is beyond verbal communication. P.A. remarks: '... I was compelled to seek asylum in fiction. Disguised as fiction, the truth occasionally slipped through' (*MF*, p. 302).

The *Memoir* and the *Zohar*

The *Zohar*, as maintained by Scholem (1961), has stood out for centuries as the expression of all that was profoundest and most deeply hidden in the innermost recesses of the Jewish soul. I do not know whether Bion had ever read the 2,400 densely written pages of the *Zohar*, although I assume he did not. However, there is no doubt that he was acquainted with parts of it through the writings of Gershom Scholem, which he cites on several occasions. Be that as it may, the similarity between the *Zohar* and the *Memoir* is striking, and it seems to me that the *Memoir*, albeit not being a mystical text, can be read as one might read the *Zohar*.

In its manifest appearance, the *Zohar* is a scriptural exegesis, i.e., a mystical interpretation of the Torah. But the *Zohar*, much like the *Memoir*, is also an epic fiction. It is written in pseudoepigraphic form, almost in the form of a mystical novel. It portrays the epic story of Rabbi Shimon and his companions, who are the fictitious or legendary embellishment of real historical persons. Its dramatis personae include other wondrous characters such as an old man, young child, donkey driver, etc., who reveal ancient secrets to the companions or describe the primordial world before emanation. Much like the *Memoir*, the author tries to capture the multidimensional transient truth through the multitude of characters. Hellner-Eshed (2009) compares the *Zohar* narrative to a jazz jam session, where a common melodic theme performed by the ensemble branches into solo improvisations that build to greater surprise, complexity and crescendo—the more virtuosity, the more wonderful and surprising the innovations. One could perhaps say the same of the *Memoir*.

I dare to think that the *Memoir*, like the *Zohar*, was written in a dream-like, at times quasi-hallucinatory state, with Bion delving into his inner world, awakening primordial sights and visions. It is an attempt to *be in* the dream rather than *talk about* it. Both texts are thus often obscure and perplexing, inclined to puns and paradoxical expressions, and should be read together in a circle of colleagues. Reading both is an emotional experience of capturing glimpses of an ineffable, hidden reality, arousing an emotional turbulence, at times bordering on ecstasy, in response to its aesthetic capacity of awakening the realm of noumena. Moreover, they both seem to be an attempt at bearing the pain inherent in the ineffability of the emotional experience.

The mystics related to the Scriptures that populated their literary world as reference points to their revelatory experiences. Similarly, by abundantly quoting classical poets such as Virgil, Milton, Shakespeare, Goethe, Wordsworth, Shelley and Keats, it seems that Bion is making a similar reference in the *Memoir* to the literary and cultural climate of *his* world, as a way of conveying his ineffable emotional experience.

The unknown author(s) of the *Zohar* make(s) use of numerous literary sources from classical Jewish writings. These sources are usually not mentioned. Instead, the author(s) content themselves, and discontent the reader, with vague references to ancient writings or mystical tracts dealing with the same topics. Thus, the discovery of the real sources, which are so carefully obscured, is one of the main prerequisites for an appreciation of the historical and doctrinal significance of the *Zohar* (Scholem, 1961).

The author of the *Zohar*, as Scholem tells us, employs the pointed language of the ancient sages although usually less successfully in terms of being understood. Not worried by chronology, the author lets imagination roam freely among the different generations. The text frequently loses itself in mystical allegorization and not infrequently becomes abstruse, but again and again a hidden and sometimes aweful depth opens before our eyes, and we find ourselves confronted with real and profound insight.

The mystic and the psychoanalyst

I would like to address the mystical state of mind of analyst and patient, whose mutual work of analysis facilitates the development of their intuitive capacity. Thus, I suggest that *mystical qualities are not reserved for a privileged, 'illuminated' few, but are part of what psychoanalysis strives to attain and develop.*

Mystics are men who by their own inner experience and speculation concerning this experience discover new layers of meaning *in their tradition*. A mystic is a man who has been favored with an immediate, and to him real, experience of the divine, of ultimate reality, or who at least strives to attain such an experience. His experience may come to him through sudden illumination, or it may be the result of long and often elaborate preparations (Scholem, 1960).

The moment a mystic tries to clarify his experience by reflection, to formulate it, and especially when he attempts to communicate it to others, he cannot help imposing a framework of conventional symbols and ideas upon it. Yet, there is always some part of it that he cannot adequately and fully express. But if he does try to communicate his experience—and it is only by doing so that he makes himself known to us—he is bound to interpret his experience in language, images and concepts that were created before him.

The mystic's attitude to religion is one of deep doubt that verbal communication can reveal divine truth. The mystic is someone who knows that real truth, meaningful truth, can never be expressed in words. And, it is not only language that the mystic distrusts. The whole range of means by which people acquire knowledge, especially the senses, logic and thought, are suspected as a cause for error and meaninglessness (Dan, 2002).

The mystic discovers a new dimension, a new depth in his own tradition. In employing symbols to describe his own experience and to formulate his interpretations of it, he transforms and *reinterprets* established religion, and his symbolism is the instrument of this transformation. He uses old symbols and lends them new meaning; he may even use new symbols and give them an old meaning. In either case, we find a dialectical interrelationship between the conservative aspects and the novel, productive aspects of mysticism (Scholem, 1960). The mystic, Bion (1970) writes, is both creative and destructive. These two extremes coexist in the same person.

The analyst's state of mind of no memory, no desire and no understanding, strives, like that of the mystic, to blur the familiar and conventional interpretations, so as to allow openness to a new impression, a fresh interpretation. Mental growth, analytic transformation and the encounter with emotional truth are made possible through a 'breakup' of the familiar meaning and a 'breakthrough' of the new discovery. The fear of catastrophic change often emerges at the point where new caesuras are created, at the place where a new incision, which is not the obvious one, is forged. The discovery of new caesuras entails de-construction, or destruction, of the familiar thought or idea and necessitates mourning the loss of the old perception. This is the potential for growth and discovery. However, this often entails a threat of catastrophic 'breakdown'.

A good illustration is Bion's (1970) well-known vignette when he suddenly hears ice/cream as I/scream. After some years when the words 'ice cream' appeared sporadically, Bion suddenly heard these words as 'I scream', cutting the syllables differently, thus discovering and forging a new meaning.

We find another illustration in Bion's paper *Evidence* (1976). The patient associated: 'I remember my parents being at the top of a Y-shaped stair and I was at the bottom and ...' That was all. There were no further associations. Bion was struck by the statement being so brief, stopping short at that point, and he thought it must have a lot of meaning that was not visible to him. It then occurred to him that the statement would be more comprehensible if it was spelled 'why-shaped stare'. However, Bion could not see how he could say this to the patient in a way that would have any meaning, nor could he produce any evidence for it. Bion said nothing, fearing it was just a pun, a fanciful free association of his or an interpretation that would be incomprehensible to the patient. The analyst had plenty of associations and possible interpretations while playing with this image. However, it was only in the next session, after 'killing time' with conventionally acceptable interpretations, that he dared to say to the patient: 'I suggest that in addition to the ordinary meaning of what you have told me – and I am perfectly sure that what you said means exactly what you meant – it is also a kind of visual pun.' And then, he gave him the interpretation. The patient replied: 'Yes, that's right. But you've been a very long time about it ...'

The de-construction of the familiar meaning, and awarding a new meaning, grants the text a mystical tenor. In this sense, a mystical interpretation is akin to an intuitive interpretation, which is often uncanny and even terrifying.

Scholem (1960) writes:

> The genius of mystical exegeses resides in the uncanny precision with which they derive their transformation of Scripture into a *corpus symbolicum* from the exact words of the text. The literal meaning is preserved but merely as the gate through which the mystic passes, a gate, however, which he opens up to himself over

and over again. The *Zohar* expresses this attitude of the mystic very succinctly in a memorable exegesis of Genesis 12:1. God's words to Abram, 'Lekh lekha' [Go thee out of thy country, and from thy kindred, and from thy father's house], are taken not only in their literal meaning, 'Go thee out'. That is, they are not interpreted as referring only to God's command to Abram to go out into the world, but are also read with mystical literalness as 'Go to thee', that is, to thine own self, away from the habits to which you are accustomed.

(p. 15)

In fact, the *Zohar* interprets every place Abram travelled to, as a psychic state of mind, and his journeys throughout the land as the inner journey of the psyche. The divine world, which was concealed from Abram, opens up before him. The verse 'And Abram journeyed, going on still toward the south' (Genesis 12:9) describes Abram ascending further and further toward encountering his own truth (Hellner-Eshed, 2009). Mystical interpretations are thus often pre-disposed toward the inner world.

London and Edinburgh

An intuitive and, to my mind, essentially mystical interpretation, re-interpreting the patient's text and directing the meaning further inwards, into the internal world, can be found in another of Bion's (1967a) seminars. The patient was apparently talking quite obviously about a particular group known to him, in external terms. As the session evolved, the analyst began to feel that he wasn't simply talking about an external group, even though it was *also* that. The patient had been talking about people, about London and Edinburgh, and Bion drew his attention to the fact that these were not simply London and Edinburgh. They were names of places where it was once a mother and a father. It was simply a way of describing not the father and mother, but the place where the father and mother were until something or other happened to them, which had turned them simply into a place. And then, that these other objects which he'd been mentioning were really felt to be the children of this pair (these two objects that had now turned into places). From that, Bion gave the interpretation that

it was in fact the patient himself, only he himself was now split up.
The parents had been attacked so that they were only places where
parents used to be, and he himself had been destroyed in the process, split up into a whole lot of particles, which could be described in
terms of these people, with names, and so forth.

Following this interpretation, the patient started on a series of hy-
pochondriac complaints. This may obviously be a controversial interpretation, but Bion contends a process by which the external objects
had been gathered *inwards* and transformed into internal objects like
his spleen, his hernia and so on. (These words are mentioned as bodily objects whereas they also have a psychic meaning, spleen meaning
hate, anger, depression, and hernia meaning a fracture or a rupture.)
Bergson asserts that the intellect has a tendency that impels us to
think on all occasions of *things* rather than movements. Bion's interpretation of London and Edinburgh transforms the places, the things,
back into movement, the inanimate back to the animate. This may
seem very similar to our ordinary work of deciphering the symbolic
meaning of the patient's repressed or displaced material. However,
we may have here, as suggested by Meltzer (2000), a distinction between allegory and symbol. Allegory is taken by Meltzer to consist
of the rather ingenious substitution of known elements for what is
mysterious and unknown; it is a kind of cheat because it pretends to
bring the unknown within the sphere of the already-known. Symbol,
on the other hand, is full of mystery, and inexhaustible however much
one digs into it. Its many levels are not just an ingenious emblem. A
symbol carries with it the gift of humility; *you know perfectly well you
will never understand it completely.*

In a lucid passage that I can imagine might have inspired Bion,
Scholem (1961) writes:

> Allegory consists of an infinite network of meanings and cor-
> relations in which everything can become a representation of
> everything else, *but all within the limits of language and expression* ...
> That which is expressed by and in the allegorical sign is in the first
> instance something which has its own meaningful context, but by
> becoming allegorical this something loses its own meaning and
> becomes the vehicle of something else ... [However] the symbol
> [is] a form of expression which radically transcends the sphere of

allegory. In the mystical symbol, a reality which in itself has, for us, no form or shape becomes transparent and, as it were, visible, through the medium of another reality which clothes its content with visible and expressible meaning ... The thing which becomes a symbol retains its original form and its original content. It does not become, so to speak, an empty shell into which another content is poured; in itself, through its own existence, it makes another reality transparent which cannot appear in any other form. *If allegory can be defined as the representation of an expressible something by another expressible something, the mystical symbol is an expressible representation of something which lies beyond the sphere of expression and communication*, something which comes from a sphere whose face is, as it were, turned inward and away from us. A hidden and inexpressible reality finds its expression in the symbol ... Where deeper insight into the structure of the allegory uncovers fresh layers of meaning, the symbol is *intuitively* understood all at once - or not at all.

(pp. 26–27, italics added)

London and Edinburgh, the symbol in the above description, much like the symbol in Jewish mysticism, is paradoxically utilized since no words can encompass the infinite meanings of the ineffable, *emotional experience* or the ultimate reality concealed in the patient's 'dream'. There is no realization that approximates the verbal description of the emotional experience concealed in the words 'London and Edinburgh'. These words do not symbolize the persons of the parental couple *per se*, but much like the characters of the *Memoir*, they evoke a caesural experience, a complex *link* that is ineffable due to its infinite dimensions. It is a constant conjunction encompassing a myriad of elements comprising the experience of the emotional link. And as Bion stressed from early on, he employs the term 'link' because he wishes to describe a patient's relationship with a function rather than with the object that subserves the function (Bion, 1959), thus rendering it unsaturated and open to infinite elaboration.

The patient's experience has never been mentalized and therefore has never been repressed. The patient could never have uttered his experience because it was never mentally registered. Nevertheless, it is burnt and encapsulated in *the unrepressed unconscious*, awaiting an intuitive, mystical moment when it can emerge as a symbol. The Kabbalistic symbol paradoxically expresses in language what the mouth cannot utter and the ear cannot hear (Scholem, 1975), thus steering us toward the unknowable navel of the dream, the noumena beyond the phenomena. This, to my mind, may be a major contribution of Jewish mysticism to psychoanalysis. It illuminates the reality of a hidden life, which can only be achieved through symbols. It sharpens our listening to the *unrepressed unconscious* and enhances our capacity to attend to the words uttered in a fresh, intuitive and mystical way.

The value of intuitive interpretations like these is therefore not in uncovering historical truth or repressed unconscious material. Nor are they evaluated for the 'correctness' of their *content*. Rather, their merit lies in their capacity for *generating psychic movement*, transforming psychic barriers into caesuras, affording a multi-dimensional view, and enabling the patient to move from a preoccupation with external reality to an observation of his or her internal reality. The patient may thus get in touch with remote, encapsulated parts of the psyche (Bergstein, 2013). *Preoccupation with external reality is finite whereas internal reality and the unconscious are infinite.* Any interpretation is only a partial representation, retaining an irrepresentable navel that will forever remain unknown, hence evoking a feeling of mystery and unknowability.

This lengthy discussion, in the attempt to give meaning to the above vignette, is brought about in retrospect, after several readings of Bion's seminar. However, my first impression of reading it was of being immensely moved, without being able to comprehend or describe in words why it was so moving. I am inclined to think that this is due to the awe generated when, paraphrasing P.A., 'one meaning turned out to have, like a many faceted diamond, a fresh, fiery brilliance of truth the [patient] did not know because it hadn't happened – when [he said] it' (*MF*, p. 234). Furthermore, it seems that by evoking an experience analogous to a mystical union, these interpretations revive our intrinsic tendency to experience the numinous. In these rare and privileged moments, the intuition is united with a conception, akin to a mystical union. Since such interpretations *evoke an experience* rather than being subject to discursive understanding, it is often difficult for anyone, other than the patient him- or herself, to sense or to comprehend the experience inherent in the interpretation.

Bion (1962a) writes: 'We have thus approached a mental life un-mapped by the theories elaborated for the understanding of neurosis' (p. 37), and this mental life, I suggest, is the realm of the ineffable.

Concluding remarks

Bion (1970) reminds us that it is often forgotten that the gift of speech, so centrally employed, has been elaborated as much for the purpose of concealing thought as for the purpose of elucidating or communi-cating thought. DU, representing a germ of an idea striving to escape from the confines of Roland's mind and create meaning, cries out: 'Words; words; words have no right to be definitory caskets prevent-ing my birth' (*MF*, p. 276).

However, I would not like to collapse to the point of abolishing the power of language. As Bion (1967a) says, 'If the psycho-analytical sit-uation is accurately intuited ... the psycho-analyst finds that ordinary conversational English is surprisingly adequate for the formulation of his interpretation' (p. 134). The analyst may interpret that part of experience at has penetrated the sensuous world and language. Any new formulation, from an additional vertex, allows us to expand our psychic world ad infinitum. And yet, any utterance is just a reminder, a pale shadow of the thing-in-itself.

The analyst should thus hover in the dialectic interplay, in the cae-sura, between intuition and conception. Intuition is essential due to the immaterial nature of psychoanalysis, and yet it must not be dissociated from a scientific outlook lest it leads to careless, wild interpretations.

Bion says:

> ... infants ... know all about what it *feels* like, but they have no concepts, they cannot write any of these great books – their con-cepts are blind. Later on they have forgotten what it is like to feel terrified; they pick up these words but the words are empty – 'I'm terrified' ... it is an empty phrase, it is a concept; it is only verbal; the intuition is missing.
>
> (1980, p. 40)

We are thus faced with the problem of marrying the *concept* of terror with the corresponding *feeling*.

So again, one must ask how can we move in the caesura between the infinite unknowable and the finite sensuous, verbalisable experience that is derived from it?

In an imaginary dialogue between Bion and myself, Bion writes:

BION: ... You must often have heard, as I have, people say they don't know what you are talking about and that you are being deliberately obscure.

MYSELF: They are flattering me. I am suggesting an aim, an ambition, which, if I could achieve, would enable me to be deliberately and *precisely* obscure; in which I could use certain words which would activate precisely and instantaneously, in the mind of the listener, a thought or train of thought that came between him and the thoughts and ideas already accessible and available to him.

(*MF*, p. 191)

In a similar vein, it is said that when God was revealed on Mount Sinai when the Torah was handed down to the people of Israel, all illnesses and handicaps were cured. Moses, who had been stammering since he was an infant, refused to be cured. When asked why, he replied that his stammer is the way he communicates with God ...

Notes

1 The concept of *evolution,* or *hishtalshelut,* as used in Jewish mysticism, refers to the metaphysical process, the chain of events, whereby the complex and finite reality of the universe unfolds out of God's absolute oneness. This evolution proceeds by ten degrees, the attributes through which God reveals Himself, called the ten Sefirot. Yet, the Sefirot themselves are only varying degrees of expression of the unchanging, all-encompassing 'Eyn-Sof' (infinite). It seems this might have reverberated for Bion the notion of transformation in O, and it is perhaps from here that he drew the concept of *evolution.* For Bion, ultimate reality is unknowable. The analyst must wait for the reality of the session *to evolve,* and he is able to know only the events that are *evolutions* of O.
2 Bion uses the word *falsity* to denote the transformation of the emotional experience into a word. A word is thus always false compared to the original emotional experience. However, falsities are distinguished from *lies,* which are conscious attacks on truth.

3 *Hasidism* is a Jewish spiritual movement founded in the Ukraine in the 18th century. It is characterized by mysticism and opposition to secular studies and Jewish rationalism. One of its aims was to popularize Jewish mysticism and to allow ordinary people access to the Kabbalah. It was opposed by the orthodox rabbinical establishment.

4 Buber's book *Light of the Hidden* (1976) is a collection of Hasidic tales in which he uses biblical interpretations, inserted into Hasidic legends. Buber stripped the legends of their magical and ecstatic elements, at the same time emphasizing a new way of seeing and experiencing reality.

5 In a striking resemblance to the role of the training and supervising analyst, Scholem (1960) stresses that

> the widespread belief that a mystic requires a spiritual guide ... He prevents the student who sets out to explore the world of mysticism from straying off into dangerous situations. For confusion or even madness lurk in wait; the path of the mystic is beset by perils. It borders on abysses of consciousness and demands a sure and measured step ... The guide should be capable of preserving the proper balance in the mystic's mind. He is familiar with the practical applications of the various doctrines, which cannot be learned from books. And he has an additional function ... he represents traditional religious authority. He provides at the outset the traditional coloration which the mystical experience, however amorphous, will assume in the consciousness of the novice ... to be safeguarded against uncontrollable emotional excesses.
>
> (pp. 18–19)

6 A 'sense of truth,' Bion (1962a) suggests, is paradigmatically 'experienced if the view of an object which is hated can be conjoined to a view of the same object when it is loved and the conjunction confirms that the object experienced by different emotions is the same object' (p. 119).

7 Bion cites only seven authors apart from himself, in his book *Attention and Interpretation*, Scholem being one of them.

8 The Godhead is a concept borrowed from the German theologian, mystic and philosopher Meister Eckhart (1260–1328). Godhead, which is infinite, is often contrasted with God, which is finite (see *MF*, p. 180).

9 Bion hyphenated the word atonement, making it into at-one-ment, which may, in the spirit of the Jewish mystical tradition, denote that there is never a complete union in this experience of being at one with ultimate reality.

Chapter 9

Psychoanalysis 'at the mind's limits'

Trauma, history and paronomasia as 'a flower of speech' in A Memoir of the Future

Clara Mucci

At the mind's limits: the position of the subject, traumatic truth and the encounter with O

In *A Memoir of the Future*, Bion provocatively acts out what happens 'at the mind's limits' (to echo Jean Amery's account of his survival after the trauma of Auschwitz; Amery, 1966), when 'wakeful dream thinking' and the language of disguise, typical of poetry and literature ('paronomasia', 'a flower of speech'; *MF*, p. 239), take hold of reality and attempt to finally express what is, by definition, ineffable and unrepresentable. The trauma of reality, after the experience of the War and towards the end of Bion's life, is investigated—enacted and worked through—intentionally by way of a kind of language and a post-modern narrational mode that explodes the limits of representation, mostly time and space, and uses a paradoxical *mise-en-scène* where the faults of reason or what Western thought considers as reasoning and truth are exposed in their limitations.

It appears that the ineffable, unspeakable, unsymbolised reality in so far as it is traumatic, has deconstructed the centre of vision and the supposed unity on which the rational mind rests, and as a consequence it has unleashed the opposite side of that rational vision, namely, the corporeal body, the un-reason, and the inversion of power categories together with the radical openness of a signification that is not univocal but polysemic and overdetermined. The moment of re-integration, or *at-one-ment* (at one with oneself but also in connection with a wider order, beyond the Self, in connection with O, which in

English has also the sense of a reconciliation), is the final destination of this movement beyond the drive in Bion's perspective. It is a trip from learning through the experience of the body (a radically painful journey through emotions, until the place of a loss is reached; see Klein, 2011; Correale, 2015) through the dream-thought of metaphorical language to its termination and possible revelations.

As Giuseppe Civitarese explains, from a deconstructive perspective in line with this new, post-modern view of psychoanalysis, the deconstruction of the binary system of signification is made real through 'the systematic use of a non-pathological, i.e., non static but dynamic, inversion of perspective' (2013, p. 2), and this inversion provokes a creative tension capable of generating thoughts and creative developments.

On the enigmatic quality of 'truth', Bion writes in *The Past Presented*, the second book of *A Memoir*:

P.A: It has often been said, and I should be claiming to be less than human if I said there was no truth in the accusation. But you will miss something if you feel that the ulterior motive is the only one; just as I think it fallacious to assume that scientific truth, or rational truth, or aesthetic truth, or musical truth, or rational truth is the only truth. Even what psychoanalysts call rationalizations have to be rational. Because I think we should be aware of the ultra- or infra-sensuous, or the super-ego or id, I do not think that one should deny the rest.

ROLAND: But, good heavens, what would happen to us if I couldn't blind myself to sidereal space or space time when I want to tell my time by my watch?

P.A: If we are to translate our thoughts and feelings into physical or corporeal fact, there has to be a certain focusing of our mental apparatus as a prelude to action. That very act seems to me–putting my thoughts into verbo-visual terms–to involve putting other elements out of focus. It is difficult in practice to de-focus–peripheralize–the irrelevant without falling in to the opposite error of permanent insensibility; blindness, deafness, repression. *That is why I talk of the 'opacity' of memory, desire, understanding.*

EDMUND: *The centre of our galaxy is hidden from us*, and though we suspect that it lies near Sagittarius we cannot see, as we can when we examine M31, the bright centre. (*MF*, p. 232, emphasis mine)

Truth cannot be seen per se, since the center of vision, the 'bright center', is precluded to us; therefore, a detour needs to be taken to pierce though it, to gaze at it without being hurt or in order to achieve a feeling or a bodily, unconscious/preverbal understanding of the experience.

I agree with Civitarese when he says that:

> 'O', similar to the sunlight, cannot be looked at without filters. A rhetoric of blindness and vision, therefore, is what forms the weave of Bion's thought, and this perhaps explains Bion's fascination with the mystical author (and poet) St. John of the Cross.
>
> (2011, p. 3)

I wonder if it is even possible to associate Lacan's *object a* to Bion's O. As for the Lacanian *object a*, and as happens for the Divine for mystics, the encounter of O for Bion cannot be experienced through the rational mind and through normal language ('the English' in the excerpt above) but might be encountered through a special disguise of language where the aesthetics and the bodily sensorial aspects of the mind are particularly awake; 'The painful, conscious learning by heart is passed on to domains which are not conscious–like muscles or nerve systems which are sub-thalamic' (*MF*, p. 239).

This kind of truth, awry and displaced, away from the comforts of a (misleading) central vision, is more appropriately traced through a sort of anamorphic vision, the decentered perspective that, through a hole on the side of the painting or even through the frame itself, a marginal site *par excellence*, achieves some kind of revelation of what the whole (the entire representation) is all about, as in the famous example of Holbein's 'The Ambassadors', analyzed by Lacan in *The Four Fundamental Concepts* (Baltrušaitis, 1977; Hamish, 1997; Broadfoot, 2002, Lacan, 1978).

As Broadfoot argues,

> In anamorphosis, what is in front of the picture plane does not locate itself in an external reality but in the real. This is what makes the image that forms itself there a presentation rather than a representation. The strangeness of this situation, however, should be acknowledged, for the real is not a reality that precedes or comes after perspective, a reality that would be outside the

symbolic order; *the real is a lack that arises from within the symbolic order itself.*

(2002, p. 88, emphasis mine)

Identifying the Real in Lacanian terms as the traumatic kernel of modern societies (major historical examples of which can be found in the extermination camps as well as in the Gulag and all the other twentieth-century genocides), we could say that trauma is the unsymbolized and unmetabolized core structure of the entire order (Lacan, 1966; Kirshner, 1994) and of what defines the uncertainties of the post-modern identity for the subject.

The centrality of perspective is illusory. It would seem that at the unattainable centre of vision lies (or silently speaks) a void, a blank space (Mucci, 1992), a sort of structuring absence, in the wake of Lacan's *object a.* The entire symbolic order, which comes to be revealed at once as an artificial construction, in a synchronic rather than diachronic understanding, through a moment of revelation, is structured on this absence, according to Lacan. And I wish to propose that it is precisely this structuring absent cause revealing the traumatic hole, the void, the blank or the black hole defining trauma that has eroded representation and rational awareness, after History encountered the devastation and the annihilation of Trauma, in the wake of the two Wars and after the Shoah and the other exterminations that took place in the twentieth century, what trauma theorist and clinician Dori Laub calls the 'empty circle' (1998). Traumatic awareness is an oxymoronic concept. Where trauma is, there is no subjectivity to record or name it: 'In this form of traumatic memory, the center of experience is no longer in the experiencing "I". Events happen somewhere, but are no longer connected with the conscious subject' (Laub and Auerhahn, 1993, p. 291). Trauma displaces the subject and his/her awareness to an extreme, to a vanishing point.

Although trauma needs to be reconstructed carefully in its historical detail for some kind of healing and recovery to come forth, for both the individual and the collectivity (for this view, see Mucci, 2013), History, has become 'an event without a witness' (Felman and Laub, 1992). We are left with pieces of corporeal understanding, 'islands' of dissociated truths (Cimino and Correale, 2005) and at the same time mental erasures of the events, dissociated fragments that we can shore up against the ruins of what used to be called civilization. It is life at the mind's limits.

This state is not too far from psychotic decompensation:

> Since structure is built up by libidinal investments and identifi-cations, we see that at its worst, trauma involves the annihila-tion, by aggression, of psychic structure and the total desolation that is tantamount to what we would experience in psychotic decompensation.
>
> (Auerhahn and Laub, 1984, p. 336)

For Bion, the reversal of perspective (RP) is therefore what can protect the subject from the unbearable pain of the traumatic experience. *A Memoir of the Future* tries to rekindle in the reader precisely the expe-rience of this 'estrangement', (and I play here on the very meaning of the concept of estrangement as 'ostranenie' from Russian formalism, a sort of defamiliarization of the familiar to introduce Freud's con-cept of the Uncanny, Freud 1919), of this alienation that can become the only productive gift of the extreme experience.

Bion in his writings predicates a reversal of perspectives, a practice similar to the continuous transformative and imaginative performativity of dreams, a concept similar to what anthropologists would call 'limi-nality'. This is a particularly creative and even revolutionary mid-phase studied in the rituals of transformation and coming of age in so-called primitive cultures, the first phase being separation and the last incorpo-ration, and involves a paradoxical notion of truth, unattainable through univocal linguistic acts. Liminality is a moment of apparent disruption of the present order and world structure, where rules and daily conventions are suspended and things seem upside down, in a realm of obscurity and unreason, followed by a moment of revelation (just as in a dream).

In liminality, anthropologist Victor Turner explains:

> profane social relations may be discontinued, former rights and obligations are suspended, the social order may seem to have been turned upside down ... Liminality may involve a complex sequence of episodes in sacred space-time, and may also include subversive and ludic (or playful) events ... Then the factors or ele-ments of culture may be recombined in numerous, often grotesque

ways, grotesque because they are arrayed in terms of possible or fantasized rather than experienced combinations–thus a monster disguise may combine human, animal, and vegetable features in an 'unnatural' way, while the same features may be differently, but equally 'unnaturally' combined in a painting or described in a tale. *In other words, in liminality people play with the elements of the familiar and defamiliarize them.*

(2001, p. 26 emphasis mine)

Like the dismantling of repression in Freud's accounts of *das Unheimliche*, liminality momentarily liberates the subject from civilization's constraints, allowing him or her to peer through the fictions of society and the constraints of rationality and political order (for this connection, which is not in Turner, see Mucci, 1995). Liminality allows one also to see through the empty structure of conventions that regulate the symbolic order, revealing the artificial core around truth. As Lacan says, 'every truth has the structure of fiction' (*The Ethics of Psychoanalysis*, p. 12; for a discussion of this point, see also Kirshner, 1994).

Here is how Bion presents his project and the tension he identifies in his Memoir/psychoanalytic treatise between what he means by 'real' (ultimately a traumatic ineffable core, unspeakable, unrepresentable if not through distortions and play) and what reality is, an inevitably distorted representation of truth:

> The whole of this book so far printed can be regarded as an artificial and elaborate construct. I myself, here introduced into the narrative, can be regarded as a construct, artificially composed with the aid of such artistic and scientific material as I can command and manipulated to form a representation of an author whose name appears on the book and now, for the second time, as a character in a work of fiction. Is it a convincing portrait? Does it appear to 'resemble' reality?
>
> (*MF*, p. 86)

The relief from the constraints of reason that he aimed to achieve is explicit. The three books represent among other things the story of characters (to start with, Alice, Paul, Robin, Rosemary, Tom) whose power position in the social structure is reversed; moments of sheer horror follow, with murder, rape, unexpected and incomprehensible violence and abrupt sexual acts, intermingled with theoretical and intellectual discussions, where Bion himself takes the parts of several personalities: Bion, myself, P.A., Captain Bion, man. They seem rather the impersonations of human features and qualities that provide a mere excuse for the description of a 'stream' of events and feelings and situations that are more important than individual qualities, similar to what modern and postmodern authors, from Woolf (especially the Woolf of *The Waves* or *Between the Acts*) to Beckett, to Joyce, have accustomed us to.

It is only through disruption of that logical order, through the apparent folly of vision, or an anamorphic intentional distortion, the relinquishing of the quest for logic, and through a language that defies univocal meaning that we can hope to arrive at a bodily experience of O, through the soma-psychotic portion of the personality, through prenatal awareness and the insights (or the hallucination, hallucinosis and delusions) of the proto-mental apparatus. As Meltzer reminds us,

> In these three methods [hallucination, hallucinosis and delusion formation] for evacuation of beta-elements, the sense data of the emotional experiences are dealt with as if the meaning and significance were already inherent in the data and need not be created by the laborious, conflictual and anxiety-laden processes of thought (alpha-function) ...
>
> One implication is quite clear, that we cannot perform this function intellectually; it requires an unusual degree of identification with the patient, an unusual depth of reverie in the session, and an unusual degree of tolerance of feeling mad oneself.
>
> (1986, pp. 35, 37)

I find here an interesting correlation with what Allan Schore in his *The Science of the Art of Psychoanalysis* (2012) recommends as the peculiarly reconstructive intersubjective practice of the psychoanalytic experience, to let oneself be disregulated by the patient, working at the disregulatory boundaries (of self and other). In a word, at the mind's limits.

The practice of 'wakeful dream thinking' (what makes psychoanalysis a practice at the mind's limits) pierces through the veil of a reality that, rather than revealing truth, eludes it and postpones the (terrifying) encounter with what is at its core, what Bion has termed

O. More than 'understood' (which is impossible, as impossible as a description or a rendering of it in normal rational language) O might only be, under certain conditions, encountered and experienced.

From this encounter and transformation might result the state of 'becoming', made possible only by the transformative state of reverie (again, wakeful sleep). The subject does not apprehend truth in the same way as he/she does not apprehend O, but O might be traversed or pierced through by what Grotstein echoing Bion has called 'a beam of intense darkness' (2007).

O conceptualizes and subsumes for Bion this passing through or piercing Truth by means of the instruments of the abandonment of memory and desire, leaving aside or overcoming the coordinates of time frame and time structure (subverted in the very title of his work, since a 'memoir' is about the past of the subject, while here it hints at the future, at the process of subjectivity itself through the relationship of the subject with his/her own Truth) as well as those of 'desire'. Consequently, what leads the subject to his/her own path of repetition, i.e., desire stands at the opposite of freedom and trans-formation or the status of 'becoming'. The tragedy of the subject lies in this being prisoner precisely of memory and desire. As Grot-stein writes: 'We are born as fateful prisoners to the quality of the maternal – and paternal – container that (who) initially contains our raw dread of "O"' (2007, p. 44).

This is similar to Lacan's concept of the Real, which is not 'reality' but precisely what resists reality and interpretation (Kirshner, 1994), therefore has a traumatic, irrepresentable and horrific core, is inef-fable and unpierceable, and a thick veil (rationality, thought without reverie, thoughts without body and bodily sensations, therefore de-prived of alpha elements) prevents us from being in touch with—or becoming one—with Truth, prevents at-one-ment, moments of reve-lations or, to use a term from modern literature, 'epiphany'. What the traumatic core of reality explodes is precisely the illusion that the sub-ject can understand and describe and peer through the Real if he/she does not put on the garments of un-reason, of aesthetics (as Civitarese has highlighted in recent years, following Bion) in the sense of being in touch with the body and the senses, or elaborating the beta ele-ments, transformed into alpha elements. If, with Freud, we could say that dreams are the road to the unconscious, with Bion we can say that it is a road of uncertainty and revelations, abiding at the margins of the rational mind.

As Grotstein writes,

> Bion pulled the positive psychoanalysis of Freud and Klein with the new, uncharted realms of *uncertainty*: from the strictures and prison of verbal language to a realm beyond and before language. Here one experiences the dread of O, the Absolute Truth about our Ultimate, infinite, ineffable, always evolving, uncertain, and impersonal Reality that supplants the putative dread of the positivistic drives.
>
> (2007, p. 44)

Only a non-linear thought processing similar to the oneiric one can account for the unbridgeable paradoxes of what existence has become after Trauma invaded the scene of History. The unconscious processes can attain truth in a way inaccessible to conscious secondary processes. Only the dreamlike disguise of truth can be peered through and hinted at without horror. Because the other side of this disguise would be, I suppose, abjection, in Kristeva's terms (1982), i.e., the other side of the Sacred (which is also part of life and the Real). The disguise (of truth) rendered by poetic language can account for Truth and leaves the Subject unhurt but transformed.

As we read in *A Memoir*,

> The dreamless sleep ended. The day was as empty of events–facts proper to daytime–as the night had been empty of dreams. Meals were served to both girls. It occurred to them that they had no memory of the food; the 'facts' of daytime and night were defective, mutilated. They were having dreams–mutilated dreams– lacking a dimension like a solid body that casts no shadow in light. The world of reality, facts, was no longer distinguishable from dreams, unconsciousness, night. Thoughts with and thoughts without a thinker replaced a universe where discrimination ruled. Dreams had none of the distinguishing characteristics of mind, feelings, mental representations, formulations. The thinker had no thoughts, the thoughts were without thinkers. Freudian dreams had no Freudian free associations; Freudian free associations had

no dreams. Without intuition they were empty; without concept
they were blind.

(*MF*, p. 33)

This is in Chapter 8, page 33 of *A Memoir*, therefore at the very beginning
of a long journey. The trip into the non-linear, multidimensional world
of psychoanalysis (and traumatic Truth or the Real after trauma) after
the linear work of Freud, a new world inhabited by obscurities, bizarre
thoughts and paradoxical truths has just started: at the mind's limits.

Bion's 'Praise of Folly' and the breach to Postmodern Truth through punning: 'through the cages of my psychoanalytic zoo'

P.A: Allow me to conduct you round the cages of my psychoanalytic zoo. Of course the names are somewhat forbidding, but the
creatures themselves are beautiful and ugly. Ah! Here is Absolute Truth—a most ferocious animal which has killed more innocent white lies and *black wholes* than you would think possible.

ROLAND: You muddle it with your puns.

ROBIN: Call it paronomasia—more scientific.

ALICE: It sounds like a very attractive flower.

P.A: Only a flower of speech. Throw here all your quaint enam-
elled lies that on the green turf suck the honied showers.

(Ibid., p. 239, emphasis mine)

Paronomasia, states structural linguist Roman Jakobson, 'reigns over
poetic art' (1960); the dictionary equates paronomasia to punning, to
a play on words. As Freud has maintained in his *Jokes and their Relationship with the Unconscious* (1905), punning or playing with language allows a return of the repressed that the rational, adult mind
rejects, imprisoning the subject in the spires of reason. Here is Freud:

The repressive activity of civilization brings it about that primary
possibilities of enjoyment, which have now, however, been repu-
diated by censorship in us, are lost to us. But to the human psyche
all renunciations are exceedingly difficult, and so we find that ten-
dentious joke [i.e., 'aggressive' jokes, jokes against authority, and
'sexual' jokes] content provides a means of undoing the renuncia-
tion and retrieving what was lost.

(*Jokes*, 1905, p. 101)

Freud attributes to what he calls the 'rediscovery of something familiar' the final reason for the pleasure we take from form, the aesthetic pleasure, but he also hints at the real reason for this pleasure we take in form: this kind of aesthetic, formal, metaphorical and disguised version of truth suggests a return to a modality of mental play that is repressed by rationality, therefore allowing the subject to express what normally is repressed, censured. It is in a word a breach to truth, a kind of truth that is collective, allowing the return of what has been repressed by the pressure of authority and the pressure of sexual containment (at least according to the Freud of the first topic, since *Jokes* was written in 1905, when the two major contending principles were reality and pleasure). He also links this pleasure in paronomasia and punning to the pleasure in nonsense, which is 'concealed in serious life' (p. 124).

The realm of literature, from narrative and novel writing to poetic language, may be viewed in this context as 'the return of the repressed made acceptable and enjoyable through its form' (Orlando, 1973, p. 25).

The pleasure jokes and literature as formal, metaphorical and metonymic disguise give the reader is due, according to Freud, to the retrieval of a modality of expression forbidden to adult rationality and that only children or poets are allowed to enjoy and use. Freud's definition of the pleasure children experience in word-play and sound-play and rhyming is strikingly close to Roman Jakobson's definition of the poetic function of language (see also Mucci, 2004, for this interpretation) based on the similarity between sound and meaning; according to Jakobson, the poetic function projects the principle of equivalence from the axis of selection [syntagmatic] to the axis of combination [paradigmatic] (Jakobson in Sebeok, 1960, p. 358).

Freud remarks: 'We notice, too, that children, who, as we know, are in the habit of still treating words as things, tend to expect words, that are the same or similar, to have the same meaning behind them' (1905, p. 120).

He goes on:

> During the period in which a child is learning how to handle the vocabulary of his mother tongue, it gives him obvious pleasure 'to experiment with it in play', ... And he puts words together without regard to the condition that they should make sense, in order to obtain from them the pleasurable effect of rhythm or

rhyme. Little by little he is forbidden this enjoyment, till all that remains permitted to him are significant combination of words ... These attempts are found again among certain categories of mental patients. Whatever the motive may have been which led the child to begin these games, I believe that in his later development he gives himself up to them with the consciousness that they are nonsensical, and that he finds enjoyment in the attraction of what is forbidden by reason. He now uses games in order to withdraw from the pressure of critical reason ... the rebellion against the compulsion to logic and reality is deep-going and long-lasting. Even the phenomena of imaginative activity must be included in this (rebellious activity).

(Ibid., pp. 125–126)

Extending Freud's consideration of 'imaginative activity' and the rebellious activity of 'treating words like things' as a rebellion against reason and the constraints of civilization for adults, I would say with Bion that the unconscious playful mechanism of punning 'treats words' not only like 'things', (as Freud underlined) but assimilates polysemic language and imaginative, aesthetic, creative activity to the protomental and the emotional unsymbolized content stemming from experience (Bion, 1962a), or in other words, 'treating words like body'. Through the creative aspect of the interventions/presence of the therapist in the field, through his/her wakeful dream thinking, the emotional experience of the patient may be transformed and find meaning.

This has several implications for a restructuring of psychoanalytic theory and Freudian metapsychology, first of all for the partial relevance of merely intellectual interpretation, if it is not sustained by a continual emotional discovery and participation in the experience of the patients and his/her somatic-linguistic experience and expression of experience (through language, dreaming, and in cases of psychotic patients, even hallucinations, hallucinosis and delirious thoughts). Language (playful, punning and creative-metaphorical language together with non-verbal communication) becomes a tool in the rendering and the understanding of the special container-contained process going on between patient and therapist. To repeat Meltzer here, this also involves an 'unusual degree of identification with the patient, an unusual degree of reverie, and an unusual degree of tolerance of *feeling*

mad oneself ...' (1986, p. 37). And, I agree with him that in the thera-
peutic interchange: 'We must set ourselves an entirely different task,
namely that of discovering the emotional experience which the patient
is unable to dream about and to do his dreaming for him' (ibid., p. 37).

What happens, then, in this continual 'praise of folly' and play on
language in which the three books consist, is the exploration of a narrative detour and the creation of a paradoxical landscape where the
inverted world of liminality (where rules are subverted and typical
expectations disattended) and the language of paronomasia takes
over through a sort of transformational state of reverie and transition, where the reader is an active participant in the continual process
of discovery and revelation. It is a way of illustrating the practice of
psychoanalysis and its revelations.

Characters in search of an author, like thoughts without thinkers,
move along through a wasteland where threatening power reversals
have taken place and atrocities have been enacted. In this trip, the
reader is not spared murder, rape, cannibalism and all kinds of allu-
sions to war atrocities, in the awareness that truth cannot and should
not be avoided, especially emotional truth, which is what the unconscious is all about. The 'ineffable subject of the unconscious', the
'dreamer who dreams the dream' and the 'dreamer who understands
the dream' (all definitions taken from Grotstein, 2007) are one and
the same when the 'veil of representation' (to quote Erasmus' *Praise
of Folly*, 1511) has been lifted and the underlying truth of deceit and
misplacement has been revealed. The subject encounters his/her own
truth only on the path of the irruption of unconscious truth, which
speaks through the disguise of a metaphorical language similar to
that of dreams and poetry, not on the route of libido and conflict.
This is the difference Bion made with his contribution to metapsychology and the reason for the strain he felt within the more traditional psychoanalytic circle surrounding him in Britain. Submerged
in psychoanalytic jargon, truth in psychoanalysis might survive only
if disguised in fiction:

P.A: I am no poet, but I succumbed to the temptation to compose
a patriotic anthem, almost a New World symphony, using the
theme – 'borrowed' of course without acknowledgement – 'My
Mind to Me a Kingdom is.'

ROLAND: How very apposite. Just right for a psycho-analyst!

P.A: Alas, no.

ROLAND & ROBIN: Really? How was that?

P.A: His Satanic Jargonieur took offence; on some pretence that psycho-analytic jargon was being eroded by eruptions of clarity. *I was compelled to seek asylum in fiction. Disguised as fiction, the truth occasionally slipped through.* (*MF*, p. 302, emphasis mine)

'A nameless dread': the reality of war, the facts of trauma and 'psychoanalysis afterwards'

Dismantling the time and space frame, and condemning the subject to an ever-present repetition (what Lacan calls 'the return of the real', as the 'ever-absent cause' (1966)), the traumatic core has the (atrocious) capacity to put the subject in contact with his/her own truth (what by definition cannot be achieved), and this encounter is effected and played out through the limits of a logical representation and the triumph of the irrational logic of the primary process similar to dreamwork, in Freud's language, or wakeful dream thinking, in Bion's words. It is an encounter with pre-verbal and pre-linguistic implicit memories, stratified in bodily sensations, which for Bion recount 'facts' and build up the path towards transformation. In the *Italian Seminars* (Bion, 2005), Bion quotes the Freud of 1926 convinced that 'there is much more continuity between intrauterine life and earliest infancy than the impressive caesura of the act of birth allows us to believe' (SE 20, p. 138). The importance of experience through senses, which he calls 'facts' is here underlined:

> My training in the British Institute of Psycho-Analysis, my experiences with John Rickman, with Melanie Klein– all of it was verbal. Are we supposed to be blind and deaf to everything except what comes in through the ears? When a patient comes to see me, there is, in fact, a body which I can see for myself, and to that extent I can fall back on the evidence of my senses and on the information which my senses bring me. I don't think that we can afford to ignore what our senses tell us, because the facts are very few anyway.
>
> (Bion, 2005, pp. 1–2)

Only the patient knows what it feels like to be him or her:

> The patient is also the only person who knows what it feels like to
> have ideas such as that particular man or woman has. That is why
> it is so important that we should be able to hear, see, smell, even
> feel what information the patient is trying to convey. He is the
> only one who knows the facts, therefore those facts are going to
> be the main source of any interpretation, any observation which
> we are likely to be able to make.
>
> (Ibid., pp. 4–5)

And he goes on equating what 'the patient feels' to 'the nearest thing to a
fact' (ibid., p. 7). And especially very sick patients are the closest to a kind
of truth we have learned to detach from: 'With regard to patients who
are described as being "psychotic" or "borderline psychotics", I think
they are extremely aware of things which most of us have learnt not to be
aware of' (ibid., 2005, p. 7). Bion carries to further consequences Freud's
assumption that between health and folly there is only a matter of degree, not of content, and that the body is the first carrier of the emotional
experience connecting him/her with the outside world and is particularly
in tune with pain and the 'brutality of reality' (Preta, 'Prefazione', in
Rugi, 2015), therefore, I would say, at the core of the Real. Without this
experience, the mind cannot work through the raw material of reality
and apprehend it (Correale, 2015; Rugi, 2015; Lombardi, 2016).

The theorization of the experience of the body, or mere flesh, as the
only (unspeakable) truth can be found in Shoah survivors and writers.

This is what Jean Améry writes describing his experience of torture:

> The pain was what it was. Beyond that there is nothing to say.
> Qualities of feelings are as incomparable as they are indescriba-
> ble. They mark the limit of the capacity of language to commu-
> nicate …
>
> Whoever is overcome by pain through torture experiences his
> body as never before. *In self-negation, his flesh becomes a total
> reality.*
>
> (Améry, 1986, p. 33, emphasis mine)

Flesh becomes the subject, a speechless subject. If, as Correale writes,
'the thing-in-itself is the object before it becomes represented in a

collective linguistic network' (2015, p. 29), here trauma has exploded any possible relationship with 'the thing-in-itself', needless to say any communication between subject and external world.

According to his second wife Francesca and to his daughter Parthenope, Bion was rather obsessed with his experience in the War as a tank officer and would buy books on the topic on every possible occasion. He also recounted his war experience, as is well known, in several writings, *The Long Weekend* (1982), *All My Sins Remembered* (1985) and *War Memories* (1997). Parthenope argues that in *A Memoir of the Future* (1991), Bion used some episodes 'carried over almost un-chewed and apparently undigested ... as though no further working-through were possible' (Bion, 1997, p. 310).

In *A Memoir*, the voice of memory of the War is evoked mostly through the stratagem of the character Captain Bion. The tone is that of an abrupt Real intruding and disrupting the futility of all the other concerns of the mind; pain strikes at truth directly; bodily sensations and concrete sensorial aspects are fundamental:

CAPTAIN BION: I stared at the speck of mud trembling on the straw. I
  stared through the front flap at the clods of earth spouting up all
  round us. I stared at the dirty, strained face of my driver Allen–
  my strained face as I sat by me; at the boomerang that Allen sent
  me from Australia. I got out and hovered about six feet above us.
  How they walked–walk! walk! They went like arfs arfing. Arf arf
  together, arfing's the stuff for me, if it is not a Rolls Royce, which
  I'd pick out for choice. (*MF*, p. 53)

This strange passage in *A Memoir* can be understood only if we jux-tapose his last Memoir (defined by Francesca Bion as his 'psycho-analytically oriented autobiographical fantasy') with what he had written right at the beginning of his first book of memories, called *The Long Week-End 1897–1919 Part of a Life,* in which the reference to Arf Arf (which in A Key to the *Memoir* written by Bion and his wife is defined simply as 'childhood version of 'Our Father'') is described as a first idea and understanding of the Divine for the child Bion in India; it conveys therefore in very oblique ways the threat to life that fighting in the War constituted for him. This brief excerpt also con-veys the sense of one of the typical nightmares of the experience of the

War, when he was dreaming of dying in the Steenbeck River flood, and his feet and his hands were sinking into the mud.

The experience of 'having been in fighting' is commented on openly not by the character CAPTAIN BION himself but also by another character, ROBIN:

> No woman, even one as sensitive as Alice, will understand that life cannot be the same for a man who has been in fighting. I remember the night when the enemy front was red with fire. I couldn't believe it was the enemy destroying their ammunition. Retreat and disaster I was familiar with; victory not – and it came too late. I had changed.
>
> (*MF*, p. 262)

It is also significant that Bion could go back to the memories of war only after he gained the security and the peace of mind of his second marriage, several years later, in the 1950s. Trauma cannot be worked through according to an agenda, but the elaboration might start when parts of the mind are strong and emotionally sound enough to start the work; it is, as I showed in *Beyond Individual and Collective Trauma* (Mucci, 2013), a process that goes on in a spiral, some movements onward followed by regressive moments going eventually further or beyond. It is in fact interesting that Bion's writing about his War experience in 'Amiens' describe events that took place in 1958, when he was writing his papers on psychosis in the 1950s and right before his major theoretical publications of the 1960s (*Learning from Experience*, 1962a; *Elements of Psychoanalysis*, 1963; *Transformations*, 1965).

It is also of interest to note that years later, in 1972, after reading what he had written in his 'Diary' as early as 1919, Bion wrote the 'Commentary' in the form of a dialogue between a character called MYSELF (i.e., Bion at the time of the Commentary) and BION (Bion at the time of the Diary). There, BION says that, during the Oxford Years, he could not work or enjoy games (1997, *War Memoirs*, p. 209), and MYSELF states that he 'did not stand up to the rigours of war very well'. And finally we have the dialogue:

BION: Of course we did not know that, though I was always afraid I would not. I think even the diary shows that as it goes on, though at Oxford I was still too ashamed to admit it, and very glad of the opportunity that Oxford gave me to be seduced into a more self-satisfied state of mind. But I never quite got rid of the sense that all was *not* well.

MYSELF: That ultimately drove me to psychoanalysis.

(Bion, 1997, p. 201)

In the *Diary*, most of the times he uses the plural form 'we' to refer to the most emotional events, and it seems that the psychic terror is described more in collective terms, or on the basis of group experiences, than in individual and personal terms. The basic incapacity to think when the mind is overwhelmed by terror is the major assumption we can make from a reading of the *Diary*, a fundamental step towards his metapsychology and his later theoretical thinking.

The connection we can make between his state of mind in war overwhelmed with terror and what he wrote in 1962 as a major contribution to psychoanalytic thinking, namely his 'containment theory' and the 'nameless terror' the mind faces when there is this lack of containment, is indeed striking:

> Normal development follows if the relationship between infant and breast permits the infant to project a feeling, say, that it is dying into the mother and to reintroject it after its sojourn in the breast has made it tolerable to the infant psyche. *If the projection is not accepted by the mother the infant feels that its feeling that it is dying is stripped of such meaning as it has. It therefore reintrojects, not a fear of dying made tolerable, but a nameless dread.*
>
> (Bion, 1984, p. 116, emphasis mine)

In Laub and Lee's convincing definition, trauma is precisely the rupture of the empathic dyad between mother and child, or between the internalized good object and the abrupt erasure of it and the invasion of the psychic by the 'horror of objectlessness' (Laub and Lee, 2003, p. 441).

A personal embodiment or incorporation of the catastrophic experience of war helped Bion in his capacity to analyze and help his psychotic patients with precisely this type of extreme and fragmented mental experience and where a total lack of containment had prevailed, throwing the mind into terror. Dissociated fragments of unmetabolized experience would still haunt the mind of Bion, as he re-worked through his memories in his last *Memoir*.

In *Beyond the Pleasure Principle*, Freud went beyond his own theorization of the dream (as given in *The Interpretation of Dreams)*, as the one to one correspondence of referents even in the over-determination of elements, so that the dream was similar to a rebus whose obscurity needed to be dispelled and removed in order for the truth (or light) to pierce through.

Therefore, a breakthrough in Freud's theory of dreams comes after World War I, when he theorized a 'beyondness' of the pleasure principle where the traumatic core of reality was repeated even in dreams as a way of mastering traumatization. For Bion, traumatization has become an epistemology, wherein light or insight is actually a beam of intense obscurity, but obscurity (at the limits of representation) is the only way to cut through O and surrender to it, the real embracement of some kind of redemption for the subject.

At the other side of a metapsychology that places thoughts over feelings and words over body, Bion re-opens a path for a psychoanalysis where the caesura (between conscious and unconscious, between mind and body, between prenatal and postnatal, between different meanings in the same word) is eroded in the direction of openness and fluidity, the fluidity of the waves, as he describes them in a passage notoriously commented upon (*Memoir, The Dream,* I, p. 193).

As Hamlet found method in folly, the reader as well as the patient and analyst for Bion can find some at-one-ment, a unique moment of revelation and oneness with one's multiple selves and at the same time some restoration and 'atonement', expiation-reparation only if he/she is capable of going through the limits of the oppositions of conscious-unconscious, mind-body, right and left hemispheres, as we would say today following Allan Schore (2012).

A Memoir of the Future shows the reader and the subject the path towards this going beyond of pleasure and the beyondness of the (Kleinian) death drive too, after the trauma of History; the radicalization of the lack of certainty and the darkness and void from which subjectivity is born point at a new 'truth drive', with its relentless work towards the irretrievability of a truth that will forever fade or escape if searched for in the direction of the rational mind (and in the guise of a language that is univocal and non-poetic, language, like the language of science). In this way, an aesthetic sensitivity or openness to ambiguity and ambivalences replaces the rational mind.

At the mind's limits, *A Memoir of the Future* reminds the reader that, as Aron Appelfeld who survived the Shoah observes, only the metaphorical disguise of art and literature can render the reality of the unspeakable aspect at the core of truth, when trauma has pierced though the surface of reality and exploded the 'thing' it posits:

> I have never written about things as they happened. All my words are indeed characters from my most personal experience but nevertheless they are not 'the story of my life' ... I tried several times to write 'the story of my life' but all my efforts were in vain. I wanted to be faithful to reality and to what really happened. But ... the result was rather meager, an unconvincing imaginary tale. *The things that are the most true are easily falsified ... I had to remove those parts which were unbelievable from the 'story of my life' and present a more credible version.*
>
> (Appelfeld 1988, p. 29, emphasis mine)

The truth of one's life after Auschwitz cannot reside in the meaning of the words of collective understanding, or belong to the 'Establishment'.

As an end, let me quote the Epilogue Bion/BION/MYSELF/ CAPTAIN BION and the other characters put at the end of the book:

> *... & EPILOGUE*
> *... FUGUE*
> *... DONA ES REQUIEM*
> *... MANY*

All my life I have been imprisoned, frustrated, dogged by common-sense, reason, memories, desires and – greatest bugbear of all – understanding and being understood. This is an attempt to express my rebellion, to say Good-bye to all that. It is my wish, I now realize doomed to failure, to write a book unspoiled by any tincture of common-sense, reason etc. (see above). So, although I would write, 'abandoned Hope all ye who expect to find any facts – scientific, aesthetic or religious – in this book', I cannot claim to have succeeded. All these will, I fear, be seen to have left their traces, vestiges, ghosts hidden within these words; even sanity, like 'cheerfulness', will creep in. However successful my attempt, there would always be the risk that the book 'became' acceptable, respectable, honoured and unread. 'Why write then' You may ask. To prevent someone who KNOWS from filling the empty space – but I fear I am being 'reasonable', that great Ape. Wishing you a Happy Lunacy and Relativistic Fission ...

(*MF*, p. 578)

In the lines right before this epilogue, in the dialogue between A and Q the page before, 577, A says to Q: 'Bye-bye – happy Holocaust!'

Bion leaves us with the riddle of transforming the language of catastrophe into that of a new subjectivity or humanism.

Chapter 10

The 'Memoir' experienced from the standpoint of contemporary art

A chronicle of a death foretold

Adela Abella

It is said that when Bion first published his *A Memoir of the Future*, his fellow analysts wondered if he had gone mad. Indeed, the contrast with the content and formal aspects of his preceding works is impressive and disconcerting. My readings of *Memoir* share this initial reaction of awe: my repeated attempts to get through it invariably failed. Over and over again, the experience of reading *Memoir* evoked in me the experience aroused by some works of contemporary art: perplexity, amazement, displeasure, irritation, rejection and ... an urge towards thinking.

A famous story concerning Marcel Duchamp comes to mind. Duchamp, often considered the father of contemporary art, was famous for his provocative work and life devoted to unrelentingly challenging the whole of the artistic and moral values of his time (Abella, 2007). Unexpectedly, in 1923, while he was not yet 40 years old, he announced his definite abandonment of all activity as a painter, proclaiming that he 'was really defrocked, in the religious sense of the word ... All that disgusted me' (Cabanne, 1971, p. 67). The shock was therefore violent when a posthumous strange, uncanny and unclassifiable work came to light: '*Given: 1. Waterfall, 2. The illuminating gas*' (1946–1966), a figurative and kitsch painting, on which Duchamp had worked during 20 years in the utmost secrecy. In fact, this astonishing and paradoxical action added an ironic, mischievous and disconcerting wink to his exuberant renouncement of painting.

A strange, uncanny and unclassifiable work: we might also apply these terms to Bion's *Memoir*. Indeed, both *Given* and *Memoir* had (and still partially have) a similar startling and enlivening effect, forcing a new regard onto a previous body of work that had, in the meantime, become canonical. (It should be noted that both Bion and Duchamp repeatedly expressed their worry that new ideas become familiar and lose their refreshing potential. I will come back to this).

A refreshing potential: like *Given*, *Memoir* adds a disquieting wink to Bion's work in such a way that other readings of his presently too familiar ideas become possible. We thought we had understood Bion. Did we really? Maybe not, suggests *Memoir*. Was Bion meaning more, less or otherwise than I thought he meant *before* I tasted the acidity of this upsetting late work? Should *Memoir* be seen as the implicit mourning for the failure of a life struggle for clear thinking and uncontaminated communicating expression? Or, from another direction, does *Memoir* represent a pro-(e)vocative invitation towards the unknowable, the unreachable O? And, in this last case, is O necessarily so irksome and ugly?

The unconventional tenor and the upsetting effects of *Memoir* give rise to two opposite risks. On the one hand, we might be tempted to put it aside and cut it off from the main body of Bion's work, as if it were an old man's silliness and a sham. On the other hand, we might idealize it, investing this unsettling work with particularly profound, far-fetched and esoteric meanings. I will try to show why, in my opinion, both extremes lead to the loss of something fundamental. Therefore, the intriguing question is, for me, what to do with this disrupting work: should we try to understand, and therefore tame, *Memoir*'s wildness, or would it be wiser to respect the refreshing potentiality of a space for impenetrability and mystery?

The end of art and the birth of a new paradigm

It has often been said that the sharp rift brought by contemporary art concerning what was previously considered art equates to a real revolution. This rift is so radical that even educated people who enjoy classical or modern art often go astray when it comes to the artistic propositions of the last 60 years. Thus, it is not unusual that using the word 'art' for certain creations arouses scepticism, bewilderment, irritation, fear of being cheated and abused. They can be felt to be shams and farces, disparaged either as profoundly ugly, disgusting pieces or as boring, senseless artefacts. Contemporary art's social and aesthetic earthquake has been compared to the one brought about by impressionism in the late 19th century. Both of them aroused similar feelings and anxieties.

Already in the 1980s, a number of critics suggested the death of painting, alluding to certain signs of exhaustion. There was a strong feeling of the impossibility of surpassing what had already been achieved in the field. No possible progress or improvement in the visual arts was to be expected. However, in the 1990s, it was in a much more radical sense that both German art historian Hans Belting (1983) and American philosopher and art critic Arthur C. Danto (1997) articulated the idea of the 'end of art'. More recently and from a different point of view, French sociologist Nathalie Heinich (2014) has come to similar conclusions, while describing the many social faces of what she agrees defines a change of paradigm. By this term, and drawing on Khun's work (1962), Heinich refers to a general structure of shared conceptions concerning a given domain of human activity at a particular moment. A paradigm, she clarifies, is not a rationally and consciously followed model but, on the contrary, a (mostly) unconsciously accepted foundation, which implicitly determines what can be considered art, what are legitimate artistic problems and what sorts of solutions can be proposed. This paradigm shift brings about a radical change in collective representation about the nature and the usage of art and, therefore, in the attitudes and expectations of artists and public.

J.-F. Lyotard (1979) developed the idea that any great discourse of knowledge is but a legitimising of a sociocultural practice. For the three authors quoted, Danto, Belting and Heinich, as well as for many others, the narratives that legitimise both classical and modern art have come to an irremediable and no-way-back final point. Briefly summed up, it can be said that classical art promoted perfect mimesis and formal beauty (as a worldly equivalent of spiritual perfection). The successive artistic periods, renaissance, mannerism, baroque, rococo, neoclassicism and romanticism, evolved gradually, often in sharp opposition to the preceding period, while keeping a degree of continuity. It must be noted, and this is a fundamental point, that this continuity was based on the fact that their central aspiration remained the faithful representation of 'nature' (be it in an idealised or in a realistic way).

A shift of paradigm was brought by modern art (which expanded since around 1880 up to the 1960s) that can be described in terms of both inward and formal turns. The inward turn: what matters is no longer mimesis of reality or formal beauty but the expression of the most personal view of the world. The formal turn: the rules of figurative representation are abolished so that the most personal expression is sought through manipulation of visual modalities of representation: form, surface and pigment. It is the triumph of pure art – the accent lies both on the appeal to the senses and on the authenticity in the expression of the interiority of the artist. Different schools (impressionism, cubism, futurism, dada, abstract expressionism) entered into acute competition, each proposing a particular formal avenue meant to allow this radical personification.

In the 1970s, we witness a second paradigm clash brought about by the agitated delivery of contemporary art. What is now at stake is neither the most faithful and beautiful rendering of reality nor the unbridled expression of the artist's interiority, but the exploration and transgression of the frontiers of art (Heinich, 1996, 2014). This questioning of the limits of art is absolute and boundless. Both the frontiers with other disciplines and the boundaries with everyday life are challenged. Thus, the interaction with other disciplines gives birth to astonishing forms of hybridisation through marriage with somewhat related fields such as video and dance but also with previously distant ones such as philosophy or science. As for the interface with everyday life, we see a two-way fecundation: in one direction, mundane objects are imported into art (Duchamp's bicycle wheel, Spoerri's dinner tables). In the opposite direction, art literally invades all sorts of social spaces, blurring and stepping outside its traditional spatial boundaries, namely museums and galleries (to which we can add the decorative and propagandistic installation of patriotic statues in places and avenues). Customary frontiers are overtaken, giving way to land art (represented by the work of artists such as Smithson or Christo) and an ever-increasing number of installations and performances in schools, parks, factories, airports and restaurants.

Still more shocking, contemporary art disrupts not only the materials used or the contexts of its presentation but also commonly shared aesthetic and moral values through attitudes combining playfulness, distancing, cynicism, mockery, scandal and provocation. The maximal originality is often sought in order to thwart any expectation and achieve greater impact. Anything goes: political protest can be instrumental as an artistic option (yielding great success, as is the case with a number of Chinese artists); traditional art values such as authenticity, disinterest and rejection of financial compromise are often explicitly dismissed (an avenue opened by Warhol and culminating in spectacular and sensationalist productions reaching unbelievable market prices, such as those by Damien Hirst or Jeff Koons); it is not unusual for good taste and common decorum to be outrageously challenged (as in Paul McCarthy's masochistic and self-demeaning performances or Piero Manzoni's non metaphorical *Artist's shit*).

Often, art lies not so much in the object but in the discourse and activities associated with the production and exhibition of the work (when it is exhibited, which is not necessarily the case with conceptual art, where the description of a work can suffice. Thus, a big collector can gather his or her collection almost entirely in a file!). What matters is not so much the pebble thrown into the lake as the waves it triggers. Therefore, art is more a question of proposing a certain experience than a question of a material object. This avenue opens the way to artistic propositions that can be depersonalised (no personal expression or implication of the artist), dematerialised (no material object) or ephemeral (no need of any permanence). The experience offered to the public can be both of an emotional nature (in the form of a quest for excitement arousing strong feelings such as amazement, desire, disgust, compassion and boredom) and of an intellectual nature (stimulating fresh thinking, as Duchamp and Cage championed). In this last case, the intellectual dimension of the work of art runs hand in hand with its capacity to foster a variety of interpretations by the public. The artist may explicitly reject any personal implication in order to avoid the seductive indoctrination of the public (an aim explicitly sought by Duchamp, Cage or Boltansky (Abella, 2007, 2008, 2012, 2015). To this aim, a textual discourse must often accompany the work of art in order to furnish an instruction manual to the disconcerted public (an introductory textual discourse that can, paradoxically, pedagogically guide the public's appropriation to the end of restraining the freedom to recreate the work of art). Thus, contemporary works of art seem to be addressed to a sophisticated and initiated public, to the exclusion of any random audience.[1] We might say that, in a similar way, Bion's *Memoir* has been, and still is, difficult to access for a random psychoanalyst, perhaps needing some sort of introduction for the approach of this disconcerting work.

In sharp contrast with the passionate struggle for hegemony characteristic of modern art, claims Danto (1997), contemporary art relies on profound pluralism and entire tolerance. It is, as Belting (1983) put it, the loss of faith in the existence of a great narrative that determines the way in which things *must* be seen. There are no rules and no values; everything can be art. We seem to be living in a period of disorganised information, of aesthetic entropy, almost of total freedom to create or recreate. In fact, adds Danto, the beginning of contemporary art can be placed in the appropriation of preceding works of art, which are diverted from the original spirit in which they had been created (for instance, works done by artists aiming for mimesis or beauty – a founding example being Duchamp adding moustaches to the Giaconda). More than a rejection of classical or modern art, we see a playful and ironic recuperation of the past. Therefore, following the line of M. Duchamp, Danto comes to the conclusion that contemporary art is more a business of intellectual understanding than a question of visual pleasure. Philosophy replaces aesthetics.

Convergences between Bion's thinking and contemporary art

There are some profound similarities between the spirit of a number of influential contemporary artists and the one underlying Bion's work (Abella, 2010, 2013, 2016). Maybe the most striking convergences can be found between him and one of his contemporaries: John Cage (1912–92) (Abella, 2012, 2015). Of course, given the contemporary boundless freedom to create, as described by Danto, these convergences between Bion and Cage are not shared by all contemporary artists. Plurality and stepping outside limits being the rule, there is no directive canon. Nevertheless, these shared views belong to the array of legitimate problems and accepted solutions that the contemporary artistic paradigm allows.

Both Bion and Cage posit mental transformation and personal growth as the central aim of psychoanalysis and music. As Cage says,

I want to give up the traditional view that art is a means of self-expression for the view that art is a means of self-alteration, and what it alters is *mind* ... We will change beautifully if we accept the uncertainties of change.

(Kostelanetz, 1988, p. 226)

This view of art meets Bion's conception of the central role of psychoanalysis: 'In psychoanalytic methodology the criterion cannot be whether a particular usage is wrong or right, meaningful or verifiable, but whether it does, or does not, promote development' (Bion, 1962a, p. ix).

For both of them, this aim can be achieved through fresh personal awareness of reality (external, sensorial for Cage; internal, mental for Bion) that is countered by habit and tradition. Thus, Cage states: 'the function of music is to change the mind so that it does become open to experience' in order to allow 'other possibilities that they had not previously considered', 'to open our eyes and our ears to the multiplicity and complexity' of life, avoiding 'what is too simple and too quickly satisfied' (Kostelanetz, 1988, p. 180). In a similar vein, Bion advocates a 'naïf-view' (Bion, 1963, p. 86) that allows openness to whatever new experience may come up in the moment, while insisting on 'the fact that any session is a new session and therefore an unknown situation that ... (must not be) obscured by an already plentiful fund of pre- and misconceptions' (Bion, 1962a, p. 39). In strikingly similar words, Cage warns against the obscuring power of 'desire, memory and taste', while Bion invites the analyst to stay free from 'memory, desire and understanding'.

Along the same lines, Cage contends that 'the function of art is to hide beauty: that has to do with opening our minds, because the notion of beauty is just what we accept' (Kostelanetz, 1988, p. 85). In a similar way, insists Bion, the truth sought by the analyst should be a personal truth, not one found in books: the analyst should respect not only the uniqueness of his patient but his own uniqueness as well. Therefore, if the experience and knowledge of predecessors is needed, they might be freely used and applied to present circumstances and context: 'Freud's papers should be read – and 'forgotten'. Only in this way is it possible to produce the conditions in which, when it is next read, it can stimulate the evolution of further development' (1967a, p. 156). In other words, accepted truths should be suspended, forgotten, hidden or used in whichever way allows new ones to come to the fore.

However, the temptation to avoid the new and take refuge in tradition and certainty is so overwhelming that both Cage and Bion claim the need of an active and sustained struggle to resist them. Thus, Bion's suggestions both of a mathematical notation and of the grid are meant to free the analyst of a saturating penumbra of preconceptions, to the end of stimulating fresh perceptions of reality and clear communication. Cage tries to counter habit and tradition through the forced introduction of chance by composing through the Chinese I Ching divination book or the star maps of Atlas Australis or by playing music through the addition of pie plates, screws, etc. to the strings of the 'prepared' piano ...

In fact, what is most feared is the depersonalising power of habit and tradition, which leads to suggestion, seduction and indoctrination, a fear shared by contemporary art (Duchamp, Cage, Boltanski and many others) as well as by contemporary psychoanalysis (Bion and many psychoanalysts). It is this fear that prompts Bion's heartfelt cry: 'Don't try to understand *me*! Pay special attention to *your emotional responses* to me!' (Grotstein, 2007, pp. 7–8) as well as to Cage's urging motto 'Get out of whatever cage you happen to be in' (Kostelanetz, 1988, p. 15).

However, the power of previous knowledge and the tendency to cling to 'a protective shell of familiar ideas' (Bion, 1967a, p. 150) are so pervasive that both of them finally resort to extreme emergency measures such as emptiness, silence, paradox and provocation. Thus, while Bion promotes a 'pro-evocative attitude', Cage multiplies shocking propositions such as his *Silent piece, 4' 33"*, a piece composed of three movements with ... no sound at all! Something of this spirit is illustrated in a famous anecdote extracted by Grotstein from his analysis with Bion:

> After many of my own analytic sessions with him, I would leave dazed and confused, believing that I had not understood much of what he had said ... During another moment in analysis, he gave me a series of interpretations which, unusually, caused me to say: 'I think I follow you'. His reply to this was an ironic: 'Yes, I was afraid of that!' It was only then that I began to realize that Bion did not want to be followed or understood, let alone idealised. He wanted me and everyone who was in his presence to be responsive to his/her own emanations and responses.
>
> (Grotstein, 1981b, p. 10)

A Memoir of the Future as a contemporary work of art?

Of course not. What I suggest is that *Memoir* arouses emotional re-actions and thoughts close to those stirred up by a certain number of contemporary works of art and, still more important, that Bion shares some central aspirations and convictions with an important trend of contemporary artists.

Among the issues in common we might point out: a focus on fresh and personal perceptions of (internal, external) reality instead of succumbing to (psychoanalytical or artistic) tradition and habit; the aspiration to mental transformation and growth; replacing the mere application and transmission of (psychoanalytical, artistic) knowl-edge by the re-discovery and re-creation of the heritage; the accent on truth and discovery instead of beauty and mental comfort; a free us-age of the knowledge transmitted by predecessors instead of submis-sion to canonical truths; profound awareness of the difficulty, even the impossibility, of achieving a 'naïf-outlook' and, consequently, the need to exercise severe discipline in order to free oneself from desire, memory, understanding and taste; finally, a desperate effort to attain this asymptotic freedom through extreme disinfecting strategies such as the use of silence, paradox, nonsense, pro(e)vocation, irony, delib-erate obscurity and the breaking of conventional boundaries; all of this ends up in the need for an instruction book in order to be intro-duced to an hermetic work.

From this standpoint, some of the disconcerting traits of *Memoir* become meaningful. A critic once said that Duchamp had 'reached the limit of the unaesthetic, the useless and the unjustifiable' (Lebel, 1959, p. 47). This is near the reaction of Bion's analytic colleagues at the time of *Memoir*'s first edition. Is this attempt to push the limits to the utmost shared by both Bion and Duchamp for the *same* reasons? That is, the unconventional and kitsch presentation of *Memoir* would aim to open the mind to unexpected truths, acting like an electro-shock on a cardiac arrest, in the same way as a work of art seeking to awake an admiring and submissive public?

The oxymoron contained in its title has a first destabilising and thought-provoking power: a *memoir* of the *future*? Is Bion just mis-chievously playing with words or is there a deeper sense? Similar to

Duchamp, is Bion attempting to subvert common language in order to uncover other possible meanings? And, if so, what might these be? Then, concerning the nature of this writing: is this really a memoir, or rather a novel, or maybe a special type of psychoanalytic discourse, or an old man's delirium or just a thought-provoking joke? What is to be found inside: Bion's personal phantasies or an esoteric message containing unexplored theoretical pearls reserved for a selected un-initiated public? Or else, is Bion forcing us to abandon the protective shell of accepted ideas by this provocative breaking of conventional limits? Is this a new version of his abrupt comment to Grotstein, aimed to remove all trace of submission and defensive idealisation? Is his baroque and acid wording the equivalent of Cage's renouncement of beauty because beauty is lulling and numbing, just as we already know? In the same spirit as Cage's passionate summons, 'Get out of whatever cage you happen to be in', is Bion suggesting that we get out of the psychoanalytical cage we might have built? And if so, what and where exactly is this cage, and how can we escape it?

When choosing the avenue of highlighting the enlivening and transformative power of *Memoir*'s wild unconventionality, a trou-bling backfire conclusion might follow. Duchamp announced the in-evitable death, not of modern art but of any particular work of art, be it the most innovative and contemporary: 'I think painting dies, you understand. After forty or fifty years a picture dies, because its freshness disappears' (Cabanne, 1971, p. 67). He develops this idea concerning his emblematic ready-mades, which he wanted to be 'to-tally and strategically unaesthetic':

> I haven't done any now for a long time ... because anything, you know, however ugly, however indifferent it is, will become ... beautiful and pretty after 40 years, you can be sure ... So that is very disturbing for the very idea of the ready-made.
>
> (Collin, 2002, p. 37)

The question might therefore be: what will be the effect of our legiti-mate efforts to penetrate the mystery and wildness of *Memoir*? Would it be possible that his shocking, and therefore enlivening, potential vanishes under the uncovering power of our attempts to understand? Once understood and tamed, will *Memoir* die, suffocated by an excess of idealisation and understanding? If this were the case, we might say that it has nevertheless fulfilled its stimulating function for a long time. I think that Bion might have accepted the irremediable death of his *Memoir,* provided that its oblivion might fecundate other analysts' minds. That is, trusting that other analysts would follow him in the struggle to be themselves, to respect the uniqueness of their personality and, therefore, to renew and revitalize our field.

Note

1 Anecdotes concerning the disorientation of the public, even those used to visiting art fairs and biennials, are common. Sometimes they are funny, at other times disquieting and even cruel. Thus, there are frequent versions of the classical case of a well-intentioned visitor who picks up a shopping-bag or something similar, thinking someone forgot it there, and is scolded and shamed because he has upset an installation. Another illuminating example: at the last Kassel Fair, 2012, a group of visitors was surprised to find the first huge museum room absolutely empty except for a bare display stand pushed to one side. What were they meant to look at? No explanatory notice, no attendant to ask. An animated debate failed to answer this basic question until a diligent tourist found the response in his book: the work was a light airstream crossing the room. The reactions of the visitors were illustrative of the variety of personal appropriations: laughter, scepticism, irritation, disappointment, shame, intense musing, blank admiration ...

Chapter 11

Reflections on 'nonsense' in
A Memoir of the Future

Duncan Cartwright

ME: 2017, are we ready for this tome yet? Did you read it? I mean *really* read it?

DUNCAN: Was it God or Satan who stole the thicket? Yes, I fell asleep 143 times. What nonsense! It's most positive attribute is its ability to take up space on my book self to show off my intelligence, although no one has heard of him. It should be admired for its potential to induce comas.

ME: You didn't understand it did you?

DUNCAN: You're not supposed to understand it! Didn't you read the end?

BION: (Waking) Oh god, has it become acceptable?

ME: No.

BION: What a relief!

SELFIE☺SELF: This makes no sense and is taking a lot of time! No one reads this stuff anymore. Just Google it or take lots and lots of pictures so you won't have to think …

PAUL S: Motherfucker! An ugly word … But ugly does have a case to make. It's not like every rodent gets a birthday cake. No, it's 'you're a chipmunk, how cute is that?' Did you hear they've found heaven six trillion light years away.

BION: Genius! Glad I woke up, he's trapped the light! Have you heard Bon Iver or Hollis? 2017 and still dancing around the same crucifix.

EMMATURE: We can only hope for something to break through before I drown in pre-mature knowledge and self-satisfaction.

A Memoir of the Future was Bion's final and most audacious attempt to explore the nature of psychic reality as a here-and-now living experience. To do so, he employs a host of literary devices, concepts, fictionalised experiences, characters, presences and registers of experience to represent a 'science fiction' of psychoanalysis. It could be seen as Bion's *Aeneid* (Symington and Symington, 1996), a freeing journey that allowed him to explore a lifetime of experience and intellectual pursuits from multiple perspectives and in a way that attempts to stay true to his vision of psychoanalysis. The trilogy draws on autobiographical experiences, literature, psychoanalysis, science, mythology, religion, the arts and history. Although its structure and style appear influenced by Socrates, Shakespeare, Goethe, Diderot and Dante (Bléandonou, 1994), as a whole, it defies categorisation. It could be read as a psychoanalytic autobiography, a speculative account of the future of psychoanalysis, a demonstration of Bion's psychoanalytic concepts, an exercise in psychoanalytic mental gymnastics, a history of 'the mind' through a psychoanalytic lens, a meditation on 'nonsense', a critique of psychoanalysis, or the incoherent ravings of an old unhinged psychoanalyst.

As is the case with many of Bion's offerings, reading him is as much an experience as it is an attempt to grapple with his ideas. Perhaps like no other psychoanalytic author, Bion engages his audience in a way that provokes and challenges the reader to experience and seek 'personal truth' as an essential part of reading or learning. It could be said that Bion is equally concerned with 'infecting' the reader or interlocutor with the problem itself, the experience, as with imparting an accumulation of facts or rationalisations. With this in mind, in *Memoir,* Bion takes his reader through periods of disorientation, confusion and obscurity in a provocative way that appears to contain an implicit appeal: dismiss the trilogy as nonsense or engage. Fall to sleep or tolerate 'something' that is unknown but 'becoming'. Choose oblivion or wisdom.

In this chapter, I consider the place and role of 'nonsense' in the trilogy. I define 'nonsense' broadly as all that flouts commonly held conventions in narrative expression and delivery. In *A Memoir of the Future*, 'nonsense' appears in many forms ranging from the idiomatic use of language and dialogue to the general structure of the works.

Its function or effect seems multifaceted. It could be seen to form the medium through which the dynamic and multidimensional nature of psychic reality is represented. Nonsense might also be understood as a device used to penetrate and disrupt the reader's desire for coherence, reason and authority. Still further, the 'roughness' of nonsense, its appeal to obscurity, could be seen as demonstrating the essential processes involved in thought formation as well as an attempt to accurately represent the experience of unconscious life and the influence of 'the formless infinite'.

I reflect on the non-sensuous nature of psychic reality as it appears in the trilogy, its relation to nonsense, the senses, fiction and psychic truth. Finally, I comment on the trilogy's currency in today's world in terms of our most recent 'fashionable' solution to psychic uncertainty: cyberspace. Here, the immediacy of 'making sense' poses new challenges in the journey towards 'mental oblivion' or wisdom. The same 'memoirs of the future' and questions remain. Will we make the mental effort, take the time, to *not* understand? As a largely dismissed piece of work, perhaps Bion's intensions remain as alive today as they ever were, still awaiting a thinker.

Multiplicity and psychic reality

Bion's use of 'nonsense' starts at the very beginning of the trilogy with the title of the introduction to the three works: 'Introduction ... prelude ... overture & beginners ... one, two' (*MF*, p. ix). It might be read as playful dream-thoughts about 'beginnings' and signals an approach set on drawing on multiple vertices or perspectives ranging from the ordinary to aesthetic, infantile to logical. The 'nonsense' continues in the introduction to the first volume, *The Dream*, with a reverie about reversible perspectives and binocular vision:

> Suppose I use my alimentary canal as a sort of telescope. I could get down to the arse and look up at the mouth full of teeth and tonsils and tongue. Or rush up to the top end of the alimentary canal and watch what arse-hole was up to. Rather amusing really. It depends what my digestive tract felt about having me scampering up and down the gut all night.
>
> (Ibid., p. 3)

The Dream leads the reader into a world of confusion and turmoil, with Bion offering little relief or orientation as to what direction or intention shapes the narrative. Characters and the setting are left undefined and vaguely represented, inducing disorientation, as the reader hears about a 'successful invasion, its details unknown' (ibid., p. 19). Two couples, Alice and Roland, Rosemary and Tom, undergo a role reversal and encounter many unknowns as they are joined by a host of characters: 'Big sister', 'Depressive Position', 'Paranoid-Schizoid', 'Memory', 'Voice', and 'Bion', to mention a few. 'Alice', a reference to Lewis Carroll's 'Alice', stands 'naked, incongruous, alien, without a point of reference that made sense' (ibid., p. 27). She occupies an upside-down world where Rosemary, her servant, has become her master or goddess. The scene is set for turbulent change.

As a representation of dream-life and psychic reality, *The Dream* challenges conventional conceptions of time, space and reasoning. Characters and background presences appear out of nowhere and remain undifferentiated. They could be understood to represent dream-thoughts at different levels of representation, past and present experiences undergoing transformation, or different aspects of a personality. All suggest a multidimensional timeless space powered by unnamable psychic turmoil:

> Rosemary and Alice have swooned away, but Rosemary still talks.
> 'Who are you?'
> (Shadowy Figures disguised as S.F. take over.)
> 'We are Science Fiction. Who are you?'
> 'I am the Artist who made the ram caught in a thicket beautiful in
>   gold ... Who are you?'
> 'I am Science Fiction. I am S.F. I am the Fiction that became Sci-
>   ence Fact ... But who now is this?'
> 'I am what I am. I am God. I am Satan' ...
> 'I am the thought that found a thinker. Who are you?'
> 'I am the robber who drugged you so you would not know you
>   were being conceptualized ... You would not know that di-
>   rection in which I was robbing you would lead from nothing
>   to unconsciousness to sleep to dream to waking thoughts to
>   dream thoughts to nothingness to O=zero, from O = zero to
>   O which is O = oh! to O which is a picture which is a picture

of a hole or greedy mouth or vagina which offers perfect freedom which is death perfect which is perfect freedom which is perfect pitch ...'

(Ibid., p. 36)

Bion was apparently very fond of the Trilogy (Bléandonou, 1994). One certainly gets the sense of Bion playing with ideas, expanding themes in an improvised and free manner along multiple dimensions. Rosemary, for instance, is Alice's servant as well as a transformation of Alice's desire. Their relationship represents masochistic or sadistic tendencies. We see the experience from both sides and in reverse. This, in turn, generates other experiences and 'eruptions' in the text. Later, Bion himself is represented in multiple forms, all transformations of the experience of 'being Bion'. Some of these characters give voice to deeply personal experiences, mostly related to the war and childhood ('Captain Bion', 'Somite thirty', 'twelve years', 'twenty years', 'Boy', to name a few). There is the more public, self-satisfied 'Bion', possessive of his own contributions. 'Myself', on the other hand, represents a more reflective state. Still further, 'P.A.' is a central, integrative character, capable of negative capability. 'The Ghost of P.A.', who died in the war, also makes an appearance.

Similar to the 'Bion' assemblage, various characters can be seen to represent differentiations or transformations in a psychic field. In keeping with this idea, they share similarities that remain fluid and undefined but suggest a sharing of characteristics that find varying degrees of representation. Manifestations of evil, for instance, can be found to exist in 'God', 'Du', 'Devil', 'Voice', and 'Man' in different ways. At other times, however, the same characters appear in more differentiated forms.

The chaotic or nonsensical elements of the text are carried by characters who interact with themselves and others, merge, imitate, resist or are transformed by each other. For instance, infantile parts of the personality can be resisted or '*imitate* the sounds that grown up make' (ibid., p. 121). Alternatively, they are transformed into more elaborate fictional characters.

The constant and chaotic movements between similarities and differences might be thought of as representing oscillations between Paranoid-schizoid and Depressive positions. This is felt in a very real way by the reader who is required to tolerate half-truths and uncertainty (Bléandonou, 1994). Aside from leaving one to general impressions, these ideas are expressed by the 'Paranoid-Schizoid' and 'Depressive Position' characters, as well as by others.

MYCROFT: The paranoid–schizoid position is itself clear and chaotic, that is, unspoiled by coherence unless spoiled by intolerance of 'mysteries, half-truths'.

(MF, p. 99)

In addition, oscillations in the text appear to reflect fractal-like qualities typically observed in non-linear dynamic systems (Marks-Tarlow, 1999). Here, different qualities in a field are repeated infinitely in different dimensions and at varying levels of complexity. The qualities or themes that are repeated are organized around 'attractor states' and share 'self-similar' attributes. One example of this in *Memoir* can be seen in the constant chatter about 'fiction' and its relation to the real. The idea or experience of 'fiction' is repeated along many different dimensions. At a 'macro' level, it is represented by the trilogy itself as a piece of 'science fiction'; the characters are fictional; its style draws the author in as a fictional character. At a 'micro' level, some characters are more fictional than others, and ideas about the relationship between reality and fiction are expressed in different ways by different characters. All these 'positions' represent ideas about fiction in multiple forms.

As Grotstein (2007) pointed out, many of Bion's theoretical concepts (e.g., ♀♂, alpha function, Ps<–>D) share some of these features and could be seen as cognates of each other. This, it could be said, is reflected in the trilogy in narrative form.

Multi-dimensionality is also reflected in the sense that dreams exist within dreams in the trilogy. Still further, the reader is given the impression that all vestiges of experience exist simultaneously, or as a potential presence, as they weave in and out of the text. In this expansive space, objects hold subjective and objective positions while, at the same time, they represent functions, forms and processes. The timeless and infinite nature of psychic reality and different 'levels' of experience often also appear embedded in the dialogue or are given a voice through different characters ('Depressive Position', Memory, Du, Voice, Soma, Albert Stegosaurus, etc.).

At different levels of abstraction, each character and represented experience, even each book in the trilogy (Meotti, 2000), could be viewed as representing 'variations' or vertices that attempt to give form to unknowable 'noumena' or 'Ultimate Reality' (Bion, 1965). For Bion, ultimate reality comprises non-conscious invariances that are universal and exist as timeless continuities. Here, interminable struggles between mind and body, pre-natal and post-natal lives, penis and vagina, omnipotence and insignificance, life and death, God and evil, reality and fiction, emerge from invariances that play out as 'memoirs of the future' and exist as part of the human condition.

The trilogy's evocative style, structure and use of 'polylogues' (Bléandonou, 1994) pay homage to Bion's (1965) idea that ultimate reality, or O, can never be known. Only its essence can be represented in imperfect multiple forms as it exists in the constant circular chatter of his characters. If we are not to see this as pure nonsense, the reader has to adopt a suitably receptive state akin to 'binocular vision' where vertices 'separate and distinct ... contribute to a harmonization' (*MF*, p. 3) and allow for an expanded view of emotional and mental realities.

All the above suggest that the trilogy is an exercise in multiplicity like no other. One wonders if it would be possible to evoke this kind of imaginative landscape without Bion's provocative use of 'nonsense', obscurity and confusion. Perhaps it is possible in the simple descriptive sense. However, my view is that *Memoir's* ability to impact the reader is precisely due to these 'nonsense' qualities. It brings to life the very movements of a living psychic system, the *feel* of chaos, turbulence and the complexity of psychic reality.

Nonsense: disrupting the dead

Bion uses reversal of perspective, paradoxical tensions, ambiguity, unresolved dialogues, de-contextualisation, punning, bizarre imagery and obscure language to generate 'nonsense' in the text. Dense referencing drawing on his favourite sources (Milton, Keats, Shakespeare, Kant, Plato, Freud, Doyle, the Bible, mathematics, Greek and Hindu mythologies), his use of neologisms and deeply personal references further add to a narrative that resists being saturated by simple understanding or interpretation. I imagine that the 'nonsense-making' aspects of the trilogy were intentional but then gained a life of their own as Bion freely engaged unconscious emergences. Space only permits a few samples. Here is 'Du', the germ of an idea, trying to escape Roland's mind.

ROLAND: You're an ugly-looking devil. Who are you? ...

DU: I am the future of the Past: the shape of the thing-to-come ... Do I grin like a ghost? How do you like these teeth? All my own. I fasten myself to you psyche–psycho-lodgement, we call it. Most amusing ...

ROLAND: I thought it wasn't a dream. Is it a psycho-drama? No?

DU: No; Psycho-sthan itself. Poor Bunyen – you remember him of course. He thought it was Vanity-Fair, but we are imaginery vain things. What the 'people' *do*, you know. They are what you will call God some day ...

ROLAND: Poor devil

DU: I told you not to use that word. Do you want you want your teeth smashed in? Or shall I have them filed away?

ROLAND: Filed away, filed away death, or is sad sigh press let me be laide.

DU: Wider yet; and wider let your jaws be set. You can have them set in a grin like mine. They're fashionable in psychosis, but some wear them that way in psycho-sthan too. As you descend the steep with our orphean Liar you can sing of chaos and eternal night ... That's hard and rare, you know, without a heavenly Muse to go ting-a-ling.

ROLAND: ... Oh death where is Thy sting-a-ling.

(Ibid., pp. 274–275)

In *The Past Presented,* Robin, P.A. and company have just finished a discussion about sex, beauty and religion:

ROBIN: You are going round in circles.

P.A: 'Circles' are a poor visual image.

ROBIN: Perhaps I should have said you are going round in a helix—

ROLAND: And should have kept your mouth shut
ROSEMARY: Roland, I told you you could go.
P.A: You might as well talk to D.N.A.
ROBIN: What's that?
P.A: Doubt, Nature, Art.
ROSEMARY: Art, Nature, Decay. You've got the order wrong.
ROLAND: I had to use my arts to prosper the crabapple before it became an apple fit to eat; fit to be turned into natural manure.

(Ibid., pp. 359–360)

Aside from the above samples obliquely referring to aspects of primary process thinking and psychic processes, the effect on the reader is confronting and disrupts attempts to make sense of the narrative using memory, desire or understanding, at least in the conventional sense. One has to take it for what it is and suspend rational sense-making. Although this is most evident in *The Dream*, it occurs throughout all three books as the dialogue moves between moments of confusion and clarity. While the three volumes appear to progress in terms of maturity and differentiation they all lack a coherent narrative structure that progresses towards a conclusion or resolution.

Bion's use of nonsense, incoherence and obscurity appears to quite incisively force a choice: reject the trilogy as pure nonsense or, 'for those willing to make the mental effort' (*MF*, p. ix), tolerate the agony of doubt, confusion, obscurity, until 'something', some personal meaning, starts to erupt or evolve. It is a choice between oblivion (or obliviousness) and wisdom. Put another way, the text appears to be as alive or dead to the reader as he or she wants it to be. Its 'nonsense value' and complexity resist saturation and induce a Rorschach-like effect where one has to allow for the emergence of their own point of view. In this way, a second or third reading often turns up something quite different. A different train of thought or point of view is discovered.

This dilemma appears to constantly challenge the reader as he or she engages in an attempt to 'make sense' or 'acquire knowledge' but is regularly frustrated by uncertainty and the circular nature of the dialogue. It disrupts the 'narrative desire' of the reader, the comfort in following a narrative that makes immediate sequential sense with a beginning, middle and end and a clearly observable intention. Bion emphasises the fact that language, grammar and the need for clear coherent narratives are modelled on the senses. In the physical world objects appear to the senses in spatial terms and move through time in logical fashion. The object can only be present in one place at a time, and our observations of its appearance and disappearance have a clear beginning, middle and end. The way we read, write and listen is serialised in a similar way, borrowed from the same preconceptions.

Memoir unapologetically lacks such comforts and requires the reader to manage and contain experiences of irritation, frustration and mental oblivion, while wading through 'nonsense'. The characters themselves express similar concerns in their constant references to the boring, soporific effects of conversation, expressions of intolerance towards nonsense and the apparent pointlessness of much of the dialogue. 'So we are back to square one?' (Ibid., p. 215), Alice asks at the end of *The Dream*.

The struggle between sense-making and nonsense represents a central interminable struggle between our desire for linear, logical thinking and articulate language, on the one hand, and embodied, 'emmature' (ibid., p. 429) psychic experiences that attempt to express emotional truths, on the other. Articulate speech and the 'Laws of logic' are poorly suited to exploring and expanding psychic reality. However, their appeal lies in the security and pleasure found in sensuous and 'sensible' experience in a way that 'gives immediacy and reality to something which might otherwise be hard to understand' (ibid., p. 172). It satisfies the 'greedy swallower of mental bait' (ibid., p. 269). The cost is the narrowing of perception that deadens the vitality of emotional and psychic experience.

P.A: The so-called laws of logic were a prescription for Chaos. They left no living space at all for vitality. Even today it would be still-born if it had not found refuge in what Alice would call craziness or—

(Ibid., p. 446)

Although we cannot escape language and thinking derived from the sensory domain, attention to apparent 'nonsense' may help keep language in good repair and buffer against the immediate saturation of meaning that leads to dead, mindless states. Therefore, in addition to 'disrupting the reader' and forcing a choice, the use of nonsense also constitutes a rebellion against certainties, facts and rational thinking. Nonsense and 'craziness' are attempts aimed at disrupting the 'cheerfulness' and apparent sanity that facts and articulate speech profess. In the closing passage of the trilogy, Bion shares some passionate parting reflections along these lines. In his characteristically obscure style, he writes:

> All my life I have been imprisoned, frustrated, dogged by common-sense, reason, memories, desires and—the greatest bugbear of them all—understanding and being understood. This is an attempt to express my rebellion, to say 'Good-bye' to all that. It is my wish, I now realize doomed to failure, to write a book unspoiled by any tincture of common-sense, reason, etc. (see above). So although I would write, 'Abandon Hope all ye who expect to find any facts—scientific, aesthetic or religious—in this book', I cannot claim I have succeeded. All these will, I fear, be seen to have left their traces, vestiges, ghosts hidden within these words; even sanity, like 'cheerfulness', will creep in. However successful my attempt, there would always be the risk that the book 'became' acceptable, respectable, honoured and unread. 'Why write then?' you may ask. To prevent someone who KNOWS from filling the empty space—but I fear I am being 'reasonable', that great Ape. Wishing you all a Happy Lunacy and a Relativistic Fission ...
>
> (Ibid., p. 578)

The sense of feeling imprisoned by reason and understanding and the idea of preventing 'someone who KNOWS from filling the empty space' are constantly present throughout *Memoir*.

Nonsense, authority and authorship

P.A: ... We want someone or something authoritative to tell us we outshine these beauties of the night.

> (Ibid., p. 255)

MYSELF: ... Here I have just written 'myself' as if I wanted to give it a status different from me. I could call 'Bion' a second-class citizen compared to 'Myself'. I indicate without definition that the opinions expressed by me, even if fiction, are worthy of being treated with respect. Those opinions are of superior status to opinions claimed as mine and spoken as if I claimed 'ownership' over them.

(Ibid., p. 95)

As well as disrupting the 'narrative desire' of the reader, nonsense appears to call into question the authority of authorship in a number of ways. Aside from this simply being related to the idea that we have limited control over unconscious life, the selfless quality of attempting to express 'thoughts without a thinker' challenges ideas of ownership and authority over ideas. From this point of view, emotional truths have to emerge, or erupt, and cannot be 'authored'.

'P.A.', 'Bion', 'Myself', 'Rosemary', 'Priest', 'Man' and many others, often engage in imaginative speculations that diverge and converge in unexpected ways. Ideas are passed through different registers of experience and viewed from different points of view, making definitive conclusions or answers difficult to find. The circular and often obscure nature of the dialogue also appears to act against certainty and ownership. As often expressed by Bion in later publications, the ownership of ideas, 'the answer', kills curiosity and the emergence of universal truths or underlying constant conjunctions that are in search of a thinker. Without an openness to speculative reasoning we descend into a 'sane' shared hallucinosis where everything is 'known' but nothing is explored: 'The "Yes I know" surface, the lifeless society, is all that is left' (ibid., p. 501).

Appeal to the 'omnipotent knower' appears in many guises in *Memoir* as an antidote to thinking about our own insignificance in an unknowable universe. Most notably, it surfaces in debates about the certainty of God's real existence, God as author, and a corresponding intolerance for mental intercourse and the confusion caused by container-contained.

MAN: God threw these presumptuous objects, ♀♂, out of eden. The Omnipotent opposes the extensions of the human ability to have intercourse.

(Ibid., p. 160)

Similarly, the proliferation of 'authoritative' jargon in psychoanalysis is often attacked for its deadening effects on the field.

ROSEMARY: Shut up! Who was that? Respectable, shoddy, worn-out psycho-analytic, mental 'reach-me-down' mental clichés for the dead-from-the-neck-up! Go to sleep I say!

(Ibid., p. 66)

Wars over the ownership of ideas, the certainty of science, cause-effect reasoning, are other representations of attempts to circumvent inevitable confusions and psychic turmoil. The desire for certainty leads to a blind following of authority, '... to the master's pointing hand rather than at the object the hand is trying to point out' (ibid., p. 266). The best we can do to counter the certainty of the author is to be receptive to the infinite and ephemeral qualities of psychic reality and the existence of multiple perspectives.

Bion's audacious appeal or desire *not* to be understood brings this to life as part of the experience of reading *Memoir*. I hear it as a deep, resounding appeal: 'Don't understand *me*, follow my fictions and nonsense'. It remains a living appeal to allow the reader to engage in a process of 'becoming' rather than deadening the process by locating the idea in the author. Once we are in search of what Bion *actually* means ('me'), we lose sight of his fleeting, always incomplete, attempts to give expression to 'thoughts without a thinker'. The former relates to assumptions that rely on a unified, common sense view of the subject where articulate speech and instrumental language assume authority and ownership over ideas. As Bion is at pains to point out, these are assumptions borrowed from the senses and the cause-effect nature of logic.

'Something more' and truth

MYSELF: What next! Someone will say that something, a configuration or pattern, might be covered and revealed by the cover. (Bion, 1991, p. 119)

P.A: The 'real psychoanalysis' to which we aspire is at best only a reaching out towards that 'real psychoanalysis'. But it is real enough to make people aware that there is 'something' beyond the feeble efforts of psycho-analyst and analysand.

(Ibid., p. 510)

Moments of clarity in dialogues among 'Bion', 'Myself' and 'P.A.' suggest links between Truth, confusion and nonsense. In response to 'Bion', 'Myself' suggests that the mental domain 'is the source of endless confusion and difficulty and in which unending confusion is an essential, not accidental, feature, I do not suppose I shall ever know escape ...' (ibid., p. 189). Although the possibility of penetrating 'true' experiences lies beyond the limits of articulate language, paying attention to nonsense is essential because it better reflects the nature of psychic reality and the manner in which 'true' personal experiences emerge from the 'formless infinite'.

ROBIN: Really – do you blame us if we don't know what you are talking about?

P.A: No, I don't. I am not surprised at your protest; in extenuation I found that if I say what I mean it is not English; if I write English it does not say what I mean.

(Ibid., p. 229)

A similar problem is posed by 'Bion': the moment one discusses something in more definitive, direct ways, we lose a more 'truthful', expansive level of experience that is obscured and narrowed by conventional language and its appeal to the senses.

BION: I want to discuss man, but as soon as I say that, I realize the word 'man' has a definite, perhaps misleadingly and frustratingly definite, meaning. I can say I want to discuss 'wilfred dr bion'. That would have a definite meaning to some, but it is not true; I don't want to exclude whatever is 'represented', signified, denoted by those letters, 'rbidefilnorw', arranged according to certain conventions, to form a visual pattern on paper. The problem is obstrusive, but not informatively displayed.

(Ibid., p. 87)

BION: O is by definition indestructible and not subject to, circumscribed by, beginnings and ends, rules, laws of nature or any construct of the human mind. Melanie Klein could not reconcile herself to the fact that whenever she had made herself understood, that fact rendered what she understood no longer 'alive'.

(Ibid., p. 88)

As the above examples suggest, apparent clarity, understanding, and pursuit of the 'right' answer violates the curiosity of an 'alive' unsaturated mind. It removes the personally felt but ineffable qualities of emotional experience that exists in constant flux. This line of thinking challenges usual associations among truth, consciousness, reasonableness and vitality. In Bion's characteristic style, the reversed perspective requires attention: conscious states largely appeal to a saturated 'groupish' mentality that is mindlessly adaptive and dead. Conversely, vitality and truth are to be found in obscure reasoning, waking dream-thoughts and nonsense.

For this, perspective nonsense thoughts, speculative imaginings and intuitions appear to represent our best efforts at penetrating experiences closer to O and expanding psychic reality. Although O remains 'indestructible', unknown to the human mind and not in compliance with the laws of nature, time, or logical thought, the best we can do is represent its essence in a very personalized way.

ALICE: Even Man thinks that by murder ... men would reach the throne of Heaven. Victory! With a capital V.
P.A: Wee, capital wee-wee.
ROLAND: Ghastly pun – even for you.
P.A: What is a ghastly pun for me may be the first step in a new language.

(Ibid., p. 465)

Whether nonsense becomes 'the first step in a new language' depends on whether it can be put to good use. The production of nonsense, when expressed with destructive intent, can certainly have the effect of obscuring mental growth. But it may also be motivated by an expression of truth and the conveyer of 'thoughts without a thinker'. As 'Myself' puts it,

Is 'Sordello' incomprehensible on purpose to make it difficult, or is it Browning's attempt to express what he had to say in the shortest and most comprehensible terms? (ibid., p. 121)

Later, this line of thought is taken further with the idea that the use of obscurity may hold a deliberate intension that aims to evoke unconscious mental activity that cannot find representation in 'sense':

BION: ... people say they don't know what you are talking about and that you are being deliberately obscure.
MYSELF: They are flattering me. I am suggesting as aim, an ambition, which if I could achieve, would enable me to be deliberately

obscure and precisely obscure; in which I could use certain words
which could activate precisely and instantaneously, in the mind of
the listener, a thought or train of thought that came between him
and the thoughts and ideas already accessible and available to him.
ROSEMARY: Oh, my God!

(Ibid., p. 191)

Being 'precisely obscure' reminds me of Ogden's (2007) reflections on
some of Bion's clinical seminars. He suggests that Bion's style as a
supervisor and analyst aimed to 'speak past' (p. 1191) the presenter
or patient so as to speak more directly to the unconscious. It aims to
stimulate more vital, creative evocations, the 'something more' that
cannot be expressed in a conventional form. There are many examples of how this is effected in the trilogy. Perhaps the most apparent
occurs through the deliberate effect of confusion and disorientation
on the reader as it connects with his or her own 'alive' internal turbulence. If Bion were to narrate the trilogy in more conventional
terms, the effect would be very different. Characters in the trilogy
also often 'speak past' each other in search of the true essence of their
experience.

Does this process bear any resemblance to the 'real' psychoanalytic
session? Do we need nonsense and obscurity as a means to get closer
to emotional truths? Certainly, non-rational emergences are central
to all psychoanalytic approaches. Although I imagine few would profess to being 'deliberately obscure' in their approach, I think the reality of the session, as it turns up 'unknowable' disturbances, leads
to *necessary* or *inevitable* obscurity as one tries his or her best to give
voice to ineffable movements in the analytic field.

Reading *Memoir* often leaves me re-sensitised to the noise of the
session, confusions, nonsense thoughts and verbalizations, chatter,
gestures, reveries that seem to have little connection to the material,
that can too quickly be dismissed, corrected, or formulated in some
'understandable' manner. I am reminded of keeping my ear in constant and good repair. I am also sensitised to the constant effort and
discipline required to adopt a stance of 'negative capability' (Bion,
1970). The thought occurs to me that although not 'real' psychoanalysis, *Memoir* would make a formidable training manual for exercising
one's capacity for 'negative capability'.

Sense, nonsense to the non-sensuous

I cannot promise communication of pure non-sense without the contamination of sense.

(*MF*, p. 429)

The experience of physical, sensuous space was not abandoned. It was clung to with such tenacity that it prevented the loss of security involved if pictorial sense where lost.

(Ibid., p. 171)

There is constant chatter about how language, conscious thought, logical reasoning, even fictions, are modelled on the senses. There is little escape in terms of communicating or envisioning non-sensuous psychic reality and transformations derived from contact with O: '... all to which the term "phenomena" applies are by definition part of the domain of the senses' (ibid., p. 203).

Problems occur when the world derived from the senses is confused with psychic reality and taken to be the 'thing-in-itself'. This halts the evolution of intuition and the non-sensuous qualities of mind. For instance, when the existence of God is taken to be a fact, intuitions about the existence of psychic forces that 'require' a god are ignored. Similarly, when psychoanalytic theories are confused with the 'thing-in-itself' other perspectives or vertices are ignored. The same confusion is responsible for debasing language and the words we use. For example, 'love' is attributed to the sensory qualities of the object instead of attending to the evolving psychic turmoil and qualities of 'loving'.

The imposition of the sensory domain on psychic qualities allows for simple, plausible, theories of causation to be settled for. That time and space no longer exist in the same way in the 'formless infinite' need not be confronted and one's truth remains unobserved. Solutions to this problem, posed mainly by P.A., involve attempts to 'augment the boundaries of perception' (ibid., p. 244). There are suggestions about using 'infra' and 'ultra'-sensory approaches and intuition for this purpose. As mentioned earlier, 'binocular vision' also enables the observation of distinct perspectives or vertices that, in turn, generate broader powers of perception and thought formation. This applies to maintaining multiple perspectives on sensuous and non-sensuous reality so as to facilitate a reflective stance that keeps language in good repair.

If this separation can be maintained the appeal of the senses might function to hold interest long enough for meaning to evolve.

ROBIN: ... The beauty of Paradise Lost made the truth last long enough for someone to receive the message.

P.A: Don't you agree that the longevity with which those formulation were endowed was a consequence of beauty? Then work had to be done to recognise the truth.

(Ibid., p. 359)

Listening to the apparent nonsense inherent in talk and language, non-sequiturs, verbal tics, the odd use of words, incomprehensible references, parapraxes, may also suggest evocative meanings or patterns beyond the senses. 'Myself' sketches out a wonderfully imaginative depiction of this process as he tries to explain this to 'Bion' who has fallen back on existing conventions:

Imagine a piece of sculpture which is easier to comprehend if the structure in intended to act as a trap for light. The meaning revealed by the pattern formed by the light - not by the structure ... if I could learn how to talk to you in such a way that my words 'trapped' the meaning which they neither do nor could express ... which is an extension of conversation into non-conversation (ibid., pp. 189–190).

Further, the work of 'nonsense' might be thought to assist in separating the over-reasoned 'understandable' use of language from truth and its non-sensuous origins. Although modelled on the senses, the obscure use of the fundamentals of language and the 'confusions' of dream states may be thought of as generating resistance to the oblivious consumption of dead 'facts'.

P.A: The night, the dream, is a 'roughness' between the smooth polished consciousness of daylight; in that 'roughness' an idea might lodge. Even in the flat polished surface there can be a delusion, or an hallucination, or some other flaw in which an idea might lodge and flourish before it can be stamped out or 'cured' ... The drunkard, like the dreamer, is less likely to be an efficient liar; he is unlikely to smooth the 'rough place'. But his inefficiency can be turned to good account.

(Ibid., p. 268–269)

Attending to nonsense or 'roughness' requires patience and a different perspective that loosens our grip on a need for logical sensuous references. It induces confusional states and emotional turmoil and gets one closer to the non-sensuous 'truth' of psychic reality. Put another way, nonsense is transformed into non-sense.

P.A: They are having an occulo-gyric crisis in unison ...
MAN: That is nonsense
P.A: No, it is Non Sense
MAN: It sounds mad to me
P.A: You have forgotten all changed here, and what was nonsense became Non Sense. The Laws of Nature are now the Laws of Un-Reason. This is the post Big Bang Era ...
MORIARTY: ... there is not Time as you used to know it. I never set much store by it – or any figments of Reality.

(Ibid., pp. 418–419)

Drawing on Bion's (1962a) theory of thinking and the dramatized transition suggested above, nonsense qualities may be thought of as creating or suggesting a negative realization. Because nonsense has a more tenuous connection to an external object, it is a reminder of objects that are not immediate, present and satisfying (a reminder of 'no-breast'). Perhaps that is why one hears one's thoughts so loudly when reading *Memoir*. In this absence, a thought is produced. To quote Bion: 'If there is no "thing", is "no thing" a thought and is it by virtue of the fact that there is "no thing" that one recognises that "it" must be thought?' (1962a, p. 35)

The absence of the satisfying object is felt as the presence of something unpleasant and requires containment if it is to lead to productive psychic growth. In this way, nonsense may be seen to precipitate non-sense. Even the very concept of 'mind' in the trilogy is based on negative realizations mediated by 'nonsense'.

MYSELF: Hitherto, the term 'mind' has proved serviceable. I propose to use it as a meaningless term, useful for talking or writing about what I *don't* know – to mark the 'place where' a meaning might be.

(*MF.*, p. 141)

Finally, fictionalisation offers another possibility that escapes psychoanalytic jargon, over-reasoned ideas and mystification. Although imaginative depictions and characters borrow from the senses, they are freed to generate nonsensical possibilities that paradoxically may bring us closer to truth.

P.A: His Satanic Jargonieur took offence; on some pretence that psycho-analytic jargon was being eroded by eruptions of clarity. I was compelled to seek refuge in fiction. Disguised as fiction, the truth occasionally slipped through.

(Ibid., p. 302)

The paradox that fictional characters are more real, alive and vital to our existence than real people is a dominant theme in *Memoir*. In the prologue to *The Dream*, Bion suggests this to be one of his intentions in putting together a work of fiction:

FALSTAFF: a known artefact, is more 'real' in Shakespeare's verbal formulation than countless millions of people who are dim, invisible, lifeless, unreal, whose births and deaths – alas, even marriages – we are called upon to believe in, though certification of their existence is vouched for by the said official certification.

(Ibid., pp. 4–5)

'Sherlock', 'Watson' and 'Mycroft', as fictional characters, often boast about their existence beyond human mortality. The vitality and longevity of good stories, from Sherlock Holmes to The Bible, is testament to the existence of invariants in human experience that seek expression in disguised form. It seems to me that their 'disguise' serves two functions from Bion's point of view. It allows for the articulation of 'personal truths' in an over-reasoned and rational world. Second, fictions help shield the individual from unbearable truths and deliver more containable representations of O. In this way, fictions are like a transitional delivery system that renders psychic objects amenable for processing and digestion.

MYSELF: I should have thought that during the course of your sojourn in my mind–if that's where it and you have been–you would have become transformed from a relatively minor, fictitious character into a somewhat major part of your more useful characteristics. If there were such a thing as a mental digestive system, I could say that the mental diet of entertaining fictitious characters has contributed greatly to my mental health.

(Ibid., p. 124)

Fictions and myths delineate an area for 'something' to evolve, just as sense in the external world signals the presence of something that can be seen (Levine, 2015b). They act like living markers or reference points that help break up the dominance of the senses. This allows for the linking of previously disparate occurrences, in turn, giving rise to new emotional experiences. As Vermote (2015) puts it, it 'leads to the witnessing of a pattern in the life of the patient, which is in constant movement' (p. 347). Simply observing this, seeing it, is itself a new emotional experience less mired in the sensory domain.

No time for nonsense

'Thoughts without a thinker' have a timeless quality that makes past and future indistinguishable. They emerge from invariances or powerful 'vogue' states (Bion, 1991a) that are part of the human condition. Although fashions in religion, culture, philosophy come and go the same human dilemmas and turbulences, irreconcilable differences between psychic and somatic states, are observable in different transformations.

One of my more persistent dream-thoughts evoked by reading and re-reading *Memoir* was 'no time for nonsense'. It seemed to represent an identification with many of the characters who express intolerances and irritation with having to endure long periods of confusion and nonsense. But it also appeared linked to thoughts about the relevance of the trilogy today. 'No time for nonsense' felt like a comment emerging from a field of experience embedded in today's 'cultural fashion': our immersion in cyber technologies.

Does the world of high-speed Internet, social networks and cell phones mediate our experience in ways reminiscent of some of the 'vogue' struggles evident in the trilogy? The Internet has made access to information and knowledge infinitely better and more available to all. The immediacy of access to others through social networks appears to create greater opportunity for connection. But how does it impact on our emotional lives and what does it say about deeper motivations from a psychoanalytic point of view? What does the 'manic googler', in search of immediate bullet-point facts, tell us about current transformations of 'memoirs of the future'? What of the seemly endless desire to mediate experiences through video, photos and messaging? Is this a version of Bion's 'greedy swallower of mental bait' (*MF*, p. 269) and fantasies related to the ownership of knowledge?

The seduction of immediacy and the rapid delivery of answers and facts seems to update *Memoir's* account of ways to avoid the noise, confusion and 'roughness' of psychic reality. It flouts the necessity of dwelling in deeply personal, messy, nonsensical reveries, and the importance of learning to bear inevitable frustrations. Is this the latest rejection of the idea that nonsense, doubt and uncertainty are required to keep the mental digestive system in a state of good repair?

The overwhelming desire for facts, 'connection', self-satisfied certainties, sensory stimulation, even interruption, perhaps points to a version of Bion's 'cheerful' sane society that avoids turbulence and the dream states required for creative, genuine thinking. Evoking the essence of the trilogy, 'the web' might be seen as the latest vessel in which we can learn how to be 'just like' a human being as a substitute for 'becoming' one. It exposes an 'articulate' world and the desire for omnipotent answers that kills curiosity and real intimacy.

Visual representations of the Internet easily conjure up an image of a world connected, networks of multiple spaces and dimensions, functions and content accessible at different levels. Ironically, it seems to reflect an image or model that is remarkably similar to a psychic reality in multi-dimensional form. Is it too far-fetched to say it is like an enticing copy of psychic reality without the messiness of the human factor? This is reinforced by the idea that connection to cyberspace or computers supports the externalisation of mental functions like memory and thinking.

There is mention of 'the machine' in *Memoir*, with reference to the ultimate need for human interpretation. Based on the above speculations, however, the latest transformation attempts to eliminate the 'experiencing' interpreter altogether through seductive mimicry. It is best expressed as the creation of a 'cut and paste' reality, a reality that looks 'just like' our abilities to think minus the nonsense and time it takes for real human connection. It might be thought of as another attempt to bring to ground psychic and emotional life by treating it as concrete fact. Although this holds great promise as a substitute for having to endure the inevitable frustrations that make genuine thinking possible, it never delivers and further exacerbates isolation, 'sensory greed', and a sense of feeling 'alone together' (Turkle, 2012). This appears no different from the 'many 'glittering' prizes offered for the greedy soul' (*MF*, p. 269). Following Bion, if we are to turn this to good use we cannot lose sight of the time it takes for the interpreter, the thinker, the perspective taker, to tolerate nonsense until awareness is expanded.

Nonsense requires a receptive state, relatively free of preconceptions and open to confusional states (PS) that have no clear beginning or end. From this point of view, we have no choice, as 'Bion' suggests, but to 'begin in the middle' (Bion, 1991, p. 197), immersed in the unknown, waiting for something to evolve. When all 'reasonable theories', science, religion, music, fail us,

> Sooner or later we reach a point where there is nothing to be done except – if there is any exception – to wait. The 'impasse' is itself a word which, in the context of this writing, is known to denote a feeling.
>
> (*MF*, p. 61)

References

Abella A (2007). Marcel Duchamp: On the fruitful use of narcissism and destructiveness in contemporary art. *International Journal of Psychoanalysis*, 88: 1039–1060.

Abella A (2008). Christian Boltanski: un artiste contemporain vu et pensé par une psychanalyste. *Revue Française de Psychanalyse*, 72: 1113–1136.

Abella A (2010). Contemporary art and Hanna Segal's thinking on aesthetics. *International Journal of Psychoanalysis*, 91: 163–181.

Abella A (2012). John Cage and W.R. Bion: An exercise in interdisciplinary dialogue. *International Journal of Psychoanalysis*, 93: 473–487.

Abella A (2013). Psychoanalysis and art: From applied analysis to interdisciplinary dialogue. In G Goldstein (ed.), *Art in Psychoanalysis*. London: Karnac, pp. 57–78.

Abella A (2015). Using art for the understanding of psychoanalyis and using Bion for the understanding of contemporary art. In HB Levine & G Civitarese (eds.), *The W.R. Bion Tradition*. London: Karnac.

Abella A (2016). Psychoanalysis and the arts: The slippery ground of applied analysis. *Psychoanalytic Quarterly*, 85: 89–119.

Aguayo J (2013a). Foreword. In N Torres & RD Hinshelwood (eds.), *Bion's Sources. The Shaping of His Paradigm*. London: Routledge, pp. ix–xiii.

Aguayo J (2013b). Wilfred Bion's 'Caesura'. In HB Levine & LJ Brown (eds.), *Growth and Turbulence in the Container/Contained: Bion's Continuing Legacy*. London: Routledge, pp. 55–74.

Amery J (1966). *At the Mind's Limits: Contemplations by a Survivor of Auschwitz and Its Realities*. Bloomington, IN: Indiana University Press, 1980.

Anzieu D (1998). *Beckett*. Genova: Casa Editrice Marietti, 2001.

Applefeld A (1988). *Walking the Way of the Survivor; A Talk with Aharon Appelfeld* http://www.nytimes.com/books/98/02/15/home/appelfeld-roth.html

Aron L (1996). *A Meeting of Minds: Mutuality in Psychoanalysis*. New York: Routledge, 2009.

Auden WH (1940). *Another Time*. London: Faber and Faber, 2007.

Auerhahn N & Laub D (1984). Annihilation and restoration: Post-traumatic memory as path-way and obstacle to recovery. *International Review of Psycho-Analysis*, 11: 327–344.

Avnon D (1998). *Martin Buber: The Hidden Dialogue*. Lanham, MD: Rowman & Littlefield Publishers, Inc.

Bahktin MM (1981a). Epic and novel. In *The Dialogic Imagination*. Austin, TX: University of Texas Press, pp. 3–40.

Bahktin MM (1934/1981b). Discourse in the novel. In *The Dialogic Imagination*. Austin, TX: University of Texas Press, pp. 260–422.

Bahktin MM (1986). Toward a methodology for the human sciences. In *Speech Genres and Other Late Essays*. Austin, TX: University of Texas, 1987, pp. 159–170.

Bair D (1978). *Samuel Beckett. A Biography*. New York and London: Harcourt Brace Jovanovich Inc.

Baltrušaitis J (1977). *Anamorphic Art*. New York: Harry N. Abrams.

Barnes J (1990). *A History of the World in 10 ½ Chapters*. New York: Vintage.

Barth J (1967). The literature of exhaustion. *The Atlantic*, 220: 29–34.

Barthelme D (1991). *The King*. Normal and London: Dalkey Archive Press.

Barthelme D (1993). Nothing: A preliminary account. In *Sixty Stories*. New York: Penguin, pp. 245–48.

Barthes R (1975). *The Pleasure of the Text*. New York: Hill and Wang.

Baruzzi A (1998). Prefazione all'edizione italiana. In WR Bion (ed.), *Memoria del futuro: Presentare il passato*. Milano: Raffaello Cortina, pp. xi–xvi.

Baudrilliard J (1994). The precession of simulacra. In *Simulacra and Simulation*. Ann Arbor, MI: Michigan University Press, pp. 1–42.

Bayard P (2004). *Peut-on appliquer la littérature à la psychanalyse?* Paris: Les Éditions de Minuit.

Beckett S (1938). Murphy. In A Samuel Beckett Reader. New York: Grove Press, 1994.

Belting H (1983). *L'histoire de l'art est-elle finie?* Paris: Actes Sud, 2007.

Bergstein A (2013). Transcending the caesura: Reverie, dreaming and counter-dreaming. *International Journal of Psychoanalysis*, 94: 621–644.

Bergstein A (2014). Beyond the spectrum: Fear of breakdown, catastrophic change and the unrepressed unconscious. *Rivista di Psicoanalisi*, 60: 847–868.

Bergstein A (2015). Attacks on linking or a drive to communicate? Tolerating the paradox. *The Psychoanalytic Quarterly*, 84: 921–942.

Bion F (1997a). Introduction to *Diary*. In F Bion (ed.), *W.R. Bion: War Memoirs 1917–19*. London: Karnac, p. 2.

Bion Talamo P (1997). The clinical relevance of *A Memoir of the Future. The Journal of Melanie Klein and Object Relations*, 15: 235–241.

Bion WR (1959). Attacks on Linking. *International Journal of Psychoanalysis*, 40: 308–315.

Bion WR (1962a). *Learning from Experience*. London: Karnac, 1984.

Bion WR (1962b). The psycho-analytic study of thinking. *International Journal of Psycho-Analysis*, 43: 306–310.

Bion WR (1963). *Elements of Psychoanalysis*. London: Heinemann.

Bion WR (1965). *Transformations. Change from Learning to Growth*. London: Maresfield Library, 1991.

Bion WR (1967a). Second seminar. In J Aguayo & B Malin (eds.), *Wilfred Bion: Los Angeles Seminars and Supervision*. London: Karnac, 2013, pp. 33–54.

Bion WR (1967b). Third seminar. In J Aguayo & B Malin (eds.), *Wilfred Bion: Los Angeles Seminars and Supervision*. London: Karnac, 2013, pp. 55–79.

Bion WR (1970). *Attention and Interpretation. A Scientific Approach to Insight in Psycho-Analysis and Groups*. London: Tavistock Publications.

Bion WR (1974). *Brazilian Lectures*. London: Karnac, 2008.

Bion WR (1976). Evidence. In *Clinical Seminars and Other Works*. London: Karnac, 1994, pp. 312–320.

Bion WR (1977a). The grid. In *Two Papers: The Grid and Caesura*. London: Karnac, 1989, pp. 1–33.

Bion WR (1977b). *Taming Wild Thoughts*. London: Karnac.

Bion WR (1978). A Seminar in Paris. 1978. Held on July 10th 1978. Transcribed by F. Bion. http://braungardt.trialectics.com/projects/psychoanalysis/bion/seminar-in-paris/

Bion WR (1982). *The Long Weekend 1897–1919: Part of a Life*. London: Karnac, 1991.

Bion WR (1985). *All My Sins Remembered: Another Part of a Life and the Other Side of Genius. Family Letters*. London: Karnac, 2009.

Bion WR (1992). *Cogitations*. London: Karnac.

Bion WR (1997). *War Memories 1917–19*. London: Karnac.

Bléandonou G (1994). *Wilfred Bion His Life and Works 1897–1979*. London: Free Associated Press.

Bollas C (2009). *The Evocative Object World*. London and New York: Routledge.

Bonaminio V (2010). Transfert prima del transfert: percorsi del lavoro dell' inconscio [Transference before transference: Journeys in the work of the unconscious]. XV Congresso Nazionale S.P.I., Taormina.

Borges JL (1949a). The Aleph. In JL Borges (ed.), *Collected Fictions*. New York: Penguin, 1980, pp. 274–286.

Borges JL (1949b). Tlon, Uqbar, Orbis Tertius. In JL Borges (ed.), *Collected Fictions*. New York: Penguin, 1980, pp. 68–82.

Borges JL (1960). Borges and I. In JL Borges (ed.), *Collected Fictions*. New York: Penguin Books, 1980, p. 324.

Botella C & Botella S (2005). *The Work of Psychic Figurability*. New York: Brunner-Routledge.

Broadfoot K (2002). Perspective yet again: Damish with Lacan. *Oxford Art Journal*, 25: 71–94.

Bruner J (1986). *Actual Minds, Possible Worlds*. Boston, MA: Harvard University Press.

Buber M (1976). *Or Haganooz (The Light of the Hidden: Hasidic tales)*. Tel Aviv: Schocken.

Butler CP (2002). *Postmodernism: A Very Short Introduction*. Oxford: Oxford University Press.

Cabanne P (1971). *Dialogues with Marcel Duchamp*. R Padgett, translator. London: Thames & Hudson. p. 136 (*Documents of 20th-century Art* series) [(1967). *Entretiens avec Marcel Duchamp*. Paris: Belfond. p. 218].

Calvino I (1959/1962). *The Nonexistent Knight*. New York: Random House.

Carroll L (1911). *Alice's Adventures in Wonderland*. London: Branden.

Cimino C & Correale A (2005). Projective identification and consciousness alteration: A bridge between psychoanalysis and neurosciences? *The International Journal of Psycho-Analysis*, 85: 51–60.

Ciocca A (2014). The late Bion. *Funzione Gamma*, 33. www.funzionegamma.it/wp-content/uploads/ing-ciocca.pdf.

Civitarese G (2011). *The Violence of Emotions: Bion and Post-Bionian Psychoanalysis*. London and New York: Routledge, 2013.

Civitarese G (2013a). *The Necessary Dream: New Theories and Techniques of Interpretation in Psychoanalysis*. Karnac: London, 2014.

Civitarese G (2013b). Bion's evidence and his theoretical style. *Psychoanal Quarterly*, 82: 615–633.

Civitarese G (2014). *Truth and the Unconscious in Psychoanalysis*. London: Routledge, 2016.

Civitarese G (2015a). Transformations in hallucinosis and the receptivity of the analyst. *International Journal of Psychoanalysis*, 96: 1091–1116.

Coetzee JM (2004). *Elizabeth Costello*. New York: Penguin.

Collin P, interviewer (2002). Marcel Duchamp spricht über Ready-mades [Marcel Duchamp talks about Ready-mades], Gallerie Givandau, 21 June 1967. In: *Marcel Duchamp*, Museum Jean Tinguely, Basel, (ed.), pp. 37–40. Ostfildern-Ruit: Hatje Cantz [(1998). Marcel Duchamp parle des ready-made à Philippe Collin. Paris: L'Echoppe, p. 22].

Conan-Doyle A (1930). The adventure of the Bruce-Partington plans. In *The Complete Sherlock Holmes*. New York: Doubleday, pp. 913–932.

Cooper A (2005). *The Quiet Revolution in American Psychoanalysis.* London: Routledge.

Corrao F (1993). Prefazione all'edizione italiana. In WR Bion (ed.) (1975), *Memoria del futuro: Il sogno.* Milano: Raffaello Cortina, pp. xi–xv.

Correale A (2015). Identifying with existential unease. In M Harris William (ed.), *Teaching Bion: Modern Approaches.* London: Karnac.

Couser G (2011). *Memoir: An Introduction.* Oxford: Oxford University Press.

Damasio AR (1999). *The Feeling of What Happens.* New York: Harvest Edition, 2000.

Dan J (2002). *The Heart and the Fountain: An Anthology of Jewish Mystical Experiences.* Oxford and New York: Oxford University Press.

Danto AC (1997). *After the End of Art: Contemporary Art and the Pale of History.* Princeton, NJ: Princeton University Press.

de Bianchedi ET (1991). Psychic change: The 'Becoming' of an inquiry. *International Journal of Psychoanalysis,* 72: 6–15.

de Bianchedi ET (2005). Whose Bion? Who is Bion?. *International Journal of Psychoanalysis,* 86: 1529–1534.

De Mattos JAJ & Braga JC (2013). Primitive conscience. In HB Levine & LJ Brown (eds.), *Growth and Turbulence in the Container Contained.* New York: Routledge.

Eco U (1970). *Il problema estetico in Tommaso d'Aquino.* Milano: Bompiani.

Eco U (1987). *Arte e bellezza nell'estetica medievale.* Milano: Bompiani.

Eigen M (1998). *The Psychoanalytic Mystic.* London: Free Association Books.

Eliade M (1968). *The Sacred and the Profane: The Nature of Religion.* Orlando: Harcourt.

Erasmus (1509). *The Praise of Folly.* Translated by John Wilson, 1668. Oxford: The Clarendon Press, 1913.

Felman S & Laub D (1992). *Testimony: Crisis of Witnessing in Literature, Psychoanalysis and History.* New York and London: Routledge.

Ferro A (1992a). Two authors in search of characters: The relationship, the field, the story. *Rivista di Psicoanalisi,* 36: 44–90.

Ferro A (1992b). *The Bi-Personal Field: Experiences in Child Analysis.* London: Routledge, 2002.

Ferro A (1996). *In the Analyst's Consulting Room.* Hove: Brunner-Routledge, 2002.

Ferro A (2002). *Seeds of Illness, Seeds of Recovery.* London: Routledge, 2004.

Ferro A (2005). Bion: Theoretical and clinical observations. *International Journal of Psychoanalysis,* 86: 1535–1542.

Ferro A (2006). *Mind Works. Technique and Creativity in Psychoanalysis.* London: Routledge, 2008.

Ferro A (2009). Transformations in dreaming and characters in the psychoanalytic field. *International Journal of Psycho-Analysis,* 90: 2009–2030.

Ferro A (2010). *Torments of the Soul. Psychoanalytic Transformations in Dreaming and Narration.* London: Routledge.

Ferro A (2015). From Freud to Francis Bacon. *The Italian Psychoanalytic Annual,* 9: 175–187.

Ferro A & Basile R (eds.), (2007). *The Analytic Field. A Clinical Concept.* London: Karnac, 2009.

Ferro A & Civitarese G (2015). *The Analytic Field and Its Transformations.* London: Karnac.

Ffytche M (2013). Investigating Bion's aestethic turn: A memoir of future and the 1970s. In N Torres & RD Hinshelwood (eds.), *Bion's Sources. The Shaping of His Paradigm.* London: Routledge, pp. 169–178.

Foresti G & Rossi Monti M (2010). *Esercizi di visioning. Psicoanalisi, psichiatria, istituzioni.* Roma: Borla.

Fowles J (1969). *The French Lieutenant's Woman.* Boston, MA: Little, Brown.

Freud S (1895/1955). A project for a scientific psychology. *SE,* 1: 283–387.

Freud S (1900). The interpretation of dreams. *SE,* 4: 5.

Freud S (1905). *Jokes and their Relation to the Unconscious.* New York: Norton Library, 1963.

Freud S (1915/1955a). Instincts and their vicissitudes. *SE,* 14: 109–140.

Freud S (1915/1955b). The unconscious. *SE,* 14: 159–217.

Freud S (1920). Beyond the pleasure principle. *SE,* 18: 1–64.

Freud S (1930). Civilization and its discontents. *SE,* 21: 57–146.

Frisch M (1954/1994). *I'm Not Stiller.* New York: Harcourt Brace.

Gaburri E & Ferro A (1988). Gli sviluppi kleiniani e Bion. *Trattato di Psicoanalisi,* Vol. 1. Milano: Raffaello Cortina, pp. 284–393.

Gallese V, Migone P, & Eagle MN (2006). La simulazione incarnata: i neuroni specchio, le basi neurofisiologiche del'intersoggettività e alcune implicazioni per la psicoanalisi [The embodied simulation: Mirror neurons, the neuro-physiological bases of intersubjectivity and some implications for psychoanalysis]. *Psicoterapia e Scienze Umane,* 40: 543–580.

Gallese V & Ammaniti M (2014). *The Birth of Intersubjectivity. Psychodynamics, Neurobiology and the Self.* New York: W. W. Norton.

Gombrich EH (1970). *Aby Warburg: An Intellectual Biography.* London: Phaidon, 1986.

Gottschall J (2012). *The Storytelling Animal. How Stories Make Us Human.* New York: Mariner Books, 2013.

Green A (1997). The intuition of the negative in *Playing and Reality. International Journal of Psychoanalysis,* 78: 1071–1084.

Green A & Duisit L (1980). The unbinding process. *New Literary History,* 12: 11–39.

Grotstein JS (1981a). Wilfred R. Bion: The man, the psychoanalyst, the mystic. A perspective on his life and work. *Contemporary Psychoanalysis*, 17: 501–536.

Grotstein JS (ed.) (1981b). *Do I Dare Disturb the Universe?: A Memorial to Wilfred R. Bion*. London: Karnac.

Grotstein JS (2007). *A Beam of Intense Darkness. Wilfred Bion's Legacy to Psychoanalysis*. London: Karnac.

Grotstein JS (2009). *But at the Same Time and on Another Level: Volume 1: Psychoanalytic Theory and Technique in the Kleinian/Bionian Mode*. London: Karnac.

Grotstein JS (2011). Bion's dream: A reading of the autobiographies. By Meg Harris Williams. London: Karnac, 2010, p. 131. *The Psychoanalytic Quarterly*, 80: 504–510.

Harris Williams M (1983). 'Underlying pattern' in Bion's *Memoir of the Future. The International Journal of Psychoanalysis*, 10: 75–86.

Harris Williams M (2010). *Bion's Dream: A Reading of the Autobiographies*. London: Karnac.

Hassan I (1971). POSTmodernISM. *New Literary History*, 3: 5–30.

Hassan I (1986). Pluralism in postmodern perspective. *Critical Inquiry*, 12: 503–520.

Heinich N (1996). *L'art contemporain exposé aux rejets*. Paris: J. Chambon.

Heinich N (2014). *Le paradigm de l'art contemporain. Structures d'une révolution artistique*. Paris: Gallimard.

Hellner-Eshed M (2009). *A River Flows from Eden: The Language of Mystical Experience in the Zohar*. Stanford, CA: Stanford University Press.

Hinshelwood (1997). The elusive concept of 'onternal objects' (1934–1943). Its role in the formation of the Klein group. *International Journal of Psychoanalysis*, 78: 877–897.

Hinshelwood RD & Torres N (2013). Conclusion. Bion's nomadic journey. In N Torres & RD Hinshelwood (eds.), *Bion's Sources. The Shaping of his Paradigm*. London: Routledge, pp. 179–189.

Hobsbawn E (1994). *Il Secolo breve*. Milano: Rizzoli.

Holquist M (1986). Introduction. In MM Bahktin (ed.), *Speech Genres and Other Late Essays*. Austin, TX: University of Texas, 1987, pp. i–xviii.

Horovitz M (2007). Transfert et vérité. In F Guignard & T Bokanowski (eds.), *Actualité de la Pensée de Bion*. Paris: Éditions In Press.

Hume D (1748). *An Enquiry Concerning Human Understanding*. New York: Dover.

Jakobson R (1960). Linguistics and poetics. In T Sebeok (ed.), *Style in Language*. Cambridge, MA: MIT Press, pp. 350–377.

James H (1908/2008). *The Jolly Corner*. New York: Book Jungle.

Jameson F (1988). Postmodernism, or, the cultural logic of late capitalism. *New Left Review*, 146: 53–92.

Jung CG (1952). Foreword to White's 'God and the Unconscious'. In *The Collected Works of K. G. Jung*, Vol. 11. Princeton, NJ: Princeton University Press, 1969.

Jung CG (1961). *Memories, Dreams, Reflections*. New York: Random House.

Jung CG (2009). *The Red Book: A Reader's Edition*. New York: W. W. Norton, 2012.

Karnac H (2008). Introduction. In H Karnac (ed.), *Bion's Legacy. Bibliografy of Primary and Secondary Sources of the Life, Work and Ideas of Wilfred Ruprecht Bion*. London: Karnac, pp. vii–ix.

Khun TS (1962). *The Structure of Scientific Revolutions*. Chicago, MI: University of Chicago Press.

King P & Steiner R (1991). *The Freud-Klein Controversies 1941–1945*. London: Routledge.

Kirshner L (1994). Trauma, the good object and the symbolic: A theoretical integration. *International Journal of Psycho-Analysis*, 75: 235–242.

Klein DB (2011). Resentment and recognition. Towards a new conception of humanity at the mind's limits. In M Zolkos (ed.), *On Jean Amery. Philosophy of Catastrophe*. Lanham, MD: Lexington Books, pp. 87–108.

Köhler W (1925). *The Mentality of Apes*. London: Routledge.

Kostelanetz R (1988). *Conversing with John Cage*. New York: Limelight. Reprinted London: Routledge, 2003.

Kristeva J (1982). *Powers of Horror. An Essay on Abjection*. New York: Columbia University Press.

Lacan J (1966). *Écrits*. New York: W. W. Norton, 2007.

Lacan J (1973). *The Four Fundamental Concepts. The Seminar XI*. London: Karnac, 2004.

Lacan J (1986). *The Ethics of Psychoanalysis 1959–60. The Seminar of Jacques Lacan Book VII*. Edited by J.-A. Miller. New York and London: Routledge, 1992.

Laub D (1998). The empty circle. Children of survivors and the limits of reconstruction. *Journal of the American Psychoanalytic Association*, 46: 527–529.

Laub D & Auerhahn N (1993). Knowing and not knowing massive psychic trauma: Forms of traumatic memory. *International Journal of Psycho-Analysis*, 74: 287–302.

Laub, D & Lee, S (2003). Thanatos and massive psychic trauma. *Journal of the American Psychoanalytic Association*, 51: 433–463.

Lebel R (1959). *Marcel Duchamp*. G Heard Hamilton, translator. London: Trianon, p. 201. [*Sur Marcel Duchamp*. Paris: Trianon, p. 193].

Levine HB (2015a). The transformational vision of Antonino Ferro. *Psychoanalytic Inquiry*, 35: 452–463.

Levine HB (2015b). Is the concept of O necessary for psychoanalysis? In HB Levine & G Civitarese (eds.), *The W.R. Bion Tradition*. London: Karnac, pp. 377–386.

Levine HB & Civitarese G (eds.), (2015). *The W. R. Bion Tradition*, London: Karnac.

Lodge D (1977). Postmodernist fiction. In *The Modes of Modern Writing: Metaphor, Metonymy and Typology of Modern Literature*. London: Edward Arnold, pp. 220–245.

Lombardi R (2016). *Metà prigioniero metà alato*. Torino: Bollati Boringhieri.

López-Corvo RE (2002). *The Dictionary of the Work of W.R. Bion*. London: Karnac.

Lyotard J-F (1979). *The Postmodern Condition: A Report on Knowledge*. Minneapolis, MS: University of Minnesota Press.

Manica M (2013). *Ogni angelo è tremendo. Esplorazioni ai confini della teoria e della clinica Psicoanalitica* [Every angel is dreadful. Explorations at the boundaries between theory and clinical practice]. Roma: Borla.

Manica M (2014). *Intercettare il sogno. Sviluppi traumatici e progressione onirica nel discorso psicoanalitico*. Borla: Roma.

Manica M (2016). *La tristezza tra fenomenologia e psicoanalisi: dalla tristezza senza-nome alla tristezza in O*. In A Ferro, ed., *La clinica psicoanalitica oggi*. Rome: Carocci, pp. 365–381.

Marks-Tarlow T (1999). The self as a dynamical system. Nonlinear dynamics. *Psychology, and Life Sciences*, 3: 311–345.

Matte Blanco I (1975). *The Unconscious as Infinite Sets*. London: Duckworth.

Meltzer D (1986). *Studies in Extended Metapsychology. Clinical Applications of Bion's Ideas*. London: Karnac, 2009.

Meltzer D (2000). Signs, symbols and allegory. In M Harris-Williams (ed.), *A Meltzer Reader*. London: Karnac, 2010, pp. 121–130.

Meltzer D & Harris Williams M (1985). Three lectures on WR Bion's *A Memoir of the Future*. In A Hahn (ed.), *Sincerity and Other Works. Collected Papers of Donald Meltzer*. London: Karnac, 1994, pp. 520–550.

Meltzer D & Harris Williams M (1989). *The Apprehension of Beauty: The Role of Aesthetic Conflict in Development, Art and Violence*. London: Karnac.

Meotti A (2000). A dreamlike vision. In PB Talamo, F Borgogno & S Merciai (eds.), *W.R. Bion: Between Past and Future*. London and New York: Karnac, pp. 155–163.

Mucci C (1992). The blank page as a Lacanian Object a. *Literature and Psychology*, XXXVIII: 23–35.

Mucci C (1995). *Liminal personae. Marginalità e sovversione nel teatro elisabettiano e giacomiano.* Napoli: E.S.I.

Mucci C (2013). *Beyond Individual and Collective Trauma. Intergenerational Transmission, Psychoanalytic Treatment and the Dynamics of Forgiveness.* London: Karnac.

Neuman Y (2010). Penultimate interpretation. *International Journal of Psychoanalysis*, 91: 1043–1054.

Noel-Smith K (2013). Thoughts, thinking and the thinker. Bion's philosophical encounter with Kant. In N Torres & RD Hinshelwood (eds.), *Bion's Sources. The Shaping of His Paradigm.* London: Routledge, pp. 124–136.

O'Brien F (1967/1999). *The Third Policeman.* London and New York: Dalkey Archive Press.

Ogden TH (2001). *Conversations at the Frontier of Dreaming.* Lanham, MD: Jason Aronson.

Ogden TH (2005a). *This Art of Psychoanalysis. Dreaming Undreamt Dreams and Interrupted Cries.* London: Routledge.

Ogden TH (2004). An introduction to the reading of Bion. *International Journal of Psychoanalysis*, 85(2):285–300.

Ogden TH (2005b). On psychoanalytic supervision. *International Journal of Psychoanalysis*, 86(5):1265–1280.

Ogden TH (2007). Elements of analytic style: Bion's clinical seminars. *The International Journal of Psychoanalysis*, 88: 1185–1200.

Ogden TH (2009). *Rediscovering Psychoanalysis. Thinking and Dreaming, Learning and Forgetting.* London: Routledge.

Ogden TH (2011). Reading Susan Isaacs: Toward a radically revised theory of thinking. *International Journal of Psychoanalysis*, 92: 925–942.

Ogden TH (2015). Intuire la verità di quello che accade: a proposito di *Note su memoria e desiderio* di Bion. *Rivista di Psicoanalisi*, 61: 843–864.

Ogden TH & Ogden BH (2013). *The Analysts Ear and the Critics Eye: Rethinking Psychoanalysis and Literature.* London & New York: Routledge.

Orlando F (1973). *Per una teoria freudiana della letteratura.* Torino: Einaudi.

O'Shaughnessy E (2005). 'Whose Bion?' *International Journal of Psychoanalysis*, 86: 1523–1528.

Otto R (1917). *The Idea of the Holy.* Oxford: Oxford University Press.

Ozick C (1971). The Pagan Rabbi. *The Pagan Rabbi, and Other Stories.* New York: Knopf, pp. 1–38.

Pieri PF (1998). *Dizionario junghiano.* Torino: Bollati Boringhieri.

Pirandello L (1921). *Six Characters in Search of an Author.* New York: E. P. Dutton.

Pistiner de Cortinas L (2009). *The Aesthetic Dimension of the Mind.* London: Karnac.

Pistiner de Cortinas L (2011). Science and fiction in the psychoanalytical field. *Bion Today.* London: Routledge, pp. 121–152.

Preta L (2015). Prefazione. In G Rugi. *Trasformazioni del dolore.* Milano: FrancoAangeli, pp. 9–12.

Rapaport D (1951). The autonomy of the ego. In M Gill (ed.), *The Collected Papers of David Rapaport.* New York: Basic Books, pp. 357–367.

Rapaport D (1958). The theory of ego autonomy: A generalization. In M Gill (ed.), *The Collected Papers of David Rapaport.* New York: Basic Books, pp. 722–744.

Rather L (2005). 'Satured-O' and 'Unsatured-O' experience: A contribution to Bion's theory of transformations. *Paper delivered at 'Hysteria and the Transformation Spectrum Conference', Northern California Society for Psychoanalytic Psychology, San Francisco, 11th June 2005.*

Reiner A (2012). *Bion and Being: Passion and the Creative Mind.* London: Karnac.

Robbe-Grillet A (1958). *The Voyeur.* New York: Grove Press, 2015.

Rugi G (2015). *Trasformazioni del dolore. Tra psicoanalisi e arte.* Freud, Bion, Grotstein, Bacon, Munch, Viola. Milano: FrancoAngeli.

Ruiz G & Sánchez N (2014). Wolfgang Köhler's *the Mentality of Apes* and the animal psychology of his time. *Spanish Journal of Psychology,* 17, e69: 1–25.

Rulli R (2015). *L'intelligenza del Sogno* (The Intelligence of Dreaming). Seminario Teorico-Clinico, Centro Psicoanalitico di Bologna.

Scholem G (1946). *Major Trends in Jewish Mysticism.* New York: Shocken Books.

Scholem G (1960). *On the Kabbalah and Its Symbolism.* R Manheim, translator. New York: Schocken Books, 1969.

Scholem G (1961). *Major Trends in Jewish Mysticism.* New York: Schocken Books.

Scholem G (1971). *The Messianic Idea in Judaism and Other Essays on Jewish Spirituality.* New York: Schocken Books.

Scholem G (1975). *Explications and Implications: Writings on Jewish Heritage and Renaissance* [Devarim BeGo]. Tel Aviv: Am Oved.

Schore A (2012). *The Science of the Art of Psychotherapy.* New York: W. W. Norton.

Schulz B (1937). *Sanitorium under the Sign of the Hourglass.* New York: Houghton Mifflin.

Stern D (2013). Field theory in psychoanalysis. Part 2: Bionian field theory and contemporary relational/interpersonal psychoanalysis. *Psychoanalytic Dialogues,* 23: 630–645.

Symington J & Symington N (1996). *The Clinical Thinking of Wilfred Bion*. London and New York: Routledge, 2002.

Tabak de Bianchedi E (2005). Whose Bion? Who is Bion? *International Journal of Psychoanalysis*, 86: 1529–1534.

Torres N & Hinshelwood RD (2013). *Bion's Sources. The Shaping of his Paradigm*. London: Routledge.

Turkle S (2012). *Alone Together: Why We Expect More from Technology and Less from Each Other*. London: Basic Books.

Turner V (2001). *From Ritual to Theater. The Human Seriousness of Play*. Cambridge, MA: PAJ Publications.

Unamuno M (1928). *Mist: A Tragicomic Novel*. New York: Alfred Knopf.

Vermote R (2011). On the value of 'late Bion' to analytic theory and practice. *International Journal of Psychoanalysis*, 92: 1089–1098.

Vermote R (2015). On Bion's text 'emotional turbulance': A focus on experience and the unknown. In HB Levine & G Civitarese (eds.), *The W.R. Bion Tradition*. London: Karnac, pp. 345–352.

Waddel M (2011). 'From resemblance to identity': The internal narrative of a fifty minute hour. In C Mawson (ed.), *Bion Today*. London: Routledge, pp. 366–380.

Warburg A (1929). *Mnemosyne: The Atlas of Memory*. London: Warburg Institute, University of London.

Winnicott DW (1969). Additional note on psycho-somatic disorder. In C Winnicott C, R Shepherd, & M Davis (eds.), *Psycho-analytic Explorations*. Cambridge, MA: Harvard University Press, 1989, pp. 115–118.

Yovel Y (2013). Introduction: The critique as a revolution. In I Kant (ed.), *Critique of Pure Reason (Hebrew Translation)*. Tel Aviv: Hakibbutz Hameuchad.

Index

non-event 126
nonsense 193–9, 201; authority and
    authorship 189–91; links between
    truth and confusion 191–2; in
    A Memoir of the Future (Bion)
    179–201; no time for 199–201
non-sensous reality 196–9
Norman domination of England
    88–90
noumena 185
noumenon 92, 106
novel: as a form of writing 23–26;
    taking place in the present 24
numinous 76–78

O (concept of) 3–5, 10, 19, 24, 29,
    30, 42, 43, 98, 106, 120, 122, 149,
    154–5, 169, 193; numinous 74–78;
    spiritual experience and 32–33
object a 149, 150
objects and ontological distance
    between concepts 5
obscurity 193–4
Ockham's Razor 87
Ogden, Benjamin 3
Ogden, T. H. 39, 45, 108, 109, 112,
    194
oneiric functions 107–10, 155–6
ontological distance between objects
    and concepts 5
The Original of Laura (Nabokov) 28
O'Shaughnessy, Edna 42
Otto, Rudolf 76
Ozick, C. 30

P.A. character 6, 12, 28, 32, 39,
    40–42, 99, 120, 126, 134–5, 183
'The Pagan Rabbi' 30
paradigm shift in contemporary art
    169–73
paradox of language 16
parallelism 18
Paranoid-Schizoid character 13–14,
    182–4

paranoid schizoid position 183–4
paronomasia 6, 147, 156–7
The Past Presented (Bion) 123,
    148–9, 186–7
patient knowing facts 160–1
permutation 27
personal growth 173
personal truth 7, 75–76, 174,
    180, 198
Pietrantonio, Violet 5
Pirandello, L. 11, 81
Plato 122
poetic function of language 157
postmodernism in fiction 26–33;
    search for transcendence 30–33
'praise of folly' 156, 159
pre-conceptions 5, 103
pressure of problem resulting in
    thinking 51–52
Priest character 6, 28, 32, 134
problem: creating pressure resulting
    in thinking 51–52; leading to the
    more interesting thought 59–60;
    not having a solution 57–58
pro-evocative attitude 175
psyche 18, 85
psychic objects amenable for
    digestion 198
psychic reality 7–8, 11, 126, 129, 181;
    multiplicity and 181–5; similar to
    the Internet 200
psychoanalysis: aesthetic 1;
    clinical dialogue and theoretical
    discussion 90; literature applied to
    40–42; narrative factor in 107–10;
    need for orthodoxy 83–84;
    negative in 125–9; relational turn
    in 86; somato-, 110–14; theories
    65–66; value of theory 91–92
psychoanalyst: being an artist 81;
    having mystical qualities 138–40;
    ignoring characters 83; negative
    capability of 127–8; suspension of
    memory and desire 128